Democratizing Global Politics

SUNY series in Global Politics

James N. Rosenau, editor

Democratizing Global Politics

Discourse Norms, International Regimes, and Political Community

Rodger A. Payne and Nayef H. Samhat

State University of New York Press

Published by
State University of New York Press, Albany

Printed in the United States of America

For information, address the State University of New York Press,
90 State Street, Suite 700, Albany, NY 12207

Production by Michael Haggett
Marketing by Michael Campochiaro

Library of Congress Cataloging-in-Publication Data

Payne, Rodger A., 1961–
Democratizing global politics : discourse norms, international regimes, and political community / Rodger A. Payne and Nayef H. Samhat.
p. cm. — (SUNY series in global politics)
Includes bibliographical references and index.
ISBN 0-7914-5927-6
1. International relations. 2. International agencies. 3. Democratization. 4. Civil society. 5. Legitimacy of governments. I. Samhat, Nayef H., 1961– II. Title. III. Series.

JZ1319.P39 2004
327.1'01—dc22 2003068660

10 9 8 7 6 5 4 3 2 1

For Siti and Gidi

and

for Chris, Claire, and Cate

Contents

Acknowledgments

From Rodger A. Payne:

Working with Nayef has been tremendously rewarding. More than two and a half years have passed since we agreed to work on this book together. Despite the occasional obstacle or delay (too many of which were my fault), our friendship has flourished through this time.

The book benefited from the able assistance of a number of graduate students over the past few years, including Adrielle Craft, Eric Crump, Dave Ellis, Sterling Hitchcock, Henry Lyon, Sophie Maier, Jeremy Morris, and Jason Renzelmann. Moreover, many of the ideas were tested on students in my courses and their responses proved helpful in shaping and reshaping the text. Financial support was provided by the College of Arts and Sciences and the President's Office at the University of Louisville. Additionally, the Grawemeyer Endowment at the University of Louisville Foundation provided important travel assistance.

Special thanks are also extended to a number of scholars who read and made suggestions about portions of this manuscript, especially Jeff Checkel, Geoff Dabelko, Jennifer Mitzen, and Paul Nelson. My colleagues at Louisville should also be recognized for their friendship and insight, particularly Julie Bunck, Anne Caldwell, Mark Frazier, Trish Gray, Dave Imbroscio, Avery Kolers, Barry Kornstein, Laurie Rhodebeck, Ron Vogel, Paul Weber, Okbazghi Yohannes, and Chuck Ziegler. Arlene Brannon has provided first-rate administrative assistance for years.

Perhaps my greatest debt is owed to my family. My parents have always encouraged me to learn and work hard and for that lifelong inspiration I am ever grateful. This book is dedicated to my wife Chris, and our daughters Claire and Cate. They were always eager to celebrate this project's completion, but were lovingly tolerant through the inevitable delays and distractions.

Chapter 1 draws from Rodger A. Payne, "Deliberating Global Environmental Politics," *Journal of Peace Research* 33 (May 1996): 129–36 (© 1996 SAGE, reprinted by permission). Portions of chapter 4 originally appeared as Rodger A. Payne, "The Legitimacy of the GEF," in *Global Environmental Politics: Institutions and Procedures*, edited by Ho-won Jeong, 161-89, New York: Palgrave (© 2001 by Palgrave/Macmillan, reprinted by permission).

From Nayef H. Samhat:

This book grew out of an unexpected convergence of research interests between Rodger and me. Intellectually and personally the collaboration has been a rewarding experience. The opportunity to share ideas with a colleague is by itself enjoyable, but to do so with a friend is uniquely gratifying.

The ideas that inform our project have been the focus of my research since arriving at Centre College. During that time I have received support from a Teagle Grant from Centre College, and successive Faculty Development Grants for summer research, for which I would like to thank my colleagues on the Faculty Development Committee. The last stages were completed while holding the National Endowment for the Humanities Junior Professorship, and I am grateful for the research assistance provided by the NEH chair.

My colleagues in the Government program, Bill Garriott, Lori Hartmann-Mahmud, Larry Matheny and Dan Stroup, deserve special recognition for their friendship and support. I would also like to express my deep appreciation to the Dean of the College, John C. Ward, for his encouragement and assistance for my work at Centre.

I am fortunate to have the opportunity to test and exchange ideas with Centre students in the classroom. Many of these strudents have enthusiastically helped with research, editing, and other general duties associated with this project. Special thanks are owed to Heather Bradley, Carrie Cutter, Colleen Harris, Greg Haskamp, Margaret Juergens, Katherine Lacy, Evan Naylor and Beth Owen.

My wife Prema and daughters Alia, Jehan and Leila have been, as they are in whatever I do, a source of the greatest inspiration and pride. This book is about the kinds of changes in our world that can provide hope and opportunity for others; it is about a world in which I want them to live their lives. Of course, such an aspiration has a special source, my parents, whose devotion to their family has made so much possible. This book is for them.

Portions of chapter 2 originally appeared in Nayef H. Samhat, "International Regimes as Political Community," *Millennium: Journal of International Studies* 26, no. 2 (1997): 349–78. Published by permission of the publisher. Portions of chapter 3 were originally published in Nayef H. Samhat, "Human Rights Regimes and the Emergence of International Political Community," *International Politics* 36 (December): 503–27 (© 1999 Kluwer Law International, reprinted by permission). Sections of chapters 1, 2 and 6 originally appeared in "Regimes, public spheres and democracy," *Global Society*, 17(3) July 2003, published with the permission of the publisher, Carfax Publishing Company, part of the Taylor & Francis Group (http://www.tandf.co.uk).

We would both like to thank Dianne O'Regan for her assistance in assembling the index and Michael Haggett, Michael Rinella, and everyone else at SUNY Press for their help in publishing this book.

Rodger A. Payne
Nayef H. Samhat

Introduction

Truly remarkable political changes have transpired in recent world history. Most prominently, the Soviet Union and its Eastern European satellite states disintegrated, ending the superpower Cold War. In South Africa apartheid collapsed, while one party rule ended in states as diverse as Mexico and Japan, and a very long list of nation-states in the Global South tossed aside military rulers or other authoritarian regimes and began to experiment with democracy. While vast literatures are devoted to explaining these changes, one could reasonably (and parsimoniously) argue that virtually all occurred because people who were affected by the prevailing political structures challenged the legitimacy of those orders. Illegitimate structures and laws, it seems, lack "staying power."[1]

By definition, legitimacy is the proper authority granted by a political community to its institutions and structures. The legitimacy of all political order thus hinges on the acquiescence of the attendant polity. Put differently, legitimacy reflects a community's broadly shared understandings about the appropriateness of authority. Obviously, an important degree of democratic accountability is implied; indeed, something like "the consent of the governed" is arguably at issue. All of the political changes mentioned in the opening paragraph, in fact, involved a shift from a less democratic order to more democracy. The Soviet Union's collapse, for example, could readily be interpreted as the logical result of a domestic legitimacy crisis.[2] The disintegration of the Soviet bloc also demonstrates that even political structures reliant upon virtually overwhelming coercive strength can be toppled.[3] Then again, the Soviet Union survived for the better part of the twentieth century, so brute force does seem to play an important role in determining the staying power of some political structures.

Recently, Ian Hurd posited that coercion, self-interest, and legitimacy are the three principal Weberian ideal types that can establish social control.[4] However, as Hurd notes, orders built on coercive force "tend to generate resentment and resistance" and "tend over time to either collapse from their own instability or reduce their coercive component by legitimating certain practices and creating stable expectations among actors."[5] He acknowledges that much more needs to be known about how such structures might be legitimated. Orders dependent upon self-interested behavior are similarly vulnerable to change because they are "contingent on the system providing a positive stream of benefits. Actors are constantly recalculating the expected payoff to remaining in the system and stand ready to abandon it immediately should some alternative promise greater utility." Hurd asserts that "long-term relationships among self-interested actors are difficult to maintain because actors do not value the relation itself, only the benefits accruing from it. . . . As a result, a social system that relies primarily on self-interest will necessarily be thin and tenuously held together and subject to drastic change."[6] Political analysts frequently explain, for example, that the current authoritarian leadership of China is secure only because it has delivered tremendous economic growth rates for more than twenty years. A prolonged recession or depression might spell political doom for the People's Republic. In the same way, some might argue that the old Soviet state was able to survive only until Mikhail Gorbachev's unprecedented reforms exposed its numerous economic failings.

In this book, we take an overtly critical theoretical stance and challenge both the legitimacy and staying power of political order built upon coercion or self-interest. Specifically, we are curious about the legitimacy (and illegitimacy) of international order. We do not dispute the empirical realist claim that "might makes right," since power obviously plays a significant role in shaping outcomes in world politics.[7] Nor do we reject neoliberal institutionalist arguments that highlight limited interstate cooperation, which can develop around mutual benefit in certain issue areas.[8] Rather, we call into question the ultimate staying power of international norms, institutions, laws, and regimes that lack legitimacy. Our position thus broadly follows the carefully reasoned argument of legal scholar Thomas Franck, who explains that nation-state compliance with international law must ultimately depend upon the law's legitimacy. Franck emphasizes that the lack of a central sovereign in world politics means that neither coercion nor self-interest can adequately explain widespread compliance with international law. "Once a norm is deprived of its legitimacy," he writes, "it becomes a dead letter."[9] However, we move beyond Franck's work by demonstrating that apparently illegitimate international order, built often on coercion, can be transformed into legitimate authority. We emphasize both the agency of numerous global actors and the power of the democratic ideals they promote. Indeed, this book examines the implications of various members of a global political community acting to challenge the prevailing orders. We argue that these community members are often helping to recast political structures so as to reflect appropriate authority.

At this point, it is necessary to explain what we mean by democracy in the context of world politics. We are not concerned with achieving the precise kind of democracy at the global level that many societies practice at the domestic level involving, for example, elections and the separation of governmental power. In global politics, the challenge is to create open and representative procedures in specific institutional contexts. Our view of global democracy is thus grounded in principles of consensual debate and public accountability. Where decision-making power is concentrated, as many different voices as possible should be heard and the result of their collective deliberations about the appropriate course of action should carry the day. Clearly then, the democratization of global politics represents an ideal—one that is quite difficult, if not impossible, to achieve in practice. Yet, we would argue that working towards such an ideal matters a great deal. We thus do not focus on some predefined concept of democracy as a necessary global end point—as some skeptics might expect. Instead, we focus on the processes of inclusion and openness that reflect democratization—the transformation to a more broadly conceptualized and potentially globalized notion of democracy.

In practice, a wide range of political actors already lament that global politics in the twenty-first century suffers from a "democratic deficit." Power over at least some substantive issue areas is shifting to political institutions above the nation-state, such as the European Union (EU), World Trade Organization (WTO), and International Monetary Fund (IMF). As this change occurs, the relative control of national governments over these issues is necessarily weakened. For Americans, this fact was highlighted in 1991, when a dispute settlement panel of the General Agreement on Tariffs and Trade (GATT) ruled in favor of Mexico and overturned a U.S. environmental law that precluded tuna imports caught without dolphin-safe nets.[10] Residents of various European countries have similarly had various domestic laws—often on controversial social policies, such as gender discrimination—overturned by the European Court of Justice. And finally, states of the Global South quite often find their domestic economic policies determined by international bankers working at the IMF or World Bank.

The potential for a deficit of democracy is established as states yield sovereign control of certain issues to international organizations or regimes, though the key concern is that the newly powerful international institutions are not democratically accountable—and are certainly not as democratic as many of the member nation-states. The problem is viewed as most acute, for obvious reasons, by long-standing democracies that cede bits of their authority to international institutions. Consider first the EU, which has attracted a fair amount of criticism even though in some ways it is a remarkably democratic institution. After all, state members are required to have democratic governments and some elements of the EU are clearly modeled after the members' national institutions. The European Parliament, for instance, includes directly elected representatives. Yet, many observers charge that important bodies of the EU, such as the Council of Ministers and European Court of Justice, are far too unaccountable, secretive, and unrepresentative.[11] Caldeira and Gibson, in their study of the European Court, claim that an institutional "deficit of democracy could well translate into a bankruptcy of legitimacy."[12]

Anyone paying attention to the "Battle of Seattle" in 1999 knows that many transnational activists and protesters are similarly concerned with the lack of democracy and legitimacy in the WTO. The litany of charges is now familiar, as the WTO mostly lacks transparent and participatory decision making structures. Trade representatives and foreign ministers cut important deals in closed meetings, often under the direct influence of corporations granted privileged access, and without the input of nongovernmental organizations (NGOs) or peoples directly affected by the decisions. For more than a decade, similar complaints about institutional secrecy and lack of accountability have been levied by many of the same activists and NGO representatives against the World Bank and IMF. Indeed, on what could have been an occasion for great celebration—the recent golden anniversary of these entities—a vast network of NGOs and social movements targeted a global campaign against the Bretton Woods institutions on the grounds that "Fifty years is enough" of such undemocratic practices.

As will be demonstrated in this book, numerous political and social actors now view the integration of NGOs and other agents of civil society into global decision-making processes as a means for enhancing institutional democracy and legitimacy.[13] The Commission on Global Governance, for instance, in its much-noted evaluation of the United Nations (UN), posited an explicit link between international legitimacy and democratic procedures, such as accountability and participation.[14] Calls for democratic procedures, however, are not merely rendered by relatively obscure international study groups. Indeed, we highlight throughout the book that a diffuse coalition of global political actors is quite apparently developing a broadly shared understanding about appropriate international practices. As a result, many international regimes and institutions are embracing relatively inclusive participation and open decision-making procedures. We do not argue that this is a process occurring simultaneously across all issue areas of world politics. Indeed, after the tragic terrorist attacks of September 11, 2001, the trend toward openness that we identify in this book has slowed considerably for institutions addressing related concerns such as transnational law enforcement and cross-border migration. Yet, the democratization of world politics continues as a dynamic process, occurring incrementally across various issue areas.

The remainder of the book is organized into six chapters. To begin, chapter 1 establishes the theoretical context for the book in two sections. First, we provide an overview of critical international relations (IR) theory, which rejects order built upon dominance, power, and patterns of exclusion. There is little hope for the legitimate resolution of contemporary global problems—such as growing inequities in wealth, ecological destruction, militarism, and intolerance—until normative order is built through consensual means. To that end, critical theory actively seeks to transform and emancipate political life. It reveals patterns of dominance and seeks to identify immanent contradictions in the current order that might be vulnerable to challenge. Ultimately then, critical theory is concerned with the building of legitimate political community.

In the second section, we briefly outline the central arguments of Frankfurt school critical theorist Jürgen Habermas. Here we are not concerned with his extensive moral, legal, social, and political theories, but instead focus on "discourse ethics," which provides a mechanism for the construction of legitimate order. Habermas promotes inclusive and public discussion of common concerns so as to assure consensual norms. This is collective "truth-seeking," or deliberation whose democratic form is itself constituted by a set of procedural norms. Many critics have called the practice utopian, and Habermas recognizes that an "ideal speech situation" is unlikely to occur. Thus, much of his writing focuses on the discursive potential of the public sphere, typically found in western democracies. The crucial point is that publicity must be a constitutive norm of the public sphere if that public sphere is to realize its full democratic potential.

In all, the first chapter situates our argument in a critical theoretical framework, on the one hand, and Habermasian principles of communicative action on the other. This provides the foundation for our critique of existing regime theory and its reconstruction in a critical theoretical mode.

In chapter 2, we argue that international regimes can be a practical source of democratic political community. We begin with a broad discussion of the idea of political community in international relations theory. Next, the chapter examines the notion of international regimes in IR theory. We briefly trace the development of the regime concept and explore recent accounts of ideas and issue-networks as elements that contribute to regime formation. This lays a foundation for our reconceptualization of regimes in a critical theoretical perspective. In particular, we discuss how legitimate international community might be constructed. We argue that inclusive and open practical elements legitimate certain regimes as forms of political community. To make this argument, we describe some international regimes as "public spheres," which can promote deliberation. Our explanation of how international regimes might reflect a legitimate and democratic political community entails an application of both Habermasian discourse ethics and international relations discussions of global civil society.

From this discussion we flesh out emerging procedural norms that constitute various dialogical communities in particular regimes. Of course, it would be impossible to precisely calibrate some measure of legitimacy in global politics. Nonetheless, norms of transparency and participation, which collectively constitute a norm of publicity, promote the legitimization and democratization of global politics.

In chapter 3, we argue that participation and transparency norms are developing in a great number of substantive IR regimes. We begin the chapter by defining more clearly what these norms mean and how they help constitute an inclusive public sphere and potentially a legitimate mode of political community. Next, several major issue areas are briefly reviewed to highlight burgeoning participation and transparency requirements, including environment, development, security, and human rights. The empirical discussion does not attempt to explain, as a detailed constructivist account might, how the discourse norms develop. At the same time, our serious attention to real world empirical experience diverges from the typical path trod by the critical theorist. Indeed, we aim to make a "dangerous liaison" between positivist forms of constructivism and abstract critical theory.[15] Our hope is to provide enough of a normative argument to make critical theorists think seriously about potential institutions for transformation of world politics and enough of an empirical argument to engage constructivists in explicit normative debate.

Moreover, the chapter briefly considers the so-called "bootstrapping problem." Participation and transparency norms themselves may not be built legitimately. On the one hand, advocates (mostly from the West) use a variety of coercive techniques to "win" contested debates about global policy and procedure. Yet on the other hand, democratically informed procedural norms could conceivably constitute metanorms that are genuinely legitimate. Ultimately, we draw on our discussion from chapter 2 on the regime as public sphere to argue that procedural norms of transparency and participation provide the conditions for deliberation that approximates the Habermasian ideal. We do not argue that this ideal is realized, rather we believe that global politics, as a dynamic sphere, is moving towards this condition.

In chapters 4 and 5, we examine two international regimes and apply our argument in greater detail to specific case examples. The empirical changes highlighted in the chapters illustrate the kinds of normative developments that are ongoing in various issue areas of global politics, but the case studies are not meant to test particular theoretical claims. For example, we make no effort to demonstrate that the participation and transparency requirements have resulted in different institutional outcomes, perhaps by constraining powerful actors.[16] After all, Habermasian discourse ethics is procedural. Thus, even though critical theorists argue that substantive changes could follow procedural innovations, we are interested first in demonstrating the extent of democratization. Indeed, simply finding that global political outcomes can be determined consensually after an open and informed discussion would be remarkable in itself. Additionally the chapters highlight the shortcomings of the regimes under investigation and identify the kinds of changes that would be needed to legitimize the institutions.

The Global Environment Facility (GEF), which is affiliated with the World Bank and is designed to promote implementation of various environmental regimes, is perhaps the most inclusive and open international organization. We have thus chosen to examine the GEF in greater detail because it is remarkable, even though it falls well short of creating ideal discursive conditions. NGOs partake directly in discussions in the important Governing Council and are granted access to virtually unprecedented amounts of information. We evaluate the democratic implications of these practices and discuss additional measures that should be pursued in the future.

By contrast, the WTO is considered an unlikely place for global democracy and community formation. The WTO is obviously one of the most important international institutions and was selected for scrutiny to demonstrate that discursive norms are not merely taking hold in remote locations in global politics. To date, the WTO has been a relatively exclusive and secretive organization that has found itself beleaguered by protesters from around the world. Many NGOs want to transform the institutional procedures and have achieved some modest success. We explore the recent history and discuss the possibilities for additional WTO democratization. Much attention is focused on the new dispute resolution procedure as a means by which the regime might be democratized. The chapter does not, however, address the substantive claims pursued by antiglobalization protesters and it would not be democratic to privilege their positions within any future deliberation—just as the current WTO is not democratic since it mostly ignores or marginalizes the voices of these activists. The key concern is how to make the WTO more inclusive and open so as to allow interested and affected parties to deliberate about common concerns and to achieve consensual decisions.

In chapter 6, we conclude by reflecting on the democratic and communal potential of ongoing global transformation, particularly how the international regime can be regarded as a site for these transformations. This provides an opportunity to discuss how the changes identified above fit with recent debates about transnational civil society and global governance.

Finally, we compare our ideas about the democratization of global politics to those proposed by other critical theorists. David Held and Jürgen Habermas, for example, imagine broadly inclusive UN-level institutions. This section contrasts the various notions of cosmopolitan democracy at the international level and, again, emphasizes the role of international regimes in this process.

1

Critical Theory, Habermas, and International Relations

Introduction

In this chapter we outline elements of critical theory and its contribution to the study of international relations theory in the belief that a critical theoretical stance offers an appropriate framework for examining the emergence of international institutions as new forms of legitimate political community. Our emphasis in the first section is on three constituent elements of critical theory: theoretical reflexivity, human consciousness, and normative purpose. In the second section, we examine the contributions of Jürgen Habermas to a critical international theory. Indeed, his ideas about communicative rationality, deliberation, and the public sphere have gone far to reinvigorate the Enlightenment project of emancipation, and the implications for international relations theory and global institutions are substantial. As we shall examine later, these institutions, particularly the international regime, commonly incorporate procedural norms of participation (or inclusion) and transparency (or openness). The consequence is that certain international regimes, by building democratic procedural norms into their design and evolution, acquire the character of incipient transnational political communities. These regimes effectively serve as public spheres whose scope for dialogic interaction amongst a wide array of state and nonstate actors reflect emerging global democratic practices on an unprecedented scale.

Critical Theory and International Relations

The turn to a critical theoretical interpretation of international relations and, specifically, international institutions, is not an argument about the failure of neoutilitarian accounts. To the contrary, neorealism and neoliberal institutionalism provide important insights regarding the relationship of power to international institutions and the role institutions, particularly regimes, have in overcoming "political market failures." Both theoretical perspectives offer insightful and helpful accounts of regime construction, maintenance and decay. Rather, we argue that a critical theoretical account is useful at this point in time for two reasons. First, the contemporary global condition is such that accounts of international politics anchored in statist forms do not accurately capture the diverse social forces and political challenges confronting the human polity. As the extensive and growing literature on the "new transnationalism" illustrates, a plethora of nongovernmental actors are excluded by state-centric formulations.[1] Moreover, we embrace Andrew Linklater's argument that the contemporary international political order has a "tenuous existence and precarious legitimacy," because decisions "are taken without considering their likely effects on systematically excluded groups."[2] Global institutions that deny the importance of nonstate actors potentially lack staying power. Second, a critical theoretical approach provides a foundation for defining alternative emancipatory purposes for international theory. We are interested in identifying the changes immanent in the global order, especially the democratic ideals promoted by the diverse array of nonstate actors contesting its current design. The status quo version of globalization often simply replicates longstanding power relations and the "discontents" associated with that material reality.[3] Thus, in the words of one scholar, globalization has too often "perpetuated poverty, widened material inequalities, increased ecological degradation, sustained militarism, fragmented communities, marginalized subordinated groups, fed intolerance and deepened crises of democracy."[4]

Taking into account the role of nongovernmental organizations and applying Habermasian discourse ethics to the study of international regimes illuminates their potential as the foundation for a new global order characterized by nonterritorial forms of political community. By dramatically expanding the boundaries of participation and open discussion in the context of universally agreed normative procedures, these regimes reflect the emancipatory aims of critical theory, approximating modes of democracy essential to constructing new identities, loyalties, and obligations inherent in a global political community. Burgeoning international norms promoting greater inclusion and openness in various international regimes greatly diminish the likelihood that the coercive strength of materially powerful actors will carry any given point, and substantially increase the prospects for compelling arguments to find consensual agreement.

The opportunity for building community is found in the immanent contradictions of the current political order. The contemporary human condition is characterized by rapidity, intensity, and extensity on an historic scale. Technological transformations are revolutionizing means of communication and production, resulting in flows of money, knowledge, and information around the globe at unprecedented rates of speed. The carrying capacity of communication networks is increasing such that the volume of flows is unique in historical time while the extensiveness of networks has left no part of the globe untouched.[5] The consequence for advocates of a "hyperglobalist" view of globalization is profound political, social, and economic change.[6] Patterns of international economic exchange are undermining the authority of states overwhelmed by the quantum leap in transnational interactions that, by virtue of their scale, demonstrate the decline of unilateral and absolute territorial governance. By contrast, for "transformationalists," it is not the decline of the state per se, but a fundamental reconfiguration of sovereignty and authority that is of interest.[7] More than simply integration and interdependence proceeding apace, the structures and centers of authority are shifting even as identities become redefined. This long-term secular trend is accelerated with networks of communication and advances in technology that, in effect, empower emerging societal actors, whether they be transnational corporations, NGOs, social movements, or other elements of a global civil society.

In either case, these profound changes are taking place within a transformed geopolitical context that heightens the salience of new issues on the one hand, and the consciousness of social actors on the other, signaling a unique era in global politics.[8] In the first instance, the end of the Cold War has increased the visibility of numerous issues on the global political agenda that were historically characterized as "low politics." Economics, certainly, but also human rights, the environment, development, and the growing gap between rich and poor are central themes of contemporary world politics. These are issues whose resolution challenges directly the politics of self-interest and particularism. The shared burdens of responsibility, the shared consequences of neglect, and the implied crisis of human experience, all suggest that the transformation brought about by globalization and the changed nature of world politics necessitates a new global agenda anchored in new conceptions of obligation, loyalty, and responsibility. To draw on Mark Neufeld's discussion, there is a recognition in popular and scholarly political discourse that the *polis*, a socially created political space intended to foster the "conditions necessary for the leading of a good and just life, a life encompassing the values of equality and freedom" requires redefining.[9] Whereas the territorial state once represented the *polis* as "coterminous with the minimum self-sufficient human reality," the scale and pace of new challenges to humanity "call out for the reidentification of the idea of the *polis* with the planet as a whole: a truly *global polis*."[10]

Such a redefinition of a *polis* emerges only with a new mode of politics. Just as the changed geopolitical context gave way to alternative issue hierarchies, that context has also opened up political space for a greater number of actors. Nongovernmental organizations and intergovernmental agencies have become integral figures in world politics. Global social movements are taking advantage of unprecedented technological developments to strengthen their capacities for mobilization, organization, and articulation of principles.[11] One consequence is that the interconnectedness of issues is increasingly made apparent through the activities of transnational issue networks seeking to construct new international norms and other institutions of global governance.[12] Loosening the historic "social bond" between state and citizen challenges claims lodged by the sovereign state to the sole possession of political authority and loyalty.[13] In sum, new global social movements and transnational issue networks are reflections of the relative shift of capacities for political action and mobilization historically contained within the state. The rise of NGOs extends the boundaries of consciousness and obligation, hence politics, thereby serving as a crucial ingredient in the constitution of an historically unique *global polis*.

Under these transformed conditions, critical theory poses a real challenge to the orthodoxy of international theory—the neoutilitarian paradigms, as it were—in that it offers new foundations for conceptualizing the discipline, both theoretically and normatively. Of course, what constitutes a critical approach to international theory remains contested. Alexander Wendt, for instance, frames a definition around the importance of social, as opposed to material, structures and the importance of identity and interests, in contrast to the narrower rationalist concern with behavior.[14] While this serves as a workable explanation of constructivism, we find it too narrow. Chris Brown, by contrast, describes critical theory as a generic term for a set of approaches arguing that the dominant discourses of Western social and political thought emanating from the Enlightenment—the discourses of modernity—are in a state of crisis. The source of the crisis is found in attacks on positivism and the presumptions of universalism, foundationalism, and rationalism of modern natural and social scientific practice.[15] In the search for a response to this crisis, postmodernism, poststructuralism, critical theory, and deconstructionism represent varying epistemological strategies for decentering modernity's commitment to an instrumental rationality that is the essence of the Enlightenment conception of progress. Jürgen Habermas bluntly opines: "After a century that, more than any other, has taught us the horror of existing unreason, the last remains of an essentialist trust in reason have been destroyed."[16] This collapse signals the emergence of a new field of action on which to construct alternative theoretical foundations. The "free play of non-foundationalist thought" offers both opportunities and dangers for the constitution of new moral and ethical premises in social life.[17]

The consequences for international relations theory are profound. The traditions of realism and neorealism, and liberalism and neoliberalism, are anchored firmly in modernity's grasp, a grasp that already spurred the field's "third debate."[18] Indeed, R.B.J. Walker notes that theories of international relations are "interesting less for the substantive explanations they offer about political conditions in the modern world than as expressions of the limits of the contemporary political imagination."[19] The constraints on this imagination are imposed by an implicit (and sometimes explicit) normative commitment to statist interpretations of the international political world, reinforced by principles of a rationalist liberal economy (and the materially self-interested being). The consequence is not innovation but repetition, progress defined not by the positing of alternative global orders, transformative possibilities, or the empowerment of new political actors and new modalities of action, but by the reinforcement of extant and unchallenged social and political forms and practices. Consider the duality of a neoliberal political economy and neorealist geopolitics, which together denote exceptionally limited bounds of imagination. In these neoutilitarian worlds, historical patterns of the moment are not taken as anything other than the reproductions of a timeless state-system. Thus, at the very point in time when the capacities, knowledge, and networks of alternative global actors are in a position to articulate concerns, assert agendas, forge new loyalties, and facilitate the generation of new norms and institutions, the theoretical apparatus of international relations is constrained from accommodating fundamental change.

To be sure, there is a danger of proceeding down a path wherein the absence of foundations finds the discipline enmeshed in a hyperpluralism of theory, method, and unresolved purpose. However, change need not involve the thoroughgoing deconstruction of existing social and territorial forms. States, in fact, are not likely to dissolve under the pressure of global civil society networks, nor is it likely that a shift in identities and loyalties will be of such a scale that territorial community and citizenship require a wholesale reevaluation.[20] To the contrary, the challenge of international theory—indeed, the thrust of a critical theory—is to pursue alternative modes of thinking that permit a reassessment of the field's assumptions about global order. Theory might then serve a higher purpose than the mere confirmation and replication of state behavior. Mark Hoffman notes that contrary to realism, critical theory

> seeks to understand society by taking a position outside of society while at the same time recognizing that it is itself a product of

> society. Its central problematic is the development of reason and rationality that is directly concerned with the quality of human life and opposed to the elevation of scientific reasoning as a sole basis of knowledge. To this extent, it involves a change in the criteria of theory, the function of theory, and its relationship to society. It entails the view that humanity has potentialities other than those manifested in current society. Critical theory, therefore, seeks not simply to reproduce society via description, but to understand society and change it. It is both descriptive and constructive in its theoretical intent; it is both an intellectual and a social act. It is not merely an expression of the concrete realities of the historical situation, but also a force for change within those conditions.[21]

Several crucial themes of a critical theory are evident in this extended quotation. There is first the theoretical reflexivity of international relations. There is also the question of human consciousness as an agent for social change. And finally there is the question of purpose. These themes offer a direct confrontation with the neoutilitarian paradigms of contemporary international relations theory, their privileging of the state, and the consequent skewed practices of inclusion/exclusion.

Perhaps the most significant departure of a critical international theory is the explicit acknowledgement of a theoretically reflexive attitude towards the process of theorizing itself. While the underlying logic is now familiar thanks to the "constructivist turn" in international relations, an essential starting point for understanding the critical theoretical component is Robert Cox's contribution to the field's "third debate."[22] His description of problem-solving theory, which takes the world as given, and critical theory, which seeks to explain how that world came about, focuses attention on the fact-value distinction in, and the normative character of, social theorizing. Viewing theory as mere problem-solving preserves the fact-value distinction, emphasizing the objective circumstances and timeless quality of the world as we find it. The reflexive position, by contrast, recognizes the contingency of social life and of our place in it. Social orders and the knowledge that both produces and describes them are historically constituted and therefore subject to reflection and reconstitution. Our knowledge of material "facts," for example, cannot be disconnected from social understandings or interpretations of those facts, despite what rationalists might lead us to believe. Broadly accepted social or political theory about material facts are of necessity anchored to sets of preconceived beliefs and assumptions. In their totality, these preconceptions reflect understandings of the social or political world containing embedded normative judgments on the existing order and the relations of power contained therein.

Thus, the core elements of the neoutilitarian paradigms in international theory—states, rationalism, and anarchy—are universalized and divorced from their historical contexts, with consequences for our understanding of who acts, why they act, and how they act, in international politics. Those instigating the field's "third debate" sought to create a space for alternative theorizing that might account for the conditions and consequences of explanations of world politics. Indeed, the critical turn, as E. Fuat Keyman offers, allows one to regard theoretical activity as a

> [cultural] criticism, a 'lens' through which one, as an active subject, problematizes the world, rather than as a neutral instrument or abstraction, (thus) it becomes possible both to critically analyze interactions between the international, the state, and civil society, and to take seriously the need to create the possibility of emancipation, either (a) through the extension of human community, or (b) through the construction of counter hegemonic discourses that constitute an international civil society, or (c) through the radical democratization of human community based on the recognition of differences.[23]

The essence of a reflexive stance is therefore to deny the neutrality and objectivity of theory, the theorizer, and the world. Mark Neufeld concludes, for example, that "reflexivity directs us to a broader debate about which 'purposes,' which 'enquiries' and which 'ideologies' merit the support and energy of International Relations scholars."[24] It is only by reflecting on the ends and means of international theory that the potential to effect change is realized. Here, the constraints on global social transformation imposed by neorealist and neoliberal interpretations of world politics are well known—the critical and neo-Gramscian positions of John G. Ruggie, Stephen Gill, Robert Cox, and Andrew Linklater, or the postmodernism of Richard Ashley, James Der Derian, and R. B. J Walker. All engage in a demystification of the past and present.[25]

For Linklater, this reflexive position challenges the "immutability thesis" in international relations theory which, as "an exercise in the politically neutral observation of independent reality (lends) vital ideological support to the status quo by denying that alternative possibilities are latent within existing social structures or by obscuring their existence."[26] The crucial consequence of the immutability thesis is that theorizing for purposes other than description is an empty exercise, rendering what are "humanly-produced circumstances into a quasi-natural condition . . . contribut(ing) to the formation of subjects who succumb to the belief that the relations between independent political communities must remain as they are."[27] Critical theory's commitment, however, to exploring human consciousness and agency allows it to overcome the theoretical closure implied by the immutability thesis. A central tenet of critical theory is that human subjects do indeed have the capacity to shape and reshape the social structures within which they exist. There is no necessary inevitability to this process, but the implications for redefining global politics are potentially profound.

The roots of this theme of human agency found in critical theory are located in the Enlightenment and the philosophical discourse of modernity.[28] Likewise, the element of critique and its consequence for a reformulation of the ends of political inquiry—emancipation—emanates from the Enlightenment movement towards autonomy in thought and action and finds expression in the Kantian philosophical tradition.[29] The Kantian position sought to assert the use of reason to throw off constraints imposed by tradition, thereby opening up unrealized possibilities for the future.[30] For Kant the Enlightenment was defined as "man's emergence from his self-incurred immaturity," a reflection that "people can and must think for themselves." This was made possibly by virtue of Reason, which, for Kant, was "that tendency, in all human thought and conscious effort, towards, at one and the same time, ever greater unity, system and necessity, and *equally* towards ever sharper and more constant self-criticism and control."[31] Kant's notion of reason found expression in two spheres: Theoretical Reason "demanded and disclosed a world of natural determinism," whereas Practical Reason "demanded or presupposed the possibility of human freedom to choose what Duty or Justice commands."[32] The former offers a completed system, the latter an "ever-open, never completed task or calling."[33] For Kant, human progress and peace followed from the application of principles of Theoretical Reason to the search for moral law. In other words, Kant's "sovereignty of reason" suggests not only that we have the capacity to produce notions of causation in a world of natural determinism, but also that we have within us the capacity to realize the "moral law" or "categorical imperative." Hence, as W.B. Gallie describes the history of man's misfortunes and endeavors:

> Might not this be construed as a succession of naturally necessitated misadventures, spiced with episodes of ostensible good luck, through which men could nevertheless learn, by trial and error, to expand the area of their own rational freedom? More specifically, might it not be that the characteristic difficulties, failures, and tragedies disclosed in the history of mankind, constituted a necessary condition for the expansion of men's capacity to cope rationally with nature's challenges, and to begin to co-operate in the face of them?[34]

In the categorical imperative, so named because it imposes an absolute injunction to act in certain ways, there is thus implied in Kant's philosophy a moral requirement of universality, realized ultimately in the rule of law. In this context, the state exists to allow people to find security for themselves, but the greatest realization of freedom can only occur with the abolition of war amongst states.[35] That is, "the same moral imperative that enjoins the creation of the lawful state" requires the formation of a world level system of laws that preserves the state within a cosmopolitan order.[36] These ends are expressed in Kant's vision of a federation of republican states arising out of a history of violence and reason, a process that reflects, as Richard Devetak describes, his "effort to break with the past . . . It constitutes a form of '*continuous renewal*' which involves the constant 'dissolution of the exemplary past' and an openness toward what Kant called 'the unbounded future.' "[37]

The willingness to break with the past and initiate a search for the "unbounded future" is, perhaps, the distinguishing element of a critical international theory. By posing a challenge to the status quo in social, economic and political life a critical theoretical stance couples political inquiry to normative purpose.[38] This normative purpose, a final theme, is found in critical theory's commitment to emancipatory ends. Such a commitment does not entail the deconstruction of foundations implied by postmodern responses to the crisis of modernity. To the contrary, the critical theory of Habermas and its application to international relations by, for example, Andrew Linklater, Marc Lynch, and Thomas Risse, has defined an agenda of political inquiry *and* action anchored in historically contextualized knowledge claims. These knowledge claims, in turn, reflect a certain type of rationality embedded in a particular social time and space.[39] As Richard Devetak notes, the project of emancipation central to critical theory's willingness to question and to reflect upon the presumed given order is a constitutive element of the Enlightenment project.[40] With this in mind, one can see that the project of critical international theory is one of reconstruction rather than deconstruction. For some, "emancipation" is, or must be, utopian for its realization entails transcending world order.[41] It is here, however, that a critical theory engages normative international theory's cosmopolitan-communitarian debate. Embedded within this debate is a contest over the ethics of place: where can the aspirations of the emancipatory project best be realized? Can an alternative world order reconcile territoriality with a universal ethics? And what forms of political community, institutions, and practices are implied by this reconciliation?

The search for a purposive politics is a response to the normative content of contemporary analyses of human practices and institutions. The crisis (and danger) of rationalist international theory is found in the refusal to acknowledge its own unspoken normative discourse, a natural refusal that follows from the absence of a reflexive stance. While ideological and value judgements constitute neorealist and neoliberal claims, this is obscured by the fact that these claims are cast in terms of objectivity and fact. Ultimately, the neoutilitarian paradigms serve to reinforce and reify prevailing global political and economic structures of power. By contrast, the explicit normative commitment of a critical theory and practice is oriented toward emancipation. Critical theorists are interested in the realization of human security through the actions of conscious subjects seeking the promotion of social justice, peace, and the removal of unnecessary constraints on human freedom, goals that are, in fact, consistent with the project of modernity.[42] As Linklater contends, knowledge of society, its practices and institutions, is of necessity "incomplete if it lacks the emancipatory purpose."[43]

The considerations of justice that inform this purpose are many—protections from inequalities of a neoliberal economy, from transnational violence, the absence of democracy, or from ecological threats.[44] A global politics that seeks both to critique the existing order and posit alternatives in the attempt to redress human injustice must first "start from the assumption that the moral relevance of the distinction between insiders and outsiders has to be demonstrated rather than presupposed."[45] It is the presence of boundaries that has generated the "Cartesian coordinates" of human existence, providing the rationale for the totalizing project of the nineteenth century. The fusion of state power, territory and identity reified principles of otherness that generated the inside/outside, society/anarchy problematic so essential to the foundations of neoutilitarian international relations theory of the twentieth century. Here, a reflective account of how we came to be, how boundaries and the logics of inclusion and exclusion have segmented freedoms, rights, obligations, oppressions, inequalities and opportunities, represents a synthesis of modernity's aspirations with a critical, post-enlightenment project. The object of a critical theory is therefore to understand how communities are formed and re-formed, how boundaries open and close, and how different conceptions of self and other evolve over time.[46]

Thus, a fundamental argument of this book is that political community need not be defined by territorial borderlines. Rather, community in world politics has assumed different forms, of which the territorial-state is only one manifestation, albeit a manifestation whose normative and ideological commitments are reproduced by the prevailing neoutilitarian paradigms. From a critical theoretical stance, however, communities reflect more than territorial borderlines; they are the consequence of shared identities, loyalties, and sympathies born of commonly held principles. The structures that govern and cement communities are human creations and therefore, given the fact of human consciousness, have no necessary permanence beyond what humans themselves define. This position is crucial for it enables a different kind of politics both locally and globally, calling into question the exclusive role of the state, its representatives, and its emphasis on narrowly defined notions of security. By offering a mechanism to reconceptualize community, global institutions, specifically the international regime, can be regarded as novel forms of political community. We address this particular institutional form in the next chapter. First, though, we introduce the work of Jürgen Habermas whose theories about communicative rationality, deliberation, and the public sphere provide the foundation for emergent procedural norms that democratize and thus legitimatize international institutions and regimes.

Habermas and International Relations

How can the concept of political community be extended well beyond the narrowly self-interested, strategic, and potentially violent domain of the nation-state? To answer this question, we briefly examine in this section the contributions of Frankfurt school philosopher Jürgen Habermas. We are primarily concerned with the way his "discourse ethics" might be employed to construct legitimate international order. His central ideas about communicative rationality, deliberation, and the public sphere will receive special attention, but given the author's prodigious output of scholarship, we cannot possibly examine in great detail Habermas's extensive moral, legal, social, and political theories. As shall be briefly discussed below, a number of international relations scholars are employing Habermasian insights to address important theoretical and empirical concerns.

Neoutilitarian accounts of international politics explain that the world of states and international institutions is shaped primarily by the strongest states employing their material power in the pursuit of relatively narrow self-interest. As we already noted, critical IR theorists examine and critique the global forms of dominance and injustice inherent in the structures and processes of contemporary world politics. Significant attention is given over to attacking the illegitimate actions of egoistic states, especially as they follow their traditional pursuits—power, security, and deterrence. One succinct statement of the analysis is offered by Neta Crawford, who asserts that "norms established through coercion, imposed by a hegemon, lack legitimacy."[47]

Of course, critical IR theorists are not merely interested in critique. They additionally explore the possibility of transforming world order, by emancipating it from current constraints. This would minimally involve, as is further explained in chapter 2, extending the concept of political community beyond its current territorial bounds. While environmentalists, human rights activists, development specialists, and others have already constructed all sorts of transnational connections, they continue to confront substantial and arbitrary barriers to action imposed by states and the state system. Critical theorists imagine a world in which the persuasive influence of a compelling argument determines outcomes, rather than the material strength or strategic action of a particular actor or set of actors. Truly remarkable change can occur, as

Linklater emphasizes, only when "dialogue and consent replace domination and force" as the central causal mechanisms in global politics.[48] This Habermasian emphasis on dialogue follows naturally from the ideas about normative agreement discussed in the Introduction. Legitimate order is "arrived at through communicative action in which participants seek consensus."[49] Dialogical processes also clearly serve the critical themes discussed in the first section of this chapter: reflexivity, agency, and purpose. People engaged in thoughtful discussions make conscious decisions about theoretical ideas. Their potential agreement, virtually by definition, reflects a shared purpose and can undergird the development of new norms.

Unfortunately, it is not at all certain that a world favoring dialogue and consent can ever exist outside the realm of the imagination. Critical theorists have infrequently offered concrete proposals and are often accused by neoutilitarian scholars of building "fantasy theory."[50] As John Dryzek has written, "It is perhaps at the juncture of model institutions that a critical theory program for political organization is currently weakest, to the point of petering out entirely."[51] This is not to imply, however, that critical IR theorists have altogether ignored questions of practice. Linklater, Crawford, Dryzek, and other critical theorists interested in global concerns have borrowed from Habermas when attempting to develop workable proposals about dialogical practice. To some extent, looking to Habermas is an odd choice since his ideas are often quite abstract and they tend to be buried in dense texts. Moreover, as we shall discuss, many critics view Habermasian ideas about practice as utopian and impractical.

In any case, Habermas has written frequently about a form of social and political decision-making based upon open discussion by the members of a community. Deliberation, or discursive democracy as it is sometimes called, is grounded in "discourse ethics," which are essentially procedural norms for dialogue that could purportedly assure genuine public accountability in modern sociopolitical settings. Deliberation features inclusive and public discussion of common concerns so that a relevant polity (or community) can work out its own consensual norms. The process is often viewed as a mechanism for collective truth seeking: inviting participants to advance claims and counterclaims so as to develop a common understanding of circumstances and solutions. Appropriately public and inclusive deliberative contexts provide advocates with a suitable forum not only for advancing their own arguments, but also for critically evaluating the points made by others. The veracity of self-interested claims can be challenged by any participant in a dialogue, which should encourage everyone to offer ideas and arguments geared toward achieving communicative consensus.

In a deliberative setting, all participants would equally find their assertions subject to scrutiny. Ultimately, if sufficiently interested in finding truth, deliberators might agree to dismiss certain claims and to accept the validity and veracity of other points. Discursive processes should not only be unaffected by the external position or rank of advocates engaged in the discussion, but should also actually reveal and thereby minimize the effects of deception, secrecy, strategic action, and other potential distortions of the communicative process. Normative consensus is ideally achieved in a forum that is free of all distortions, including threats, secrets, and lies. Because deliberations are inclusive, public, and oriented toward consensus, at least some participants in a discussion should be able to provide good reasons to challenge and reject deceptive or self-serving arguments. By contrast, arguments supporting the community's "generalized interests" should be quite difficult for anyone to refute and relatively easy for everyone to embrace.

Put differently, deliberative participants engage in what Habermas calls "communicative action" that creates the possibility of "communicative," or "argumentative," rationality.[52] Habermas sees communicative rationality as an important critical alternative to the instrumental rationality he finds to be so destructive. Communicative rationality results when a community's members discover or develop intersubjective agreement after probing and challenging publicly presented arguments and evidence. Decisions would reflect generalizable, or collective, rather than particular, interests—and their authority would be based on the ideational force of a better argument rather than some other arbitrary and likely distorted cause. Indeed, sound ideas and arguments, advanced and refined in an appropriately open and inclusive discussion process, should lead participants to construct mutually agreed, and thereby authoritative, answers to fundamental questions about truth and justice.[53] Deliberation is a pathway, in other words, to the construction of legitimate normative understandings and order.

As should be evident, deliberative democracy is constituted by several basic procedural norms. While Habermas lists a number of specific requirements, we would argue that two are clearly the most important. First, the dialogue must be open to all interested parties—especially individuals and groups likely to be affected by any decision of the community. Linklater, for instance, calls for a wide-open "universal communication community."[54] In the literature on Habermas, this procedural norm requires that every community member enjoy "equal access to the discourse." Second, the discussion must be public so that everyone involved in the discussion has the opportunity to evaluate everyone else's arguments and evidence. This norm, which is in important ways intrinsically linked to the norm of access, is commonly known as "publicity."[55] When all the necessary conditions for deliberation are in place, Habermas would consider that context an "ideal speech situation."

Many critics consider deliberative democracy to be hopelessly utopian, and Habermas recognizes that the ideal speech situation generally cannot occur in practice. Realistically, it would be impossible for all members of a community to engage in open debate about virtually every issue that affects their common lifeworld. Meaningful deliberation would seem to be especially problematic in international contexts, which are typically dominated by a very small number of powerful states and regularly feature coercive rather than communicative action.[56] Deliberative democracy is quite distant from the day-to-day reality of international affairs. Rather, global politics typically features secretive, exclusive and coercive state action that is fundamentally inconsistent with discursive democracy and communicative rationality. Even current international organizations, which might feature somewhat open forums for diplomatic discussion, such as the United Nations or European Union, would fall well short of Habermasian ideals. James Bohman observes that existing international institutional arrangements "do not have anything like the sort of accountability that public access to global processes requires."[57] Most students of international relations, in fact, would likely find the globalization of democratic discussion a virtually inconceivable prospect. Even among scholars attentive to communicative concerns, "operationalizing Habermasian notions" and applying them to "real world settings" are viewed as "difficult" or "daunting" tasks.[58]

Much of Habermas's writing thus focuses on the discursive potential of the public sphere, typically found in western democracies, but now also arguably developing in world politics.[59] The public sphere is simply the "shared space of common language, political argument and experience," which allows members of a polity to engage one another in a public debate.[60] In Western democracies, basic rights of free speech, association, assembly, and free press together help constitute a public sphere. Elected government likewise creates the conditions for some semblance of public accountability. While critical theorists can readily expose all sorts of arbitrary limits on freedom even in Western liberal democracy, Thomas Risse explains that political actors seeking normative consensus in a discursive setting behave counterfactually "as if" they are in an Habermasian ideal speech situation.[61] Advocates advance arguments and criticize opponents in the hope of providing a convincing rationale for political action, social action, or both. Relatively typical public discussion thus provides a potential—though flawed—means for endogenously discovering and creating norms even in nonideal settings, such as world politics.

Empirically, Marc Lynch directly employs Habermasian public sphere theory to explain how international normative understandings can be built through public discussion of actor interests and identities. Much of his work specifically examines the historic operation of public spheres in the nondemocratic Middle East, though he has also explored whether U.S.-Chinese relations might be transformed through "communicative engagement."[62] Risse's research employs a somewhat different approach, though he too finds Habermasian insights important for explaining some elements of international relations. After reviewing evidence from numerous human rights cases, Risse finds that "argumentative rationality and persuasive processes constitute one of three causal mechanisms by which international norms become socialized into domestic practices."[63] These constructivist IR scholars sidestep the practical problems that might seem to preclude implementation of Habermasian ideas about discursive democracy in global politics by more narrowly employing his notions of the public sphere and communicative rationality in specific regions or issue areas. Lynch's work on global pursuit of a "dialogue of civilizations" rather than a "clash of civilizations" is something of an exception here.[64] Even without discursive democracy per se, the existence of an international public sphere has apparently allowed for the development of arguably legitimate norms. Indeed, constructivists define international norms as shared understandings about appropriate behavior and frequently assert that they reflect "legitimate social purpose."[65]

A truly deliberative world society, for many obvious reasons, seems impractical and utopian. Neither Risse nor Lynch view international relations as particularly inclusive or open to public deliberation. As Risse notes, for example, "the Habermasian condition of 'equal access' to the discourse . . . is simply not met in world politics."[66] Internationally, he argues that the sovereign equality of states might serve as a "functional equivalent" for the norm of equal access to a discourse. However, it is quite debatable whether constructivists should relax this Habermasian requirement, as Risse claims, since international politics quite often features hierarchical arrangements determined by differences in the material power of states.[67] Lynch, moreover, recognizes that "serious power inequalities are likely to stand in the way" of meaningful dialogue.[68] Relaxing the standard would mean, moreover, that nonstate actors would be excluded; thus, sovereign equality cannot assure anything like the kind of inclusion that critical theorists discuss. Risse also acknowledges that public spheres "vary dramatically in international relations" because secretive international negotiations may well limit access about many important decisions exclusively to nation-states.[69] This is a fundamental problem since secrecy has historically been a powerful norm in world politics, especially in security affairs, but it can also have a broad scope in financial matters.

Skimming Morgenthau's *Politics Among Nations*, for example, one quickly notices how important secrecy and disguised intentions are supposed to be for statesmen. Morgenthau specifically addresses the problem of distinguishing between policies that are status quo oriented versus those that are imperialistic, given that statesmen are naturally going to disguise their intentions and behavior behind political ideology and rationalizations. He also sharply criticizes the "vice of publicity," since he believes it inevitably causes diplomacy to degenerate "into a propaganda match."[70] Morgenthau's understandings of nation-state behavior, while perhaps momentarily out of favor in some academic circles, almost certainly continue to resonate powerfully with policy actors. Indeed, since the terrorist attacks on New York and Washington on September 11, 2001, the U.S. government has quite obviously increased its efforts to control its secrets. Among other measures, various agencies and departments established more restrictive information policies and "sensitive" data on government internet websites was removed.[71]

What then can be made of the prospects for global transformation? Habermas and other critical theorists embrace open dialogue and consent, but those are qualities often missing in world politics. While constructivists find that some international norms are built legitimately, international relations is for the most part dominated by powerful states who use their strength to pursue their own interests, even as they limit the political participation of other actors. Secrecy, rather than publicity, seems to be a more commonly embraced norm of these states.

To return to the notion stated earlier, the opportunity for building a more democratic community, according to the critical argument, is actually found in the immanent contradictions of the current political order. Any normative structure not grounded in legitimate authority may well prove unsustainable, ultimately inviting disobedience and change. This book explores the immanent possibilities of discursive democracy in world politics.[72] Specifically, we discuss the construction of participation (or inclusion) and transparency (or publicity) norms in various international regimes and institutions. We argue that these norms can effectively function as discourse norms in world politics. A major reason they are burgeoning within numerous international regimes and institutions is that norms of exclusion and secrecy, which effectively preclude access to discourse and vitiate the possibility of publicity, are now typically viewed as illegitimate by a substantial set of global political and social actors. Thus, we find that all sorts of institutional foundations are being altered to allow for greater participation and transparency in world politics. Once in place, these norms provide opportunities for transformative deliberative practices—decisions based on dialogue and consent rather than force and coercion.

The evidence explored in this book differs rather dramatically from the empirical insights pursued by constructivist IR scholars. Fortuitously, our research dovetails nicely with the other research by filling an important gap in the literature. Risse and Müller, for instance, may well find that state representatives successfully employ arguments in certain international negotiation contexts, or Checkel may be able to isolate argument structures by studying the content of micro-debates within agencies of the European Union.[73] However, their findings will be inherently limited because the specific contexts under scrutiny are relatively exclusive and secretive. Individual agents may experience an epiphany thanks to a specific persuasive argument, but the resulting norms would remain quite vulnerable to critical scrutiny. Some excluded non-state actors, for example, would almost surely find the results less than satisfactory, and their concerns could well be appropriate if agents were convinced in secret meetings by distorted arguments that would not withstand public scrutiny. By contrast, open public debate democratizes norm construction. Constructivists who claim that norms reflect "legitimate social purpose" should be keenly concerned about this point. As we wrote in the Introduction, our work attempts to build a bridge between relatively abstract critical theory and constructivism, in part by raising normative questions that should be central to any understanding of constructivist research.

In the end, our argument owes much to the critical theorist Dryzek, who searches for "incipient discursive designs" that might be taking hold in various institutional arenas—even in global politics.[74] Indeed, Dryzek argues that the international system provides a "golden opportunity for discursive designs" because there is no central world state to serve as a compelling authority.[75] Once a deliberative foothold is established, institutions are more readily viewed as legitimate, and they can act authoritatively on certain social and political issues. Logically, similar processes should begin to "invade" a variety of other institutional contexts since those would now be viewed as illegitimate. In this way, genuinely deliberative democracy might begin to permeate global politics.

2

International Regimes and Political Community

Introduction

In this chapter we argue that certain international regimes are in the process of becoming legitimate political communities. Drawing on Stephen D. Krasner's "consensus" definition of international regimes as "sets of implicit or explicit principles, norms, rules, and decision-making procedures around which actors' expectations converge in a given area of international relations," we depart from the discipline's practice of validating the efficacy of regime theory through substantive case study.[1] Instead, our argument is that some regimes constitute a public sphere that facilitates the emergence of legitimate global political community in various issue areas. In particular, those regimes incorporating procedural norms of transparency and participation foster a public sphere that creates appropriate conditions for open dialogue and inclusion that considerably enhance the prospects for emancipatory outcomes. It is our contention that these procedural norms are evident in institutionalized dialogical practice, and in the activities of nongovernmental organizations (NGOs) whose participation lends voice to excluded constituencies in global politics.

The first section of the chapter explores forms of political community found in international relations theory. The territorial state traditionally prevailed as the only legitimate form of community principally because it offered the closest approximation to matching national identity and territory in the European experience. Since the institutionalization of the State, the idea of political community anchored to territoriality has become a fixture in international political life. An alternative concept of community, however, is found at the level of "international society." Here, political community is constituted by states; thus, achieving the emancipatory aims of the critical project is constrained by the enduring tension between the order assured by sovereignty and the pursuit of justice. Finally, the growing literature on interdependence and integration offers a third version of "community," most recently the notion of security community explored by Emanuel Adler, Michael Barnett, and others.

The next section very briefly examines the literature on international regimes, arguing that neoliberal and neorealist accounts limit the transformative potential of this particular institutional form. Indeed, because of these limits the need for a critical theoretical approach outlined in chapter 1 is manifest. The purpose in offering a critical account is to formulate an alternative analysis of regimes according to the procedures whereby they are constituted. In particular, a critical method entails an analysis of discourse—who speaks, what they say, and the effects of their words. This requires understanding that the space within which discourse is occurring is a sphere of political and social action that constitutes and is constituted by identities and interests. For much of critical theory, seeking out the ideal speech conditions for these dialogic processes is a central task. However, scholars recognize that ideal conditions are implausible. Rather, the object is to attain a level of public interaction and communication that ensures an effective voice for relevant persons or groups so as to affirm the principle of inclusion. Interpreting regimes through discourse ethics and the role of nonstate actors, we believe, facilitates public accountability. Hence, the last section discusses international regimes as a form of political community with specific reference to these factors. The chapter concludes by linking our conception of regimes as political community to the procedural norms of transparency and participation, both of which are evident in the practice of discourse ethics.

International Community and World Politics

Political community in international relations is characterized by practices of inclusion and exclusion that accentuate differences among people and peoples. Consequently, those principles, values and ideals containing the potential for forging cosmopolitan bonds of loyalty and obligation across human communities are too often subordinated to the narrow interests of particular groups. Overcoming these practices is, according to Andrew Linklater, the central task of the next stage of the critical theoretical project.[2] The most common form of political community is the state. In theory and practice, states constitute an international system whose precise definition of citizens and aliens and conception of sovereignty and territoriality form the basis for rigid practices of inclusion and exclusion in the world polity. A second communal form is found in the idea of a society of states cohered by a system of international norms and moral principles. Yet this system engages in exclusion through references to "the standard of civilization" that distinguish modern societies from backward ones.[3] Andrew Linklater discusses a third type of political community anchored in a "moral conviction that individuals belong not only to their respective sovereign states, but to a more inclusive community of humankind."[4] This last form is most elusive, in part because of the enduring commitment to the prior two communal forms in both theory and practice. However, the normative implications of this third type have been expressed theoretically in the functionalist literature and, we shall argue, in practice through the formation of certain international regimes.

In the first instance, community as territorial state has its origins in ideas of citizenship and obligation, forged from the conflagration of warfare that determined not only the constitution of sovereign authority—struggles over the kind of units—but also its configuration, or boundaries of units as well.[5] A centralizing administrative apparatus facilitated the expansion of sovereign authority necessary to prosecute warfare successfully, and aided in the management of property rights and mobility of capital necessary to the spread of capitalism and economic growth.[6]

The effects of these materialist elements of sovereign nation-state building were reflected in ideas that wedded authority to the individual. As absolutism gave way to decentralized patterns of governance, the fusion of national identity and political community was expressed in terms of Rousseau's "general will" in which citizens possessed a collective interest in the well being of the community.[7] By making the citizen body the only legitimate "sovereign" of a political community, Rousseau drew a distinction between the people as "sovereign" and "government" as an agent of the popular will, thereby laying a foundation on which to build a collective consciousness that promoted responsible and moral citizenship through shared obligation.[8] With the spread of democratization and nationalism during the nineteenth century, the nation-state gradually acquired a "personality and character" that promoted particularist forms of political community.[9]

This theme is taken up in international theory by "communitarians" who assert that the individual, as a socially embedded agent, requires social context in order to develop a moral personality.[10] In this view, a state is morally relevant if "it protects, enhances or makes possible the national life that people value."[11] It becomes a place where the individual can realize fully her or his potential as a citizen by pursuing valued ends and goods that constitute a state's social tradition. It is this tradition, notes Molly Cochran, which provides and enables "the ethical discourse in which social judgements are possible."[12] Of course, not all states share the same traditions—nor may all states meet the criteria of moral relevancy, particularly those of a totalitarian vein. Yet, the community within each state is unique and therefore arrangements that satisfy this criterion are, too, particular.[13] Indeed, this particularism is, as Michael Walzer contends, the one commonality of humanity that makes sovereign borderlines, along which exclusive notions of political community can be formed, both natural and necessary to the conduct of international relations.[14]

Reconciling particularism was the purpose of post-World War II explorations of political integration and the formation of broader community pursued by functionalist writers such as David Mitrany, Ernst Haas, and Karl Deutsch.[15] In response to the nationalist sentiments that ignited the devastation of World Wars I and II, E.H. Carr urged a cautious attempt at forging functional organizations based on common principles.[16] The future order, he argued, was not to be a society of free and equal nations, but one built on the establishment of a freedom and equality that "will express themselves in the daily lives of men and women."[17] Carr was reluctant to endorse a careless internationalism, contending that the plea for "emancipation of the individual must not be interpreted as a plea for a sentimental and empty universalism."[18] Hence order could be realized through a balanced structure of international or multinational groupings for the maintenance of security and the development of geographical areas.[19]

This approach became the analytical core for writings on integration generated by Haas and Deutsch, whose notions of political community were actually anchored in different assumptions about politics. For Haas the kind of political community offered by neofunctionalism was the result of an intensely political process where institutional development preceded sentiments of community. This is because the refocusing of people's loyalties and attentions was a response to new international institutions. On the other hand, Deutsch described a sense of community as a "belief on the part of individuals in a group that they have come to agreement on at least this one point: that common social problems must and can be resolved by process of 'peaceful change.' "[20] Integration, which Deutsch argued might range from amalgamation—the formation of a common government among two or more previously independent units, to pluralism—in which units retain formal legal independence and separate decision-making centers, was dependent on the existence of a sense of community.

The distinction between Haas and Deutsch is significant, particularly in methodological terms. Haas explains a pluralist process involving "numerous political actors, pursuing their own interests, pressuring governments, or, if they are governments, pressuring one another to negotiate toward international policies that are collectively beneficial because they are individually beneficial for all concerned."[21] By contrast, Deutsch's approach argued that functional integration could not proceed effectively unless identities were reconfigured in such a way as to give meaningful purpose to new institutions. The weakness of the latter approach, as Donald Puchala suggests, is that "his formulation makes statements about people's attitudes and sentiments, individually and in the aggregate . . . [but] what remains undisclosed is how, when, and why changes at the social-psychological level are converted into changes at the governmental level."[22] There is, in other words, no articulation of how these sentiments, attitudes and dispositions originate, evolve and insinuate themselves into a political process.

The recent work of Emanuel Adler and Michael Barnett seeks to extend Deutch's argument by refining the conditions for the formation of security communities.[23] They employ a constructivist approach to understanding the circumstances under which states and their peoples will have "dependable expectations of peaceful change."[24] Mutual trust and collective identity formation are the core conditions fostering these expectations, deriving from structures of knowledge and power on the one hand, and processes such as transactions and social learning on the other. Yet their emphasis on security communities downplay what in our argument is a crucial element of community—channels for and patterns of interaction that facilitate the kind of access approximating democratic participation. In part, the formation of a security community can enable other modes of interaction, but the security community itself is not intentionally constructed for these other modes. Rather, to the degree that traditional security issues are of concern, the community described by Adler and Barnett remains state-centered with limited opportunities for the formation of civil society networks. In other words, security communities might help us to understand peaceful change among states, but do not offer insight into social processes that are necessary for the construction of transnational political community, which of necessity seeks to broaden participation beyond states to account for the needs of constituent populations.

In a less demanding vein is a view of political community as being bound to a society of states. Interactions within an international society are built around three principle tenets: the existence of common interests of states, of common rules accepted by states, and common institutions employed by states. The effective functioning of these principles facilitates the preservation of order in the international system.[25] The tradition thus encompasses a corpus of norms that foster a sense of community among those entities recognized to have fulfilled certain criteria. Historically, those criteria relied on a particular "standard of civilization" in which aspiring state members would be found to have achieved a degree of development justifying their inclusion in an international society—itself a dynamic construct that originated in Europe and expanded around the world.[26] An essential goal of this position is to find grounds on which to reconcile international order and justice within the sovereign states-system.[27]

Terry Nardin's description of an international society as a "practical association"—"a set of considerations to be taken into account in deciding and acting, and in evaluating decisions and actions"[28]—makes clear that the pursuit of social justice is something best undertaken on a local rather than global scale. The members of this association "share no common goals other than a desire to co-exist in peace and security" on the basis of accepted practices of international law and diplomacy.[29] Hence, the "practical association" of international society falls short of suggesting a transnational project building toward global political community. As Hedley Bull discusses, it is the normative character of the rules of this international society that identify states as the members who are competent to carry out political tasks within it. This fundamental rule distinguishes a society of states from other notions of community such as an empire, or a cosmopolitan community of human beings.[30]

Balancing a state-centered view of the world with order as a primary goal against a commitment to a progressive style of global politics fosters a unique tension in this perspective. On the one hand, threads of cosmopolitanism are evident in the discourse of human rights. Yet, this discourse is keenly aware of the principles of sovereignty that constitute international society. To assert a fundamental role for human rights in foreign policy is to subvert the very notion of order in that society.[31] Rhetorical references to the interests of an "international community" often serve to reconcile this tension by placating cosmopolitan aspirations while minimizing threats to the principle of non-intervention, a phenomenon that is frequently demonstrated in the realm of human rights.[32] But because advocates of an international society are much more concerned with order, the control of violence and threats to the existing system, than they are with fundamentally transforming that system by acting on rhetorical admonitions, the possibility of reconstituting political community on universal moral and ethical foundations is limited.

Alternative frameworks for thinking about new and evolutionary forms of political community in world politics are found in what Linklater refers to as "post-Westphalian" societies. This notion radically departs from the present, reflecting not only a commitment to shared moral and ethical values and the institutions through which these might be achieved, but also a decision to relinquish elements of sovereign power altogether.[33] Notions of power, territoriality, national identity and citizenship become subordinate to larger cosmopolitan commitments that transcend historic territorially-bound conceptions of community. Perhaps because its intellectual supporters imagine unprecedented global change, this theoretical abstraction currently seems of little use to the world of political practice.

Our argument certainly does not go so far. We seize the middle ground, between a pluralist and post-Westphalian international society, to argue that certain international regimes can be construed as emergent forms of political community.[34] Such a global society reflects an agreement among its state and non-state members on a set of moral principles and shared duties that they believe they should collectively promote. In Linklater's words, they work to achieve "some consensus about the substantive moral purposes which the whole society of states has a duty to uphold."[35] In contrast to a post-Westphalian order, a global society does not reflect the decay of sovereign authority per se, only the internalization of moral and ethical principles of conduct as expressed in international institutions. Such expressions are not inconsistent with territoriality and sovereignty, nor with the concept of political community advanced here, because political community can be rearticulated on foundations other than discrete boundary lines. In other words, on the basis of universal acceptance by state and non-state actors working together in an international regime, authoritative and legitimate principles are sufficient foundations for the emergence of political communities at a level of analysis other than the territorial state. While other criteria are required in order for one to make a claim for the presence of community—inclusion, democracy, and civil society, for example—the existence of a global society would be the necessary context to give that claim legitimacy.

As the scope of political community shifts from the nation-state, to an international society, to functional institutions and regimes that transcend the state, the very concept of community is increasingly lost from view. The prevalence of realism couples any meaningful idea of political community to the state, rendering other potential forms of community on the margins. Yet the growing attention devoted to interdependence, international organizations, and institutions offers alternative possibilities for conceptualizing world politics, recognizing, in particular, the growing role for social and economic processes and transnational actors beyond the reach of the state. As a consequence, Linklater has suggested that the bonds which tie people to the state are weakening as those elements that it once monopolized—war making, production and identity—are becoming reconfigured with the growth of subnational cultures and movements, the obsolescence of major power war, and globalization.[36] Rethinking international regimes reveals underlying transformations in the fundamental nature of world politics that reflect these new forms of political community.

Regimes and International Relations Theory

The debate between neoliberal and neorealist interpretations that dominates the discourse on international regimes has reenergized efforts to problematize the state and move away from the oversimplified presumption of states as unitary actors in international politics. Yet, neither approach has sufficiently discussed the potential for global political and social change as a result of the presence of certain regimes. For neorealists, the only "meaning" derived from a regime is the distribution of power among states and their respective interests.[37] Therefore, regimes are epiphenomenal forms of interstate interaction. States seeking to survive in an anarchic international system are not engaged in a fundamental reordering of global relations. Rather, they merely engage in the instrumental use of an institutional form.[38]

In contrast, neoliberal institutionalism aspires to explain international cooperation. In *Power and Interdependence*, Joseph S. Nye, Jr. and Robert O. Keohane described a world with "multiple channels of communication," embracing both the informal and formal links between societies.[39] At first glance, it would seem as if multiple and complex patterns and processes of international interaction could be decentering the prominent role ascribed to states in world politics. Keohane and Nye, however, have since lamented that their original "concept was left hanging" and was "bypassed or misinterpreted." Their greatest shortcoming, the authors concede, was accepting state-centric assumptions. They defined complex interdependence "in terms of the goals and instruments of state policy."[40] Keohane and Nye acknowledge that their utilization of system-unit concepts "weakened the prospects for deeper analysis of complex interdependence" and left it "incapable of being developed without relaxing the systemic perspective" so commonly applied.[41] Rather than advancing the study of transnational connections, *Power and Interdependence* ended up spawning neoliberal institutionalism, which emphasizes state cooperation in international organizations and regimes. In Keohane's later work, *After Hegemony*, the state clearly assumes a central role in explaining persistent patterns of international cooperation.[42] Other scholars, such as Mark Zacher, similarly note that networks of international regimes enmesh states and constrain their behavior.[43]

Recent scholarship, much of it by social constructivists, has sought to examine the role of "ideas" in transforming international politics. This literature has renewed interest in epistemic communities and transnational actors as important elements in explaining the emergence of global norms and institutions, and thereby penetrates the hard shell of the state.[44] Scholars developed these concepts to understand why actors, such as states, but also organizations and individuals, move from acting on their self interest to the detriment and expense of other actors, to sustaining cooperation, perhaps grounded in strongly held principles, between distinct and diverse nations and cultures. Emanuel Adler and Peter Haas, for example, argue that the rise of epistemic communities offers guidance in how preferred and alternative visions of world order are formed, and how these visions change in response to new technologies and understandings of cause-effect relationships.[45] Margaret Keck and Kathryn Sikkink suggest that the proliferation of "advocacy networks," by which they mean transnational relations motivated by shared values or principled ideas—beliefs about what is right or wrong—are altering and reconstituting understandings of the scope and limits of sovereignty, and, as a consequence, of sovereign practices.[46] In addition, Alexander Wendt has described the "internationalization of political authority" through a process of collective identity formation.[47]

These accounts go far in recognizing the possibility for change by moving away from the presumptions of stasis implied by Kenneth Waltz's structural theory.[48] Yet the scholarly work employing epistemic communities and transnational issue networks reflect what Andreas Hansenclever, Peter Mayer, and Volker Rittberger characterize as "weak cognitivist" approaches that, rather than presenting a fundamental attack on neoliberalism and realism, actually fill an "important theoretical gap by explaining preference and interest formation."[49] The epistemic communities model is, for example, dependent on the capacity of these knowledge-based communities to acquire influential bureaucratic positions within states or the international organizations they form.[50] In the case of global warming, Matthew Paterson notes that relevant groups' influence lacked staying power as members achieved only a "tenuous and erratic foothold in national bureaucracies," which in turn reduced their ability to influence negotiations.[51]

Transnational issue-networks work across state lines to reshape domestic practices, thereby potentially reflecting what Ronnie Lipschutz describes as the emergence of a kind of global civil society,[52] But Keck and Sikkink are reluctant to posit the existence of such a global civil society, and acknowledge only the presence of transnational actors, such as advocacy networks, which are involved in contentious struggles about their roles and goals.[53] Advocacy networks can contribute to the formation of new political communities, but their use of material levers and strategic framing raise important questions about the legitimacy of their actions.[54] Moreover, much of the work on transnational norm entrepreneurs highlights the influence of these agents on target states, both to construct new international norms and to affect domestic compliance.[55] While we agree that these networks are often important engines of change in an international society of states, our intent is to take this argument farther by outlining the potential for legitimate transnational political communities anchored in dialogic processes.

Wendt's constructivist account of the international system sometimes contains the possibility of transcending the state, but he seems reluctant to go too far, restricting the necessary shifts of identity to states rather than the variety of agents who participate in social life.[56] It is difficult to discern the degree to which the motives of states depart from strategically self-interested behavior (perhaps, especially, of ruling elites). As Keohane has argued, merely joining institutions is not the same as sharing the burdens of institutional goals. The gap between practice and fairness does not necessarily disappear with the "international state."[57] From these perspectives, then, the creation of an international regime or world state may constitute a rearticulation of sovereign authority, but apparently does not reflect an alternative notion of political community. The consequence is that these new descriptions of international relations offer outcomes that are, as John G. Ruggie contends, "substitutable for the state."[58] The patterns of authority may be partially reconfigured, but the individuality and the sanctity of the state, the states-system, or both are preserved. Thus, there is little reflection on the social possibilities engendered by the construction of communal interests or norms that could inform radically new regimes and institutions. Even worse, from our point of view, Wendt notes that "as states pool their de facto authority over transnational space, they remove it from direct democratic control."[59] This yields the so-called democratic deficit, which is the subject of much of our analysis of international regimes.

Neither neoliberalism nor neorealism have challenged their own foundational assumptions, nor has either sought to articulate mechanisms for fundamental changes in the nature of the international system. However, the search for political community in international regimes can express the idea of "social possibilities" by recognizing the capacities of agents—states, political networks, organizations and individuals—operating within a given social sphere, to reconfigure that sphere through dialogue and the collective commitments that result. It is our view that the critical approach outlined in the opening chapter, which explicitly seeks to challenge traditional modes of inquiry, can help us also to move beyond the conceptual limits of current debates about regimes to explore other modes of community that might be constituted within global politics.

International Regimes as Community

The international regime as a form of political community reflects a unique kind of global society that is capable of reconciling claims of sovereignty and moral universalism in the promotion of emancipatory goals. In other words, the norms and principles of certain regimes can reflect larger ethical and moral tenets that enhance human freedom and security. The procedures for agreeing about these principles must be inclusive in nature, for a fundamental assumption of a critical theoretical approach is that boundary lines provide illegitimate moral and ethical constraints. Any attempt at enhancing human freedom and security can only be achieved if practices of exclusion give way to a genuinely inclusive means for seeking consensual normative understandings. Mechanisms to express pain, injury, or injustice are essential to insuring that agreed principles are upheld. In one sense, this role is taken up increasingly by nongovernmental organizations. In another sense, and perhaps most significant for conceptualizing regimes as community, that accessibility or capacity to express voice is the cornerstone of democratic accountability.

A crucial distinction must be made, however, between the substantive issue areas regulated by regimes, and the democratic procedures potentially employed by those same institutional forms. Any given international regime could govern behavior in one of any number of diverse issue areas in world politics. Trade, transportation, nonproliferation, and communication, for example, have proven suitable subjects for international regulation. However, it is arguably even more important to recognize that the governance models employed by these various regimes may well differ dramatically. Each regime could have unique decision-making and accountability mechanisms. A critical perspective would identify and critique the procedures in these regimes through which power is exercised, discipline imposed, and stratification reinforced.[60] We argue in the next chapter that regimes employing certain dialogical procedures promote the construction of genuinely intersubjective understandings among the diverse members of a transnational society. The norms agreed in these regimes, we would argue, are more likely to reflect the global community's general interests and moral principles.

This is the essence of the emancipatory aim of a critical theoretical stance. Genuinely democratic decision-making provides the foundation of a cosmopolitan commitment, which is, as Janna Thompson notes, "the notion that there are values which everyone in the world ought to accept, whatever their personal interests or community loyalties."[61] This cosmopolitanism, however, must be responsive to communitarian concerns. Political institutions at the domestic level, for example, are arguably better positioned to assure the application of principles of justice. The challenge is a dual one. First, while it is necessary to articulate moral principles according to which world society might be ordered, regime-makers must remain conscious that those moral principles, however desirable, are not likely to be accepted as the basis for transnational political authority if local or particular identities and loyalties are threatened. The second challenge is that those political institutions constructed to promote a democratic global society will only succeed in building loyalties and bonds if they express the motivations and sentiments of people in particular communities.[62]

Thus the foundations for international regimes as political community can be established at the intersection of the institutional form and the articulation of applicable moral principles that promote what Thompson calls "world citizenship" through new political identities. It is not the existence of a regime that promotes emancipatory ideals that permits a claim to political community. Many types of functional regimes are already present in international relations.

Rather, genuine political community is reflected in a concern for the ways in which the political will to implement the principles come into existence:

> Cosmopolitans cannot be content with putting forward a moral position or with constructing blueprints for a cosmopolitan society. They must turn their attention to the creation of community. . . . Whatever form it takes, the political realization of cosmopolitan values will require that individuals come to identify with transnational communities in a way that so far has not happened. This does not mean that existing social commitments will have to whither away, but it does require that these other allegiances sometimes take a subordinate place in a global framework in which new loci of political authority become more prominent and are able to command support on crucial issues.[63]

New forms of political authority are essential to the emergence of global political community. But these authorities and the rules they offer must be internalized by actors in order to be perceived as legitimate. Rules should not merely arise from self-interest or coercion; indeed, the mode of internalization is a vital point for cosmopolitan claims.[64] Arguments for the presence of community rest on the degree to which political authority can be said to be legitimate across sovereign borderlines.[65] In this regard, deep and broad legitimation of principles capable of constructing community identities can occur through democratic processes that encourage individuals to "think as citizens and to take responsibility for the decisions that they have collectively made."[66] A world, or global, citizenship analogous to domestic conceptions of citizenship may well represent an unrealistically high standard for community, impossible to attain in a world of sovereign territorial states. But a notion of global citizenship defined by the duty to uphold consensually agreed principles would satisfy the cosmopolitan commitment to enhancing human freedom and security. It would extend the boundaries of community beyond the territorial state for the defense of general interests, such as protecting human rights or the natural environment.[67]

The practice of citizenship, however, occurs within a specific space or sphere of action that offers opportunities for inclusive participation and representation in open debate. In international relations, one potentially exciting institutional form of this space is the regime, which as an entity acquires the characteristics of a political community by virtue of the dialogic and participatory processes it can make possible. Put differently, international regimes can serve as public spheres, depending upon the norms that constitute them.

According to Mark Lynch, "a public sphere approach builds on a conception of action in which a public claim on identity or an argument made in the public sphere is an action."[68] The public sphere itself is "that site of interaction in which actors routinely reach understandings about norms, identities, and interests through the public exchange of discourse."[69] For James Bohman, the modern public sphere is distinguished by its role as a site for social and cultural criticism, and as a unique form of communication across a diverse audience.[70] This audience, according to Bohman, need not be individuals, but can instead be participants of representative institutions or transnational civil society. The nature of the audience is significant because global democracy cannot be expected to assume the same participatory requirements as the domestic democratic practice of one-person, one-vote. Lynch further elaborates on the global-domestic difference by distinguishing between a public sphere for deliberation and a political subsystem for decisions and administering their enforcement. In the international realm, no structure exists to impose decisions; rather public spheres serve "as locations for norm formation, and for deliberation over the shared interests of international communities."[71] The weight of the public sphere follows not from enforcement mechanisms to ensure that states are complying with agreed upon rules and norms, but from the creation and maintenance through deliberation of consensual norms. Lynch notes that not all deliberation will be free of strategic interests, but as he argues:

> The point is not to find interest-free, power free behavior but rather to identify the conditions under which the need for public justification oriented toward shared norms, goals or identity produces behavior different from behavior absent such demands. . . . The more that a public sphere provides the expectation of ongoing deliberation, and the greater the sense of belonging to shared identity and institutions, the more that states must justify their behavior with reference to shared norms.[72]

Jennifer Mitzen maintains that international public spheres have transformative potential by virtue of the solidarity generated among a diverse group of actors. This sense of community, forged through public deliberation, reconfigures authority in world politics. Accountability in a global public sphere, indeed its inclusive and democratic character, is achieved through publicity of both a direct and mediated mode.[73] The former entails state-to-state discussion while the latter is, for Mitzen, "what turns a decision-making or political group into a public sphere . . . by expanding the critical audience for state actions and for decision-maker arguments."[74] The patterns of mediated publicity facilitate the participation of global civil society actors such as NGOs in processes of global governance in a variety of forms, such as agenda setting, articulating ideas and knowledge about goals and practices, or monitoring and revealing compliance (and noncompliance).

We believe that an international regime can serve as a public sphere featuring dialogic processes intended to establish shared rules, norms, and principles for governing a specific issue area of world politics. Such a regime is potentially a viable political community within which its state members and non-state affiliates jointly express and defend higher principles. In broad terms, our argument is concerned with the prospects and potentialities of change in the international system, recognizing in particular the capacity of actors other than states to constitute and reconstitute the social structures within which they exist.[75]

The challenge is to reconceptualize traditional notions of political community. There is a difference, for example, between political community defined by bounded political institutions and structures of governance one finds in discrete municipalities or territorial states, and a political community where such boundaries are irrelevant to the identity central to the meaning of community. Indeed, the presence of discrete boundary lines often has little connection to communities contained within, as evinced by the numerous instances of ethnic conflict in Africa, Asia, and the Balkans. In cases of ethnicity or religion, forms of community transcend boundary lines. It is in this sense that a critical theoretical approach can argue for the evolution of alternative forms of political community to that provided by the state. Institutions and the ideas that inform them have the capacity to foster loyalties to and identities with emerging normative principles of global life, and can thus be the basis for defining an alternative notion of political community in world politics.

The possibility of constructing new boundaries of community that are anchored in moral and ethical principles, that recognize and account for diversity, that engender transcultural sympathies, and that give voice to those on the margins within and across territorial units, is found in commitments to the "ideal of a universal communication community."[76] In synthesizing Kantian cosmopolitanism with Marx's revolutionary project, Linklater identifies the progressive force of modernity residing in dialogic processes, as formulated by Habermas:

> Collaboration across the frontiers to produce arrangements which are more universalistic, more sensitive to cultural differences and more committed to reducing social and economic inequalities than their predecessors is entailed by commitments to domination-free communication. A global narrative of universal emancipation which aims at this, the triple transformation of political community, is immanent within the dialogic ideal.[77]

The Habermasian emphasis on dialogue and communicative action is an essential quality of the "thin universalism" of political community. This kind of universalism is not about inscribing absolute ethics or morals onto the practices and principles of what might constitute the "good life." Rather, it is about insisting on the condition whereby all voices have the opportunity to be heard, where dialogic engagement permits an expanding range of difference to be incorporated into discussions "to determine the principles of inclusion and exclusion which govern global politics."[78]

In practice, this dialogue can be facilitated by NGOs, social movements, and their transnational networks, which often provide voice to those on the margins and thereby bridge the divide between local experience and global process. Indeed, it is in these observable patterns of contemporary global politics that new forms of community consistent with a "thin universalism" may be taking shape. The international regime, viewed as a public sphere, fostering an expression of principles that govern relations of global society, is a reflection of the kind of dialogic potential inherent in the practice of world politics. These institutions evolve from discursive and ideational interaction among state and nonstate state actors that provide the rationales for the need to regulate spheres of global life.[79] Interestingly, John S. Dryzek argues that these kinds of discursive designs should be more readily developed in global politics, rather than in domestic contexts, because of the opportunity provided by international anarchy.[80] In domestic politics, the state can hierarchically impose all sorts of arbitrary barriers to open and inclusive discussion. No ultimate authority can similarly restrict global possibilities.

The democratic potential of international regimes, as Bohman notes, is in their location as "a political space in which effective freedom emerging in the public sphere and civil society can be exercised transnationally." Furthermore, these institutions legitimate principles that ensure voice through direct and mediated publicity thereby creating what Bohman calls an "egalitarian distributive effect: they can at least widen the range of political actors with access to influence."[81] By providing a public sphere for what amounts to growing networks of transnational associations, international regimes strengthen a global civil society within which actors advance or oppose ideas, values, and principles through argument. The ideas debated and justified directly and in a mediated form can undergird principled norms, once these are identified.[82] Hence, the international regime that is a public sphere acquires the quality of a community within which civil society networks can extend participation and inclusion in search of cosmopolitan principles, thereby moving towards a global democratic ideal.

A fully developed conception of a regime as political community hinges on an essential question: how are standards of universal moral foundations and universal inclusion attained? We offer a two-part answer. First, Habermasian discourse ethics provides a useful means to explore processes whereby contending principles can be harmonized and legitimized. And second, the role of global civil society networks operating within the public spheres created by regimes serve as a mechanism for representation, internalization and implementation of principles in the absence of universal democracy.

Discourse Ethics

Establishing the necessary principles on which to build community entails a kind of engagement where the outcome is regarded as consensual rather than coercive. A consensual outcome presupposes a recognition of, and accounting for diversity, the engendering of transcultural sympathies, and the provision of voice to those on the margins. As Linklater argues, the construction of commitments that satisfy those ends are found in the "ideal of a universal communication community" that reflects the dialogic potential inherent in modernity's emancipatory project.[83]

The dialogic ideal of which Habermas writes is oriented to the validation of norms through the force of the better argument. In the so-called "ideal speech situation," no moral position or no person can be arbitrarily excluded from participation, for the purpose is to "create social arrangements which meet with the consent of all."[84] Indeed, the establishment of a communicative procedure for building intersubjective agreement allows Habermas "to claim universal applicability for his thesis in the belief that, in being value-free, it is sensitive to cultural difference, while providing the possibility of reaching rational consensus through the force of the better argument."[85] Democratic deliberation is intended to identify those principles through unconstrained participation that can be generalized without sacrificing difference and diversity. In other words, because norms have been consensually agreed by "those affected in their capacity as participants in a practical discourse," they are legitimate.[86]

In this regard, two important constraints on the application of a discourse ethic appear. One is in the form of the assumption of the difficulty of achieving an ideal speech situation and the other is in the normative judgement implied by the procedure itself. Lynch and Mitzen, for example, separately highlight the first constraint, by noting that public spheres contain elements of communicative and strategic action. Deliberation is a truth-seeking exercise, and if participants, especially powerful ones, are intentionally evasive, secretive, or manipulative, then the dialogue may well not produce the desired result. The challenge, as Neta Crawford suggests, is to expand communicative action while limiting strategic action.[87] Two responses follow from her suggestion. First, the context in which dialogue occurs is reconstituted by interaction. A discursive context, in other words, is what the participants make of it. Actors are not fixed in their perception of interests and identities, they are reflexive agents capable of responding to reasoned arguments in such a manner as to promote understandings in accordance with collectively defined and evolving norms. Individuals may move from strategic towards communicative action in the process of dialogue. The dialogue itself can facilitate this transformation since some participants in an inclusive discussion are apt to challenge the truth and veracity of strategically-motivated claims. Secondly, the expectation of absolute consensus derived from an ideal speech situation is, as Charles Beitz argues, "too stringent a requirement to place on the justification of moral principles."[88] And, indeed, to the degree that a basic consensus can be secured on abstract foundational moral goals, their particular application should be expected to vary according to specific cultural and social contexts. That is the essence of a discourse ethics that seeks to reconcile universalism with particularism, a practice that has, in fact, informed contemporary debates on issues such as human rights and sustainable development.

The second constraint entails limits on the capacity of actors to participate in dialogue in various contexts, including formal political institutions and processes and civil society networks. Linklater notes, for example, that discourse ethics can be realized only in societies that are sensitive to the diversity of forms of life.[89] While noting that Western liberal democracy is one model that can accommodate this sensitivity, Linklater suggests that many other systems of governance may also be capable of this standard of inclusion. However, societies that tolerate extreme inequalities, which practice exclusion on any number of criteria, such as race, religion, or ethnicity, are not capable of participating in the dialogic ideal.[90] At issue then is the existence of other types of governance systems beyond the liberal democratic model that can satisfy the standard of freedom and participation in social and political life sufficient to approximate a dialogic ideal.

Here, it is necessary to make a distinction in discourse ethics between "moral questions, which can in principle be decided rationally in terms of criteria of justice or the universalizability of interests," and "evaluative questions, which fall into the general category of issues of the good life and are accessible to rational discussion only within the horizon of a concrete historical form of life or an individual life style."[91] Though the latter set of questions reflect particular issues and interests within a private sphere, they are not inseparable from the moral questions settled in a public sphere that, by protecting the individual, necessarily protect the well-being of the community to which he or she belongs. This differentiation offers an opportunity to reformulate the role of discourse ethics in the constitution of a political community.

If an international regime provides a public sphere within which argumentation and norm testing can occur, the new norms in need of validation can be held up against the prevailing normative framework and evaluated against the moral criteria appropriate for particular contexts. Some skeptical discussions of discourse ethics fail to address adequately the role of international institutions and the plurality of actors operating at both the local and global level. Charles Rustin, for instance, emphasizes the necessity of a transition from a mythical conception of politics to a global liberal democratic society before universal norms such as social justice and human rights can effectively be realized. However, specific international regimes are already providing contexts for debate, argumentation, and transmission of consensual principles. And the growth of nongovernmental organizations and transnational social movements is serving to couple the moral principles articulated at the global level to concrete experience at the local level, often challenging where necessary the low standards of freedom and participation in social and political life found in many domestic contexts. These efforts meet with mixed success, and the kind of communicative conditions regimes provide are not necessarily ideal in the Habermasian sense. Yet, inclusion of non-state actors enhances the legitimacy of international regimes. Their participation is therefore the most effective means at hand in contemporary world politics to give voice to the marginalized and to build cosmopolitan democracy essential to new modes of political community.

Transnational Civil Society

The role of non-state actors in world politics is well established in the complex interdependence literature. More recently, however, interdependence has given way to explorations of a global civil society that Paul Wapner describes as "that slice of associational life that exists above the individual and below the state, but also across national boundaries."[92] For Wapner, this realm of civil society is composed of institutional and ideational structures that are constitutive of intersubjective understandings. Therefore, following the constructivist argument, global civil society shapes transnational social practices and is, in turn, shaped by those practices. Ronnie D. Lipschutz notes that the spatial boundaries of this civil society are different from those of the state. They are "delineated by networks of economic, social and cultural relations, and they are being occupied by the conscious association of actors, in physically separated locations, who link themselves together in networks for particular political and social purposes."[93]

Of course, the existence of transnational civil society networks is not, in itself, sufficient reason to forecast the development of global democratic political community. Christoph Görg and Joachim Hirsch, for example, describe the role of NGOs in international political processes as "soft," meaning that these groups merely engage in lobbying, consultation and the dissemination of information. Additionally, the role and influence of NGOs hinges on the cooperative will of state apparatuses.[94] Other skeptics note that these global civil society organizations proliferate in only a limited number of issue areas (the environment, human rights, and developmental rights, for example). Worse, the groups and networks themselves lack democratic accountability and therefore popular legitimation. Though claiming to act on behalf of the global good, in many instances, NGOs are seen as elitist organizations that effectively reproduce relations of social and political power. This is particularly the case in regards to the transnational corporation as a form of NGO and its representative agents participating in negotiations over issues related to, for example, property rights, trade, and investment. On any given issue area, nongovernmental organizations can acquire the character of what Emery Roe calls "artificial negativity," giving the appearance of opposition though ultimately reinforcing elitist and technobureaucratic governance institutions of the existing political-economic order.[95] Thus, as Blaney and Pasha contend, a true global democratic society entails "resisting not only the oligarchical organization of global life, but also the impulse to rectify that situation with a prefigured set of global values sponsored by the transnational extensions of actors from advanced industrial societies."[96] Viewed in this way, global institutions and regimes are inherently antidemocratic and unable to pursue genuine democratic community even in the face of countervailing pressures from an array of nonstate actors.

These criticisms raise serious issues about the validity of relying on NGOs and civil society networks to ensure representative practices at the global level. Yet, the growing recognition of these criticisms, together with some serious self-assessment, has led to some promising new initiatives by NGOs. This is increasingly evident in the formulation of codes of conduct by NGO collectivities that seek to address relations on several dimensions: between Northern and Southern groups and global and local organizations, and among civil-society, state, and international institutions.[97] Moreover, the growth of NGOs and their enhanced capacity to network, both globally and locally, generates an extensive scope of countersystemic pressure, which Görg and Hirsch associate with real democratic potential.[98] For example, outcomes of the Uruguay Round of trade negotiations reflected less an overwhelming transnational corporate power promoting extensive commercial globalization than it did a "patchy and uneven triumph of private authority" that was often subject to broader social interests.[99] And the campaign against the Multilateral Agreement on Investment was greatly facilitated by alliances and information generated through technologies such as the internet.[100] In other words, the diversity of NGO goals, structures, resources, and modes of action contributes to patterns of democratization in global politics.[101] Furthermore, critics like Görg and Hirsch acknowledge that a form of democratization is realizable in international regulatory organizations—as long as these entities embrace procedural reforms that foster broader inclusion of previously unexpressed interests and voices.[102] Blaney and Pasha, who are similarly skeptical about the development of transnational civil society, likewise emphasize the need for an inclusive "global conversation and global deliberations," as a means to overcome the obstacles imposed by existing governance networks.[103] In effect, NGOs and global civil society networks, while operating within a particular political economy, have the potential to serve as effective voices of reform and democratization given procedural transformations within international regulatory networks.[104] This is likewise our central point—procedural norms that enhance open and inclusive debate are significant because they allow an increasing number of voices with more diverse goals and geographic representation to be expressed.

The associational relations that give effect to a global civil society function at the local, national and global level, signifying the existence of multiple public spaces within which dialogic engagement can occur. What differentiates this civil society from political community is the role of a specific institutional form—the regime—that can serve as a "web of meaning" whose norms and principles cohere and give purpose to this diverse group of actors. International regimes express specific principles agreed by states and thereby serve as a public sphere for a discourse by those states. The genuine inclusion of nonstate actors in the dialogue democratizes and legitimizes the regime and thereby helps build global community. The agreement of states to certain principles of conduct is in and of itself not novel; it is the inclusive participation of NGOs and other actors ordinarily excluded that is significant for the emergence of political community. On the one hand, regimes are constructed, in part, by the efforts of associational networks of civil society. On the other hand, regimes also mobilize, enhance and legitimize the activities of these networks by promoting public and inclusive discourse. The consequence of these relations is to strengthen global democracy arguments based on the "cascading effect" of regimes. Bohman, among others, argues that the lack of (or unwillingness of states to support) centralized international institutions has led to a network of decentralized governance structures—to governance without government:

> As the product of political activity at various levels, regimes provide the basis for a democratic process of institutionalization. Once implemented, further institutions are needed to monitor and organize compliance and cooperation. . . . Moreover, the procedures that these regimes [human rights and rights of the child] have established "are open to public inspection and to NGO influence in both standard setting and monitoring." . . . Thus the democratizing effect of regimes

> is not directly the content or even the control over global processes that they produce. Rather it is that they create new structures of accountability and locations for the exercise of political influences and the regulatory effects of accountability.[105]

Thus, in the interpretive struggles over the kinds of issues to be regulated, how they should be regulated, and the moral quality of the norms and principles it embodies, "the regime itself reflects the intermingling of aspirations belonging to decentered local actors represented by civil society networks as well as the goals of particular states."[106]

It is through the mode of dialogic engagement that these associations can be said to facilitate the kinds of collective identity that fosters transnational obligation, raising consciousness and providing a voice to those on the margins of social, economic, and political life. An active politics of argumentation and mobilization represents a shift toward a global politics of inclusion and representation. Indeed, as Warren Magnusson suggests, it is the drawing together and connecting of diverse local peoples in a common purpose that redefines political community.[107] Absent this nexus, the expression of norms and principles at the global level would have little effect on the concrete experience of local communities or networks of NGOs.

NGOs and social movements additionally serve a unique discursive function in world politics by facilitating the socialization of ethical norms articulated at the global level into domestic practices. Thomas Risse has examined this process in the human rights issue area. Specifically, he applies communicative, or as he prefers, "argumentative," rationality to the internalization of norms.[108] The existence of a common lifeworld among actors is acknowledged as an important prerequisite for such internalization because it "provides arguing actors with a repertoire of collective understandings to which they can refer when making truth claims."[109] As Risse notes, given the diversity of political, social, economic, and cultural systems, there is little at the global level to identify the existence of a common lifeworld. But at the same time, in those areas of international life where there are some common frameworks of understanding or mutually understood foundational moral principles, there may exist the minimum conditions for a common lifeworld. Risse contends:

> A high degree of international institutionalization might substitute for the absence of a "common lifeworld" in terms of a common history and language providing a crucial background condition for argumentative behavior. . . . From a communicative perspective they [international institutions] also create a normative framework structuring interaction in a given issue area. They often serve as fora or arenas in which international policy deliberation can take place.[110]

Two additional conditions for successful argumentative rationality are the existence of a public sphere and the need to recognize actors as equals. In the first instance, we have already discussed that the framework established by an international regime, in which certain procedural norms and principles are secured, provides a public sphere for nongovernmental actors to assert arguments in an institutionalized context. The latter condition, however, is more problematic in a state system. Nonetheless, as the practical experience of various NGOs and social movements demonstrates, over time and in a given context, the relationship between states and non-state actors can evolve to overcome inequalities in deliberation. NGOs often do have at their disposal the power to mobilize global opinion, media attention, and consciousness, and state actors eventually begin to respond to their arguments as the norms defended acquire greater validity in particular contexts.[111] The transformation of the character of the dialogue from rhetorical exchange to true argumentative rationality is a reflection of the "civilizing effects" of public deliberation.[112]

The role NGOs serve as a nexus between local and global politics and society is therefore crucial to an argument that regards these associations as a form, albeit rudimentary, of global democracy. For example, John Boli and George Thomas place them at the core of a world polity perspective.[113] In this view, NGOs contribute to a world culture characterized by similarities in the way in which "definitions, principles and purposes are cognitively constructed . . . throughout the world," and in its universality, or the fact that certain goals are said to be applicable everywhere: economic development, schooling, healthcare.[114] As these scholars argue, a form of diffuse world citizenship is embedded implicitly in the cognitive framework of this world polity and culture. The explicit expression of this citizenship is found in the body of agreements, conventions, and covenants that articulate rights and protections for individuals. The tension that inheres between states and world citizenship principles can be reconciled by NGOs, which help translate "diffuse global identity and authority of world citizenship into specific rights, claims, and prescriptions for state behavior."[115] World citizenship thus endures on the basis of common needs and obligations, infusing "each individual with the authority and agency to pursue particularistic interests, preferably in organizations, while also authorizing individuals to promote collective goods defined in largely standardized ways."[116]

In a similar vein, James Rosenau describes the emergence of a nonterritorial "Globalized Space," "created by the lessened governance capacity of states and the growing porosity of the boundaries separating local, national and international affairs." In this new sphere of politics, the global polis, "processes of representation and responsibility normally associated with (territorially anchored) democratic institutions are of little relevance." Thus, under conditions of decentralized governance structures and nonterritorial politics, democratic modes of participation can be sustained through what Rosenau calls "functional equivalents," such as nongovernmental organizations and social movements.[117] NGOs and global civil society networks expand the boundaries of inclusion. They partake in a public sphere institutionalized by the international regime, laying the foundation for new political communities anchored in shared concerns for the well-being of humanity.

Conclusion

This chapter sought to outline a conception of regimes as legitimate global political community. A legitimate political community features consensual norms and principles that have been openly debated by all relevant members of global society. We argued that by conceptualizing certain regimes as public spheres it is possible to apply and interpret practices of discourse ethics to this institutional form. The consequence is that these regimes are in the process of generating an alternative type of political community to that anchored in the territorial state. Both the potential for and transformative effects of dialogue within this sphere offer participants the opportunity to articulate emancipatory principles. This becomes increasingly likely as regime legitimacy means accounting for the needs and interests of vast segments of the global polity whose interests might otherwise be excluded. We do not suggest that the ideal of global democracy has been attained, only that the international regime provides a plausible current institutional form to realize these goals.

Legitimate regimes must incorporate certain foundational procedural norms that insure the promotion of a discourse ethical dialogue constituted by principles of inclusion. We specifically argue in chapter 3 that the effective incorporation of participation and transparency procedural norms in a regime makes meaningful and democratic deliberation in this public space possible. These practices allow the global community to foster collectively defined goals whose protections extend across borderlines and cultures. In the absence of participation and transparency, the substantive principles of international regimes too often promote exclusion and thereby enhance the needs and interests of one actor or group over others. Such an outcome is detrimental to the promotion of human freedom and security that is the essence of the critical theoretical project. The minimal conditions for the existence of a legitimate global political community that seeks to advance emancipatory ends are realizable only by the institutionalization of democratic procedures that secure public accountability.

3

Participation and Transparency Norms

Introduction

In the previous chapter we argued that certain international regimes could serve as public spheres and thereby reflect emerging forms of international political community. These new political communities are characterized by discourse ethical practices, including the participation of nongovernmental organizations and transnational social movements in open discussions about important global issues. In this chapter we extend this reasoning by arguing that the incorporation of the procedural norms of participation and transparency embody a more fundamental norm of publicity in international regimes. As international regimes build publicity into their processes, the opportunities for inclusive, open and equitable dialogue among the full range of actors in world politics are enhanced considerably. Thus, publicity is essential to making international regimes more democratically accountable than they have ever been. Ultimately, we believe the effective application of the norms that constitute publicity are a precondition to realizing cosmopolitan aspirations and a global emancipatory politics of the sort implied in new, legitimate forms of political community.

The concept of publicity has garnered increasing attention from international relations scholars of late. It is an often unrecognized but nonetheless crucial factor for critical theorists who emphasize communication under ideal conditions as a prerequisite to reflection, understanding, and social progress. Jennifer Mitzen explains the normative and practical importance of publicity, noting that as it expands in a social system, "everything can be seen and nothing is off limits to outside assessment. Publicity allows actors to constitute events as shared problems and to form opinions on what should be done."[1] James Bohman similarly argues that publicity can create conditions for meaningful public input and accountability in international contexts.[2] Indeed, he calls for new "norms of cosmopolitan publicity" to facilitate democratic accessibility and responsibility within international agreements or regimes.[3] Publicity can even help overcome the problems associated with large material differences in power among different actors, which Andrew Linklater and others identify as a significant international barrier to genuinely inclusive political action.[4] As Thomas Risse explains, "the more an issue is subject to public scrutiny the more likely it becomes that materially less privileged actors have access to the discourse and that their arguments carry the day and convince an audience."[5] As a norm, then, publicity requires that processes and policies are open to public participation and inquiry, thereby permitting interested and affected actors to contribute to substantive debates.

Attaining this ideal at the global level is problematic, to be sure. Unlike the domestic realm where constitutions and courts, at least in democracies, can ensure a high degree of public access to institutions, international politics traditionally features participation only by nation-states. Yet, the gap between articulating emancipatory goals at the global level and their implementation at the local level is gradually being filled by civil society networks whose growing capacities enable them to represent disaffected segments of the global polity. It is our contention that achieving more democratic global politics requires an institutional form, such as the regime, and the incorporation of norms of publicity that provide for participation and transparency. In this way, movement toward the global democratic ideal symbolizing the construction of new modes of political community can be realized.

We begin this chapter by defining what we mean by participation and transparency norms and then overview their development in a broad array of issue areas. We argue that burgeoning norms of participation and transparency, which are clearly present in various global institutions and regimes, reflect norms of publicity and the emergence of Habermasian communicative rationality in world politics. Thus, they not only help make possible the construction of legitimate international regimes, but they also promote the conditions whereby these regimes acquire the character of new forms of political community. The brief empirical sections offer examples to illustrate the real-world potential of discursive designs, though we should note that these do not serve as scientifically selected empirical cases suitable for testing hypotheses. Chapters 4 and 5 focus on more thorough case illustrations.

Following the discussion of issue areas, the next section of the chapter addresses the so-called "bootstrapping" problem. Many scholars have pointed out the dilemma of developing and promoting Habermasian norms in political and social settings that do not already meet his ideal conditions. In this case, how can norms of publicity be constructed legitimately, given that existing international institutional arrangements often lack the kind of participatory channels and equitable access required of global democratic processes? Indeed, as James Bohman notes, norms of publicity are most urgently needed in those institutions and issue areas where the opportunity to shape decisions is most limited.[6] Resolving this dilemma demands reflection on the nature of global politics and, in particular, the potential efficacy of those nonstate actors who are most likely to challenge exclusionary practices. However, this issue is discussed in the abstract since, unlike positivist constructivist accounts, it is not our purpose to demonstrate that specific normative changes followed from political campaigns led by NGO networks. Empirical investigation of this question is a task for supplemental research projects.

Finally we conclude by exploring the relationship between transparency and participation norms and their contribution to a meaningful public sphere. Ideally a public sphere assures public accountability and access for all interested potential participants. We reiterate our belief that international institutions and regimes constructed so as to assure publicity generate patterns of dialogic engagement and inclusion essential to new forms of political community.

Participation and Transparency Norms

In the following two subsections, we explain what we mean by norms of participation and transparency. As will be evident from the discussion below, these norms are closely related—the effectiveness of one generally requires the incorporation of the other in an international regime. No claim about global democracy can be credible without participatory decision-making. For participation to be meaningful and substantive, actors must have access to information and decision processes, as implied by transparency. Similarly, the value of transparency is realized when actors are able to utilize information and observation to effect outcomes.

Participation Norms

Historically, of course, international politics has been viewed as the near-exclusive domain of nation-states. Theoretically there has developed a continuum of sorts to account for the relevant actors in world politics. At one end are realists who have traditionally argued that scholars should study the world as it is, rather than as it perhaps ought to be. Therefore, they and most other IR scholars focused almost all their attention on the interests and behavior of states. Only nation-states, for instance, possess sovereignty, wield military power, and engage in warfare. These sovereign states, on a very basic level, can reasonably be viewed as the central "participants" in world politics. In fact, a relatively small number of materially powerful states tend to dominate international politics, typically using their coercive strength to shape important outcomes to their liking. As Kenneth Waltz writes, "The theory, like the story, of international politics is written in terms of the great powers of an era. . . . [They] set the scene of action for others as well as themselves."[7] Thus the domain of world politics is characterized by exclusion—not only in terms of privileging powerful over weak states, but also in practices that deny the relevance of persons and groups. Indeed, this exclusion was historically institutionalized in the form of international law, which, on the one hand reflected the needs and interests of the most powerful states and, on the other hand, assigned legal standing only to sovereign states.

Closer to the other end of the continuum are neoliberals who also accept the centrality of the state but emphasize the importance of international institutions in the regulation of world politics. Within these institutions, power is acknowledged to assume distinct forms and to vary asymmetrically across issue areas.[8] Hence, Saudi Arabia is an influential state when it comes to petroleum politics even though it found itself dependent on a coalition of American backed forces to protect it from the apparent threat of Iraqi invasion in 1990–1991. In a world increasingly reliant on international institutions, participation has come to imply the regular inclusion of all states, weak and powerful, in the formation of universally applicable rules, norms and principles. To a lesser extent, neoliberals recognize the contributions of nonstate actors to world politics, particularly their role in constructing, monitoring and changing international regimes or norms. In the most inclusive version of this perspective, reflected perhaps in the complex interdependence literature, participation means that virtually all parties with a stake in an outcome utilize multiple channels of contact to pursue their own interests and to make "government policies in various countries more sensitive to one another."[9]

Yet, neoliberal theories have not been particularly concerned with the transformative potential of institutions, regarding them in instrumental terms as solutions to the failure of political markets. Their sense of inclusion extends to all relevant states and not only the most powerful ones, but neoliberal thinking about even international political economy remains centered on the mutual vulnerability of interdependent states. Moreover, the means of participation and the nature of the outcomes continue to be defined primarily by material levers. Finally, though neoliberals account for a role for nonstate actors, including influential transnational corporations, and though this represents an important contribution to IR discourse, neoliberals are not inclined to remove these actors from the shadow of the state and the national economy.[10] In effect, participation of the sort that strengthens global democratic practices can only be realized if special consideration is given to the idea of a global civil society, which functions with a high degree of autonomy from the state. In the absence of such autonomy, networks of NGOs cannot truly represent the interests of persons and groups; rather, they come to be seen as instruments of the state system itself.

It is the case, in fact, that on any given issue a wide array of social and political actors are concerned about whatever happens in global politics and would want to have some say in these matters if they could. In this regard, critical IR theorists like Linklater note that overlooking and silencing the diverse array of actors affected by a decision is clearly unjust and perpetuates structures of domination.[11] Indeed, as explained earlier, exclusive and nonconsensual international decision processes are illegitimate and potentially unsustainable over the long haul as the disaffected challenge prevailing norms that undermine their sense of freedom and security.

Obviously, the possible participation of nonstate actors with global interests, such as transnational nongovernmental organizations, poses a quite interesting question. How can these nonstate actors participate meaningfully in global politics that are apparently dominated by powerful nation-states (and to a lesser extent by affluent corporations)? The response to this query depends, at least in part, on the findings of some recent innovative empirical work. Through the past decade or so, numerous scholars have been documenting a tremendous amount of global political activity by a wide array of nonstate actors.[12] The literature on the "new transnationalism" builds on work from the 1970s that often focused on the global reach of corporations.[13] The latest empirical literature, however, highlights the impressive and growing involvement of NGOs, especially social movements and nonprofit organizations, in numerous international regimes and formal institutions.[14] The scope of NGO political activity now extends widely across the gamut of regime and norm-building processes, ranging from lobbying and protesting efforts in the agenda-setting stage, to information gathering, and to monitoring treaty compliance.[15] Furthermore, participation norms legitimize the activities of NGOs in the implementation of regime goals—humanitarian efforts, local human rights representation, and sustainable development tasks, are all undertaken by literally thousands of nongovernmental actors throughout the world. While research on NGO political activity tends to focus on the global influence of organizations headquartered primarily in affluent states, it is worth noting that there has been a similar boom in recent years in the number and variety of NGOs that have formed in the Global South.[16] Use of new information technologies, especially by groups headquartered in the Global South, allows NGOs to stretch their scarce material resources much further than they otherwise might.[17] Bisi Ogunleye of the Country Women Association of Nigeria noted that:

> In 1969 . . . most governments just viewed the NGOs in their traditional role of voluntary support. In 1995 . . . the role of NGOs has been transformed worldwide, especially in the developing countries. Today NGOs are the ones giving impetus to processes of social change and economic change in many parts of the world. Even in the UN itself, NGOs are no longer mere silent observers or transmitters of information. They have become relevant political actors.[18]

Many of these actors have even become directly and indirectly involved in world politics as evinced by their growing role in various regime issue areas. For example, the number of international NGOs dedicated strictly to human rights has grown from 103 in 1970 to 325 in 1996.[19] The number of NGOs granted consultative status by the UN's Economic and Social Council (ECOSOC) rose from forty-one in 1948 to approximately one thousand in 1992. An important indicator of the mobilization capacity of these networks is the fact that over 1,500 organizations attended the NGO forum at the June 1993 Vienna World Conference on Human Rights, while more than 9,000 organizations participated in the UN Conference on Environment and Development in 1992.[20] The growth reflects both the formation of coalitions and communication linkages within and across states, and the rapid blurring of distinctions across issue areas, which has effectively amplified the influence and extent of networks. Given the large number of NGOs dedicated in one way or another to sustainable development goals, the number of NGOs in the Global South is calculated to exceed 30,000.[21] Keohane and Nye recently reported that the number of globally active NGOs grew from about 6,000 to over 26,000 in the 1990s.[22]

NGOs are capable of helping states construct more legitimate regimes in a deliberative process. Indeed, John S. Dryzek considers even partisan groups, such as Greenpeace or Friends of the Earth International, as potentially valuable participants in a collegial global community, which could also include professional (or epistemic) groups, government representatives, immigrants, and so on.[23] These relatively independent actors can generate and provide potentially overlooked information so that states and the institutions they sometimes constitute might come to recognize not only their shared problems, but also the need for consensually agreed solutions. This does not mean that NGOs should serve merely as outside advisors to official state-to-state negotiations. Rather, to extend the parameters of dialogue, they should bring their own perspectives to a genuinely open discussion. Nor does it mean that NGOs should automatically "win" debates, especially by trumping the views of other actors. Consensual policies would generally reflect a diverse array of voices and will therefore better reflect a community's needs and aspirations.

Skeptics, of course, might point out that a norm opening regimes to some NGO participation does not come at all close to fulfilling the Habermasian ideal. Inclusive participation is a centrally important precondition for meaningful deliberation and NGO representation in various regimes and institutions would not appear to approach an ideal level of inclusion. As Habermas has written, "no one may be excluded in principle; all of those who are possibly affected by the decisions have equal chances to enter and take part" in discussions.[24] No international institution currently allows for such open participation. Bohman argues, however, that deliberative participation might reasonably involve representatives.[25] Even if they are headquartered in advanced industrial states, NGOs can represent at least some of the most important interests of peoples affected by global governance institutions. In practice then, NGOs organized around issues, such as the environment, or the rights of native peoples, would bring a new perspective to forums that have previously been dominated by states and corporations. Transnational NGOs can, for example, champion the interests of parties affected by decisions, who currently have no input whatsoever. In any case, Northern-based NGOs have concerns of their own about global issues and therefore have a legitimate claim to participate in discussions as well. The greatest challenge is to find innovative ways of including appropriate representatives of marginalized peoples, often from the Global South. Broad NGO input would legitimize regimes because inclusive participation promotes genuinely consensual politics.[26]

Transparency Norms

IR scholars, NGO advocates, and policymakers commonly use the word "transparency" to explain an assortment of obligations. Ann Florini, who has done extensive work on the norm of transparency, notes that it can be most simply defined as the "opposite of secrecy."[27] This is clearly a broad definition with distinct implications that should be clarified. In his work, for example, Ronald Mitchell focuses on "information regarding the operation and impact of a regime." This is the most common usage of transparency and an extensive literature already explores the way that information disclosure requirements might facilitate state compliance with international regimes.[28] Such neoliberal requirements do matter for our purposes, since even basic regime compliance information can be important in fashioning public accountability. In the security field, arms control advocates and governments have for decades been addressing transparency issues in the form of substantive questions about monitoring and verifying treaty compliance. Reporting requirements make it possible for observers to demand that the parties to an agreement live up to their obligations.

Much less attention, however, has been directed at the prospect of opening global governance institutions and regime decision-making processes to outside inspection. Yet, as Mitchell acknowledges, the idea of transparency includes the "openness" of "political system[s] and decision-making procedures to external observers."[29] This relatively underexplored notion of transparency is of greatest relevance for our purposes because it not only requires that various actors have access to information about regime effectiveness, but also that they are able to observe—if not participate in a strict sense—political and decision processes. This is a much more direct and inclusive form of scrutiny that is crucial for assuring public accountability. It should be noted, however, that scholars who study negotiations, as well as policy practitioners, often specifically embrace secrecy as a means to assure agreement between parties. As Mark Lynch explains, however, this view of diplomacy excludes the public as both an audience and actor and allows parties to pursue strategic misrepresentation and other potential communicative distortions.[30]

The burgeoning international norm of transparency clearly has an impressive scope, encompassing both deep and broad information disclosure requirements for institutions and regimes on the one hand, and on the other, an expectation that at least some actors who are not parties to a given international institution or regime should be able to monitor its decision-making processes. In the first instance, as Florini points out, the norm obligates states "to provide vast quantities of information to other states" and that "treaty after treaty now requires states to report information about their capabilities and activities."[31] Moreover, these transparency obligations are not merely felt by states. International organizations like the World Bank, International Monetary Fund, and European Union also face similar kinds of reporting requirements. In fact, even private transnational corporations are increasingly required to disclose information about their pollution emissions or labor practices. Virtually all new international obligations require parties to disclose some important information about their behavior in the relevant issue area. Historically, this information would have been kept secret.

For international institutions, such as trade and finance agencies, transparency additionally means making public much information about the inner workings of the organization—exposing their internal operations to the "bright light of scrutiny."[32] In practice, this shift is perhaps most evident in the growing role of nongovernmental actors as observers of global governance. However, the institutions are often additionally required to make important decision documents and meeting notes available to NGO observers or others who might request them. Whether in the daily deliberations at the United Nations and its specialized agencies, or at major world conferences, or even within relatively isolated decision making arenas, NGOs are often now present as informed observers. Indeed, because of NGO inclusion, coupled with document disclosure, there is now an expectation of openness at many international proceedings. The cumulative effect of these requirements is genuinely remarkable. World politics is experiencing "a rapidly evolving shift of consensus among observers and actors" toward transparency and away from secrecy.[33] Put differently, a transparency norm has been constructed and is becoming ever more pervasive in global governance.

These developments are quite interesting for the application of Habermasian ideas because transparency norms can make the policies and practices of global governance actors and institutions far more accountable to interested, affected, and weaker political actors. By contrast, when information is tightly controlled, states and international institutions can freely pursue policies that have significant, and potentially adverse, effects on specific individuals and groups. At the very least, if information about governance is made public, or if deliberations and procedures are opened to observation, the various agents that might be harmed by secretive practices can become knowledgeable critics. In other words, the new norm promotes exactly the kind of open dialogue imagined by proponents of discursive democracy: "Transparency provides a basis for a highly democratic, albeit non-electoral, system of transnational governance based on the growing strength of global civil society."[34]

Collectively, norms of participation and transparency arguably constitute publicity, an essential prerequisite to fostering the democratic potential of international regimes. We do not argue that this potential arises merely from the fact of international cooperation in a regime. Rather, this potential follows when institutions such as regimes stimulate political activity at a variety of levels that create new locations for public accountability. The degree to which these various centers of accountability are monitored, how information is provided and applied, and the effectiveness of these processes, largely depends on the extent to which norms of participation and transparency are upheld within the regime. Absent these norms, a regime can become a vehicle for exclusion and privilege.[35]

Participation and Transparency in Practice

In the following sections, we overview the formation of participation and transparency norms in the environment, development, security, and human rights issue areas. In all these cases, the examples we discuss stand in for a plethora of other arrangements that assure greater participation and transparency in global governance. Of course, not every claimed move towards participation and transparency is genuine—nor would all changes necessarily be steps towards global transformation. Many institutions are more likely to employ democratic rhetoric than uphold open and inclusive procedures. This likelihood serves to remind observers of the wide range of practices imaginable between exclusive and inclusive or closed and open political systems. Deliberative global community will most likely be achieved via ongoing normative development, though it is certainly worth noting that political actors might "entrap" themselves into more-extensive-than-intended commitments by employing and acknowledging certain kinds of arguments.[36] For example, as those who fight democratic deficits challenge the legitimacy of various international institutions, it becomes quite difficult for those vested in the current system to defend secrecy and exclusion.

It is also apparent that there is considerable overlap between these normative ideas; yet, it is also evident that participation alone does not ensure transparency and vice versa. In the next two chapters to follow, we offer a pair of much more detailed empirical cases of publicity in specific international regimes and institutions.

Environmental Regimes

Scholars have thoroughly documented far ranging political activity by NGOs in numerous environmental regimes.[37] Moreover, these regimes typically contain a wide array of transparency requirements. To begin, global environmental institutions and regimes are now commonly required to include NGO participants in various aspects of their operations.[38] We argue that these practices constitute a norm of participation in this issue area. According to Kal Raustiala, who has done extensive legal research on a wide variety of international environmental agreements, even states recognize the benefits of NGO participation and usually incorporate inclusive language in all new environmental accords and institutions.[39] Though Raustiala notes that NGOs cannot yet claim an "inalienable right" to participate, he demonstrates that states typically make NGOs "a regular part" of ongoing international environmental cooperation.[40]

NGO activity in this issue area is well documented and the research generally supports our argument about democratization of world politics. Michael Zürn, in his recent survey of the international environmental politics literature, points out that a consensus of studies demonstrate that transnational NGOs have had "a significant influence on international governance by shaping the agenda, by playing a role in the negotiation process, and by improving implementation."[41] Quite simply, regimes and institutions now commonly feature fairly broad NGO participation in a variety of functional capacities, including decision-making. Though it may be premature to argue that a full-fledged global civil society has emerged, even scholars who find important limits on NGO global political activity nonetheless acknowledge that "new rules facilitate their expanded participation" in UN conferences and international agreements.[42]

For example, Article 7.6 of the Framework Convention on Climate Change grants NGOs the right to participate as observers in the ongoing negotiation process. This normative commitment was adopted after NGOs had already been intricately involved in global warming negotiations leading up to the Earth Summit. Several years prior to that seminal meeting, regional groups of NGOs formed a Climate Action Network in order to influence the interstate bargaining on the FCCC. Networked groups provided background information and documentation about global warming and possible solutions, published a daily bulletin (*ECO, the Daily News*) that covered working group discussions and highlighted unresolved issues, organized seminars, forums and meetings to exchange views, and lobbied members of national delegations. More importantly, many NGOs also attended plenary sessions of the Intergovernmental Negotiating Committee (INC) as officially sanctioned observers. Upon the invitation of states, NGOs were even able to express their views during official INC meetings. Indeed, NGOs were invited to make a formal statement at each INC session. Apparently, NGOs first debated important issues behind the scenes so that these statements would reflect their consensus on substantive issues and negotiation strategy.[43] States, of course, retained their ability to control access to negotiations and did limit final stage FCCC bargaining sessions to "representatives from thirty (or so) key states. Consequently," as one scholar has written, " when the chips were down, the NGOs' representatives were not in the room."[44]

Nonetheless, the global warming regime reflects what has become standard practice. NGOs have long been involved in helping to make climate change policy, and their regular participation has been formally institutionalized within the convention. Similar evidence of NGO participation in environmental regime building is pervasive throughout the literature—and most new environment commitments contain language about formal NGO inclusion. For example, NGOs were said to be "key players" in establishing a global ban on ivory trade, which was achieved in 1989 under the Convention on International Trade in Endangered Species of Wild Fauna and Flora (CITES).[45] Under Article XI of CITES, NGOs have the right to participate in meetings of the Conference of the Parties. NGOs were also integral to the development of International Tropical Timber Organization and can likewise "be seen as central actors in effective environmental policy implementation."[46] In the ITTO, NGO observers are formalized in Article 15, but the provisions of Article 14 seem even more striking for regime implementation:

> The Organization shall, to the maximum extent possible, utilize the facilities, services and expertise of existing intergovernmental, governmental or nongovernmental organizations, in order to avoid duplication of efforts in achieving the objectives of this Agreement and to enhance the complementarity and the efficiency of their activities.[47]

Even when NGOs have had fairly minimal apparent influence on the negotiation of specific regimes, the state parties to the agreements now nonetheless readily agree to allow them to participate in the ongoing regime-building process. Such measures, for example, are institutionalized throughout the Convention to Combat Desertification, which encourages all sorts of linkages between affected country governments, NGOs, local populations and developed countries.[48]

In regard to transparency, global environment institutions and regimes now frequently demand remarkable disclosure of various kinds of information by state members and by international organizations.[49] Indeed, almost all new environmental agreements now impose meaningful transparency requirements. For example, new substantive regimes commonly include reporting provisions in service of data collection and scientific exchange. These are often, in fact, among the very first commitments in environment regimes. States are typically asked to calculate and make public their contribution to pollution and resource exhaustion. The global warming regime, to name one case, calls for states to determine and publicize their various greenhouse gas emissions. While these disclosures instrumentally facilitate the operation and potential impact of any given regime, they also contribute to the openness of decision-making procedures. States can even be asked to account for their future emissions in a public plan to address substantive regime goals. Thus, even narrow informational requirements that seemingly only contribute to verification and compliance ends can help make a regime more publicly accountable. NGOs can more readily assess and critique regime processes when armed with this kind of data.

Even better, NGOs are able to act as informed critics when meetings are made transparent to them. "NGOs play a vital role" in observing the Consultative meetings of the London Dumping Convention, for example, which allows them to make reasoned arguments to attempt to alter state behavior or to embarrass parties by later reporting criticisms made against specific states during the meetings.[50] As noted above, it is becoming common practice for environmental regimes to authorize the inclusion of NGO observers, who are allowed to interact with state representatives at the formal conferences and meetings that consider ongoing regime issues such as compliance or implementation. While few of these regimes currently authorize far-reaching NGO access to decision-related documents, this seems to be forthcoming in the immediate future. Consider the so-called Åarhus Convention, which is the recent Economic Commission for Europe Convention on Access to Information, Public Participation in Decision-making and Access to Justice in Environmental Matters. The Åarhus Convention was adopted in June 1998 as part of the "Environment for Europe" process. It featured extensive NGO participation in the negotiation process, and was explicitly designed to promote active engagement of civil society in ongoing environmental decision-making by mandating specific kinds of participation and transparency—toward the explicit end of public accountability and democracy. It specifically grants far-reaching NGO access to environmental policy discussions and provides for disclosure of decision-related documents. Though the Convention was negotiated in a European context, it is open to accession by all UN members and has been mentioned as a possible model for future global action. The reach of participation and transparency requirements in the environmental issue area will be further demonstrated in chapter 4, which focuses on the Global Environment Facility.

Development Regimes

Participation and transparency are now important procedural norms within development regimes. To begin, consider the rules assuring involvement of grassroots and transnational organizations in the World Bank, which is the central international institution charged with promoting development. NGOs and scholars have long argued that the World Bank has been an aloof and exclusive organization. Just over a decade ago, for example, Eric Christensen of the Natural Resources Defense Council pointed out that "public involvement in Bank operations is almost non-existent."[51] Indeed, in words that could have been written by a critical IR theorist, international attorney Jonathan Cahn argued that the Bank's top-down management of development projects made for an "extraordinarily powerful" lender that was "fundamentally unaccountable."[52] Grassroots and transnational advocacy NGOs, of course, typically reject the so-called top-down development model and have convincingly argued that people affected by development projects should have a much greater voice in the selection and planning of them.[53] Indeed, the Bank's own published documents now almost fully embrace this notion. NGOs also recognize the leadership role taken by the World Bank in establishing rules of procedure in this issue area. Regional development banks, for example, usually copy its procedural guidelines. For this reason, pressure groups have devoted substantial resources in the past fifteen to twenty years securing changes in World Bank operations.

At least on paper, many of these campaigns have been successful, as the World Bank has now adopted significant procedural reforms that have, among other things, meant more extensive NGO inclusion in the identification, design, implementation, and monitoring stages of development projects.[54] The Bank is now compelled by its own policies to encourage more inclusive participation in its lending practices. Some legal scholars go even further, arguing that basic "principles of international human rights law" additionally oblige multilateral development institutions like the World Bank to open their operations to participation by nonstate actors.[55] In any case, whether this right becomes widely recognized or not, both grassroots and transnational NGOs are now regularly granted unprecedented access to development processes. The Bank itself keeps track of and reports NGO participation in various stages of the development process, though some external observers claim that the Bank greatly inflates the extent of progress. As Paul Nelson asserts, "participation is a virtue much praised" in development institutions, "but practiced only occasionally."[56] For the most part, however, critics do not dispute the claim that the current situation is markedly better than the past. The Bank's practices are now so well established, we would argue, that they constitute a participation norm.

During the late 1980s and through the 1990s, the World Bank likewise adopted fairly extensive information disclosure policies. Unsurprisingly, the organizational culture of the Bank historically embraced secrecy in the form of financial confidentiality for borrowing governments. NGO critics quite reasonably argued, however, that much greater transparency is needed to assure a semblance of institutional accountability. Charges of waste, fraud and abuse fueled some of the campaigns against Bank practices. Moreover, environmentalists and social activists noted that exclusive Bank control over information meant that important political and social questions about sustainable development could not readily be answered. In the end, the Bank adopted an Information Disclosure Policy that purports to assure unprecedented access by nonstate actors to project-related information. Hypothetically, this might include access to environmental impact statements, cost-benefit analyses, and other important data previously held tightly by the Bank. However, critics argue that the formal changes do not assure an adequate level of disclosure.[57]

The World Bank's new participation and transparency requirements are discussed somewhat more thoroughly in chapter 4, which focuses on the Global Environment Facility. Though the GEF is an environmental institution, it is embedded in the World Bank, and thus serves at the intersection between various environment and development regimes. While recent World

Bank procedural reforms are flawed in important ways, we argue in chapter 4 that the GEF goes much further in assuring inclusive participation and openness—and that World Bank reform was a vital step on the way toward this progress. The chapter discusses the transnational advocacy campaigns that led to the changes, as well as the implications of reform.

As expected, regional development banks have literally followed the World Bank's lead and embraced relatively similar participation and transparency requirements. Sometimes their formal commitments to these practices are weaker, but they can also be stronger because of various organizational idiosyncrasies. Nelson, for instance, has specifically compared the participation and transparency requirements of the World Bank to those at the Inter-American Development Bank.[58] He finds that the IDB's transparency provisions are weaker because it allows borrowing governments greater discretion to limit information access. However, NGO participation at the two institutions varies a great deal, in part because of the differing organizational structures. "Critical, uninvited participation has been stronger at the World Bank," Nelson writes, but Latin American civil society organizations have sometimes gained unparalleled access to national strategy processes in the IDB.[59]

Potentially, the information and perspective that NGOs bring to development debates can dramatically transform the regimes. Given enough time, even a historically detached institution like the World Bank might become substantially more democratic and accountable.[60] It seems apparent, then, that publicity norms in this issue area promote inclusive dialogue.

Security Regimes

Security issues are traditionally viewed as "high politics" by states and the scholars who study their affairs. Indeed, neorealists like Waltz consider security to be the most important goal of states. With few exceptions, states are said to be self-reliant for their security, so they do not make or seek significant international commitments. The disparate relative gains that states might achieve in international cooperative endeavors like regimes should preclude their successful organization, operation, or both.[61] For this reason, realists argue that international regimes and institutions are insignificant forces in world politics.[62] Even alliances, which rely upon a modicum of interstate cooperation, are viewed as temporary, contingent associations made merely to balance threats.[63] Once the threat is mitigated, alliance commitments should dissolve. John J. Mearsheimer famously argued, for example, that NATO should collapse (or be disbanded) once the Soviet Union disappeared.[64]

Realists are also concerned that participation and transparency might undermine national security.[65] States should centralize security decision making, according to the realist logic, because democratic forces like public opinion are likely to impede a state's ability to pursue its interests. Non-state actors, such as NGOs, have not generally been viewed as active parties in the most important debates about security—which, according to realists, appropriately occur within a relatively tight inner circle of national leaders. Additionally, secrecy allows states to hide their intentions—and sometimes even their power resources, such as weapons—from other states. Indeed, deception and uncertainty often play important roles in security planning. Consider, for example, the longstanding ambiguity surrounding Israel's alleged possession of nuclear arms and American unwillingness to confirm or deny the presence of nuclear arms on particular naval vessels visiting allied ports. Since September 11, 2001, the United States and other states have increased secrecy measures in the name of security. In sum, neither participation nor transparency should be considered important elements in the realist account of security politics.

Nonetheless, recent research on domestic and transnational politics reveals that, in fact, non-state actors have been important in shaping security outcomes, and have helped construct international regimes. Thomas Risse-Kappen, for example, demonstrated that various scientists and arms control advocates acting transnationally played a meaningful role in ending the cold war.[66] In the 1990s and since the turn of the new century, numerous NGOs have additionally been quite active in the formation of various security regimes that require significant, binding commitments from states. Kenneth R. Rutherford, Richard Price and other scholars have separately examined the most prominent case—the Landmine Ban Treaty, which was placed on the international security agenda by NGOs.[67] Indeed, the International Campaign to Ban Landmines, under the coordination of Jody Williams, won a Nobel Peace prize for its work leading the campaign to produce a landmine treaty. Michael Barnett argues that nonstate actors concerned about human rights similarly pushed for new international norms of humanitarian intervention at the United Nations and that these norms reflect a "changing definition of security."[68]

Though the NGO grasp on security policymaking is not nearly as firm as it is in the environmental issue area, it is clear that NGOs concerned with security affairs are attempting to extend their reach. Rutherford, for instance, points out that NGOs are now actively involved in security-related campaigns to stop the use of child soldiers and to limit the proliferation of small arms and light weapons. Arms control groups have likewise been active on the nuclear nonproliferation regime, the comprehensive test ban, and the chemical weapons accord. Increasingly, in fact, NGO involvement is sought even by states and their participation in regimes is becoming formalized—just as it is in the environment and development issue areas. Price notes, for instance, that NGOs were included on official national delegations during the landmine treaty review process in various international conferences. He notes that "with such seats at the table, civil society has participated at even 'closed' government negotiating sessions."[69] Many analysts refer to NGOs positioned in this fashion as Trojan Horses. Membership on a state delegation places NGO representatives inside exclusive meetings where they are then free to speak and act according to their organizational goals.

Additionally, new security regimes seem likely to provide for regular NGO participation in future international conferences addressing regime maintenance, implementation and amendment. Consider specific provisions of the Landmine Ban Treaty. According to Article 12(3), "the International Committee of the Red Cross and relevant non-governmental organizations may be invited to attend each Review Conference as observers in accordance with the agreed Rules of Procedure."[70] Similar wording is repeated in the document concerning other potential meeting types and processes. The UN Preparatory Committee members have also agreed to allow NGO participation in ongoing negotiations concerning the Illicit Trade in Small Arms and Light Weapons in All Its Aspects. At minimum, groups deemed " 'relevant and competent' with respect to the scope and purpose of the conference" are able to participate.[71]

As noted earlier, provisions to assure verification of arms control regimes constitute specific forms of transparency. Florini, in fact, has written a great deal about transparency and security. She argues that there has been a "massive shift toward transparency" over the past few decades in this issue area.[72] Essentially, states have long recognized the power of disclosure to assure compliance with bilateral and multilateral security agreements. Traditionally, arms control treaties have included specific measures to assure compliance. Some allow verification by national technical means, such as space satellites, others require even more intrusive forms, such as on-site inspections or data-gathering and reporting. Still other proposals, moreover, have explicitly focused on transparency as an independent security measure. During the Eisenhower administration, the United States and the Soviet Union seriously considered an "Open Skies" proposal which would have allowed each superpower to have relatively free access to the airspace over the other for the purposes of verifying armaments and military activity. The more recent UN Register of Conventional Arms obliges states to record conventional weapons transfers in an international setting.

Florini emphasizes that the UN Register of Conventional Arms is especially significant because of its democratic potential. The registry is a public resource, unlike the verification measures used by many regimes, which limit access to information to member states. Security field NGOs like the International Institute for Strategic Studies and the Stockholm International Peace Research Institute have already made great use of the registry in order to monitor and critique the international arms trade.[73] These groups are free to utilize newly acquired information when they write reports for experts in the field, testify in public hearings, or communicate with their broad membership. This is precisely the kind of regime accountability made possible by publicity measures.

Though security regimes are more inclusive and open than ever, many scholars remain skeptical about the ultimate meaning of these changes. For example, even during the Ottawa process, NGOs working to ban landmines found their behavior significantly limited by states, which directly controlled access to negotiating sessions.[74] Additionally, the overwhelming majority of NGO representatives who participated in the process was from Europe or North America and were primarily English-speakers. In regimes that address weapons of mass destruction, state roles are especially strong and NGOs face even more barriers to entry. While NGOs may be "pushing the envelope," many scholars and activists caution against "fairy tale" stories that overstate their influence.[75] Similar warnings could be sounded against making too much of current transparency measures, which certainly do not yet provide significant access to military information that is often considered top secret. Nonetheless, as demonstrated in this section, some new security regimes are much more democratic than their predecessors were and this development seems likely to continue. When states, whether on their own or because of NGO pressure, impose bans on weapons or behavior, publicity promotes compliance. Presumably, this is desired by the states that agreed to the norms.

The Human Rights Regime

Formal participation in the human rights regime typically occurs through UN mechanisms; therefore, NGO activities can be severely circumscribed by the desire of states to shield transgressions. On the other hand, implementation and monitoring of state practices often fall to the nongovernmental organization, which is regarded as neutral actor whose primary goal is to secure the rights of individuals and groups. In addition, the scope of participation has grown as the mandates of NGOs have shifted from narrow issues concerned with political oppression—an arena in which Amnesty International has been most prominent—to a more complex and integrated debate about what constitutes fundamental human rights.[76] Henry Steiner notes the frustration felt by some NGOs who historically responded to the symptoms rather than the causes: "Participants in these NGOs have come to feel the need to examine the contexts of and linkages among human rights violations, and thus the need to pay attention not only to cases of individual abuse but also to patterns of cases and their explanations."[77] These changing mandates reflect a dialectical process between the growing empowerment of nonstate actors in world politics to represent the unrepresented, a fact that has allowed them to assert particular agendas and influence governments at the local, national and international level, and the evolution of an expanding body of human rights instruments. The consequence is that human rights NGOs, broadly defined, are acquiring a degree of legitimacy in world politics that challenges the unquestioned place of the state. In particular, at the forum that serves as an important space for the development of global governance norms, the United Nations, NGO human rights activities are absolutely vital. For example, NGOs often drive review processes in the Commission on Human Rights by monitoring compliance with treaties and providing information for specific decisions.

The UN system formally integrated NGOs into its deliberative procedures through the 1968 ECOSOC Resolution 1296 (XLIV), but the growing numbers of NGOs and the elastic nature of the issues necessitated a recent revision. The new resolution vastly improved the status of NGOs within the UN machinery, reflecting then-Secretary General Boutros Boutros-Ghali's view of a world characterized by " 'participation' and 'globalization' in which the 'activity of non-state actors has . . . become an essential dimension of public life at all levels and in all parts of the world.' "[78]

In an issue area of world politics that most states would prefer to avoid, the July 1996 revision permits national and sub-national human rights NGOs to apply for consultative status and to participate along with international NGOs in UN world conferences and in sessions of ECOSOC and its subsidiary bodies, such as the Commission on Human Rights, the Commission on Sustainable Development, and the Commission on the Status of Women. The recent reform draws attention to the intense interdependency characterizing contemporary global civil society wherein the interests, agendas, and activities of international and local NGOs are increasingly interwoven, enhancing the linkages between global and local politics. In addition, two other changes reflect the evolution of NGOs in world politics in general, and human rights in particular. First, a new paragraph 50 acknowledges an important role of NGOs in the preparatory process and conferences, merely formalizing what had often become common practice.[79] And second, accredited NGOs may now represent interests of specific groups of persons as opposed to having only "a general international concern with human rights."[80] The consequence of this new language is that human rights within international fora were redefined from a general, even universal, approach to the issue, to a more particular approach that recognizes those NGO activities addressing *specific* circumstances or groups of people. These changes do not promote relativism, but rather reflect a strengthening of the edifice of global civil society that couples ethical commitments at the global level with localized practice.

While these changes represent a significant step forward for NGOs in the evaluation of human rights violations, the basic procedural mechanisms for the protection of human rights within the UN remain closed to nonstate actors. Patrick James Flood distinguishes between treaty-based and charter-based mechanisms for assuring human rights.[81] In the former case, each of the International Covenants on Economic, Social and Cultural Rights, and on Civil and Political Rights, provide specific procedures to assess violations by states. On the other hand, charter-based mechanisms are built around the activities of the Commission on Human Rights. The CHR historically operated under the "1503" procedure in which charges of and defense against violations of human rights are conducted in strict confidentiality, although the Chair of the CHR has, since 1978, announced the names of the countries under examination. Here, the lack of participation is compensated by increasing the transparency of the process, albeit minimally. An alternative procedure under the charter-based mechanisms is the establishment of thematic and country *rapporteurs*, representatives, and working groups. Intended to investigate violations of human rights in specific countries or in terms of a general practice—disappearances, for example—these mechanisms provide opportunities for non-state actors to contribute to the fact-finding process, though the final report and follow-up is the responsibility of the *rapporteur* or working group. Thus, even though particular processes often impose limits on the formal role of NGOs in the fact-finding and evaluation process, the expanding mechanisms for the definition and investigation of human rights reflects a gradual decentralization and diffusion of opportunities to engage states at the global level. Indeed, with the formation of new institutions at the global level, such as the International Criminal Court, or specific war crimes tribunals for gross violations of human rights in places such as Bosnia, Central Africa, or Sierra Leone, or at the national level as the UN focuses attention on the formation of state human rights institutions, access for NGOs to at least bring complaints or provide information continue to expand.[82] Ultimately, these opportunities heighten the awareness of governments to human rights violations around the world which, by drawing attention to the transgressions of states, serves as a fundamental method to encourage changed domestic behavior on the one hand, and influence the nature of interstate relations on the other.[83]

Within this institutional context NGOs are able to perform three crucial functions: standard-setting, monitoring and implementation. Consider first that NGOs commonly serve as observers in and contributors to international conferences. For instance, at the World Conference on Human Rights in Vienna in June 1993, the considerable presence of NGOs influenced the debate on whether or not human rights were universal. As Felice D. Gaer notes, all governments paid "lip service" to the idea of universality. Representatives from states such as Iran and Indonesia, the latter speaking for the Non-Aligned Movement, expressed support for the "universal validity of basic human rights" or the fact that human rights are "inherent in human beings . . . (and) cannot be subject to cultural relativism."[84] This position was strongly supported by NGOs and was eventually reaffirmed by the 171 states at the World Conference in the Vienna Declaration, which recognized that "the promotion and protection of all human rights is a legitimate concern of the international community."[85] In the recent cases of Bosnia and Kosovo, NGOs such as Amnesty International and Human Rights Watch, among others, attract attention to practices of ethnic cleansing and massacres of civilians. At the same time, other organizations like the International Helsinki Federation for Human Rights, and its affiliate the Helsinki Committee for Human Rights in Bosnia and Herzegovina, work to facilitate the development of a durable civil society in the region that will institutionalize human rights practices. Some of these activities include creating the conditions for assisting local NGOs in providing reliable, accurate and objective reports on the human rights situation in the region; strengthening the capability of newly emerging human rights groups and activists to monitor, evaluate and document the authorities' compliance with international human rights standards; enhancing the capability of human rights groups and activists to initiate and effectively carry out specific projects that promote human rights, democracy, and the rule of law; and promoting the integration of human rights groups and activists into the international human rights community.[86] Finally, NGO attention is not restricted to states, of course. NGOs have also been effective in shaping the practices of transnational corporations, particularly in the areas of child labor and environmental protection.[87]

NGO activities are now widely viewed as credible and legitimate, and this status is reinforced by the existence of a growing body of human rights instruments that are acquiring the standing of law in world politics. Importantly, the NGO network that extends from the global to the local can help ensure that what Vincent calls "basic rights" are upheld across boundary lines, for humanitarian intervention by other states does have its limits. The consequence is that the participatory and representative function of many nongovernmental organizations can promote protections based on global norms and principles. Further, because these regime mechanisms function as a public sphere that fosters accountability, the human rights regime can be argued to contain elements of global democratic practice.

The problem of transparency in the human rights regime is characterized by the demand for confidentiality by states under review. For example, as we noted above, the core "1503" procedure of the Commission on Human Rights is entirely confidential in both fact-finding and deliberation. Though the Chair of the Commission has disclosed the states under investigation, there is no obligation to do so. And the country-mechanism used by the CHR is often regarded as a vehicle for the targeted attack against specific regimes rather than a more general commitment to a particular human rights principle and therefore can be regarded as a less effective means to investigate transgressions.[88] Given the inherent defensiveness of states to accusations of violations—a defensiveness that also testifies to the growing efficacy of the norm—the barriers to transparency are considerable.[89] Despite demands for greater openness and participation at the World Conference on Human Rights in Vienna, the Final Document of the Vienna Plus Five Global NGO Forum on Human Rights held in June 1998 identified the need for increased transparency and called for improved dissemination of information from, and strengthening NGO relationships with, working groups and special rapporteurs in both their country and thematic mandates.[90]

Yet the "cascading effects" of human rights institutions has balanced in part the reluctance of states by not only increasing opportunities for participation, but also by broadening the scope of transparency as well. For instance, the formation of new institutions such as the international war crimes tribunals in Yugoslavia, Rwanda, and Sierra Leone, and the International Criminal Court reflect a commitment to more open processes of determining the kind and extent of human rights violations. Truth Commissions in Latin America and South Africa serve the same basic function. While the dispute over the effectiveness and legality of these institutions is profound, their very presence serves as an important milestone in enhancing publicity in the human rights regime.[91] In these cases, violators are no longer simply states and governments, as the institutional reach extends to specific individuals who may or may not have served in official capacities. The ICC refines the institutional apparatus for the protection and defense of human rights by filling important gaps in existing coverage of national and international institutions.

In addition, the increasing emphasis by the United Nations on national mechanisms for human rights provides alternative channels for publicity in general and transparency in particular. These mechanisms, which may appear in the form of a commission or ombudsman, investigate charges of discrimination or human rights violations by public or private actors, publicize transgressions and serve as a focal point for education efforts in particular societies. And in some instances a commission or ombudsman may have the ability to impose legally binding decisions on the violating party to a dispute.[92] In an attempt to further develop local channels and following the recommendations of the June 1993 Vienna Declaration, national plans of action for human rights have been prepared by various states, which outline principles, commitments and strategies to strengthen the protection of rights. Indeed, the world conference stimulated not only national approaches but regional designs as well. For example, workshops at which NGOs served as observers in Tehran,

New Delhi, Bangkok, Tokyo, Sana'a, and Beijing between 1998 and 2000 sought to outline strategies for regional, national and local implementation of broad human rights programs. One of the central goals of these plans is to increase the availability and flow of information among interested parties.[93]

The increasing volume and velocity of information available to actors other than states fosters transparency. In certain cases international regimes are specific about the documentation, procedures and actors permitted access to information and deliberation. Naturally (though unfortunately), in the area of human rights, as in development and security, the sensitivity of states precludes unlimited transparency and participation. However, the conditions that permit communication and inclusion on a relatively equal basis are developing through the proliferation of mechanisms for the investigation and redressing of human rights violations around the world. Ideally, public institutions would assure inclusive access to formal procedures that define rights and evaluate claims and counterclaims of states and victims. More practically, publicity can be assured when NGOs are regarded as legitimate actors who can reliably monitor regime compliance and present evidence in various forums. Their role has become such that there is now an expectation of some NGO presence in human rights deliberations and, further, that confidentiality will become the exception rather than the rule.

THE "BOOTSTRAPPING" PROBLEM

So far, we have described procedural norms that promote the kind of dialogic engagement necessary for the emergence of international political community and global democratic practice. Obviously, the participation and transparency norms that are being constructed in world politics do not yet encompass all issue areas and are not even fully implemented in the regimes discussed above. Thus, we must ask how norms promoting democracy can be developed given the nondemocratic nature of current decision processes? James Bohman refers to this initiation issue as a "bootstrapping" problem.[94] Critical theorists could justifiably question the means employed to date by successful advocates of participation and transparency norms because their strategies differ little from the behavior expected by realist or neoliberal theories. Indeed, even NGO norm-builders have often used coercive strategies and material levers to achieve their goals. Empirical work by constructivists, in fact, demonstrates the capacity of actors to behave strategically and employ material pressure to change state policy towards preferred norms. Consequently, those norms are not internalized by elites.[95] As Keck and Sikkink note, advocates often make "implied or explicit threat of sanctions or leverage if the gap between norms and practices remains large. Material leverage comes from linking the issue of concern to money, trade, or prestige, as more powerful institutions or governments are pushed to apply pressure."[96] To put it bluntly, even though norm advocates often act out of a deep sense of commitment to their principles, they often do not seek shared consensus so much as policy change.[97] Emancipation and justice thus remain elusive goals in so far as the procedures of their realization are equally important for global democracy as their attainment.

In response to these concerns, Dryzek claims that progressive change can and should occur incrementally. He specifically argues for the creation of "norms of free discourse" which would "help constitute a world increasingly hospitable to truly discursive designs and to the participatory process of discursive design."[98] Somewhat similarly, Habermas acknowledges that institutional deliberative frameworks can plausibly be delineated from "ideal procedures."[99] Drawing this distinction is essential if the critical project is to engage with and thereby reform existing institutional processes. Scholars who develop dialogical models of decision-making, for example, typically emphasize the importance of inclusive and open processes in particular issue areas or for specific situations.[100] Indeed, the idea of the public sphere, explored in the previous chapter, represents a suitable approach for addressing the "bootstrapping" dilemma. The public sphere is a place wherein global civil society can organize for the promotion of substantive norms, in opposition to the actions of the state, or assert appeals to it through communicative interaction. Further, the institutionalization of participation and transparency norms in regimes fosters publicity and accountability and can, over time, be strengthened by the ongoing deliberative practices in the public sphere.[101]

A more compelling dilemma of the deliberative process may be the emergence of antidemocratic feedback.[102] Promoting norms of publicity provides ample opportunities for those tendencies that undermine global democratic practice, creating a kind of tension between competing visions of what constitutes emancipatory goals and how institutions can fulfill their goals. Two points can be offered in this regard. First, a public sphere provides the conditions for networks of transnational actors to assert contending points of view in a deliberative fashion. Interaction within and equal access to this public sphere generates a far more cosmopolitan publicity that ensures greater accessibility and accountability in the constitution and functioning of formal institutions. Nonetheless, those who seek to broaden publicity and work towards emancipatory ends must confront and overcome resistance from antidemocratic forces. The objective in this regard is to create suitable conditions for deliberation on the assumption that those conditions will entrench democratic practices. This certainly does not require supporters of deliberative procedures to embrace (or reject) particular substantive claims advanced by antidemocratic forces—perhaps on questions of immigration or preservation of jobs.

Rather, those arguing for exclusion and secrecy face a legitimacy problem that is evinced by the deliberative process itself. In the environment, development, and human rights issue areas, nongovernmental actors are now generally assured a place in the decision process leading up to the establishment of a regime. They serve in an advisory capacity to states, mobilize states and institutions to act, and participate in parallel global conferences. Of course, the fact that public spheres exist or are formalized in the first instance is often a reflection of the ability of civil society actors to bring to the global agenda issues of concern to various communities in the world polity.[103] And while initial outcomes may not duplicate the exact demands of these actors, the *process* for dynamic change is established. Those who challenge that process must utilize it—and thus counterfactually demonstrate the importance of argument—even as they seek to limit debate.

Second, international regimes both reflect and stimulate political activity and institutional structures at a variety of levels, at once globalizing particular norms while decentralizing their implementation. To the extent that norms of publicity have been incorporated into the regime, the activities of nongovernmental actors are regarded as legitimate and often necessary to realize particular institutional objectives. This decentralization facilitates accountability and accessibility for civil society networks as well. Again, this does not mean that particular policy outcomes will always reflect the emancipatory goals of global democracy advocates, only that those outcomes were produced from relatively inclusive and open processes characteristic of democratic practice. In the issue areas described above, transparency and participation norms enhance the roles of NGOs in a variety of ways at the local, state and global levels. Project implementation and evaluation in the case of development and local monitoring of and participation in national and global human rights mechanisms provide channels for representation that are innovative and transformative. So long as those channels are preserved, the opportunity to at least contest antidemocratic tendencies is secured.

The bootstrapping dilemma does pose a considerable challenge for regime formation and the construction of global democratic community. Yet, the insights provided by critical theorists and their emphasis on deliberative or dialogic engagement suggests that progress towards incorporating participation and transparency norms into formal institutions, if only in an incremental manner, is possible. These norms promote publicity and provide at least some opportunity to transform dominant structures in the pursuit of emancipation and justice. This argument is consistent with the basic constructivist claim that any given context will be what the participants make of it.[104] A particular discursive situation is socially constructed and might approach ideal conditions if the shared understandings and practices of participants make them appropriate for the situation.

Conclusion

Global democracy does not arise directly from the elements of publicity present in international regimes. But publicity, constituted by transparent and participatory processes, is an essential part of any conception of global democratic practice. We have generally treated them as separate notions in our discussion in this chapter. Yet, it is apparent that transparency and participation are deeply connected and not easily disaggregated in a regime. For transparency to be meaningful, participation is essential. Perhaps more importantly, participation is only effective when access to information is freely available to all. In the examples discussed above, it is clear that degrees of participation and transparency have been attained. However, global democratic practice cannot be achieved until norms of publicity have become widely embraced and implemented. To this end, we noted that at the very least, even the initial acceptance of publicity norms could encourage global democracy within international institutions by virtue of creating the condition for their entrenchment and expansion.

Thus, because opportunities to voice environmental concerns or human rights grievances are increasing, the volume of information is rising and the nature of proceedings is changing dramatically. Networks of NGOs, virtually independent of states, seek to identify, articulate and implement objectives that are often emancipatory in nature. They are operating at the local, national, and the global levels with explicit recognition from states and intergovernmental bodies such as the UN system, enabling their claims to be publicized through these channels as well as through other informal means such as the news media. Under these conditions demands for accountability—an essential element of global democratic practice—are intensified as states become "targeted" by international organizations and nongovernmental actors. NGO voices should not be privileged, of course, nor should every utterance even be taken at face value. Nonetheless, NGO perspectives deserve a fair hearing in global politics, an opportunity typically denied in a world dominated by powerful states and well-connected transnational corporations.

As we have argued, the development of global civil society reflects an important transformation in world politics. Throughout this chapter, we have essentially identified processes that promote legitimate forms of international political community. We do not assert that the development of community is global in the sense of international cooperation that transcends all issue areas. Rather, our argument is that certain international regimes are the institutional locus of global democratic practices that mirror transnational community. In effect, a universal democratic community could potentially be constructed, but only in an incremental fashion through the establishment of international institutions and regimes featuring various democratic procedures.[105]

We make this claim on the basis of the formation of international public spheres that enable demands for norms of publicity to be institutionalized in regimes, on the basis of the effects of these regimes for local, state and global governance in particular issue areas, and on the basis of expanding calls for placing universal emancipatory goals at the heart of global politics. On these grounds, we believe that global democracy is a project in the gradual process of realization.

4

The Democratization of the Global Environment Facility

This chapter considers the deliberative potential of the Global Environment Facility (GEF), a relatively youthful entity that functions within several related international environment and development regimes. We argue that GEF decision-making processes are unusually inclusive and transparent and that these procedural conditions promote democratic accountability, if not discursive democracy.

The Institutional Context

In the late 1980s, many affluent states considered and debated the need for international institutions that could help poor countries finance projects that would address global environmental problems. In part, the impetus emerged from the high profile follow-up negotiations to the Montreal Protocol.[1] In that agreement, northern states agreed to limit industrial and consumer uses of manmade chlorofluorocarbons (CFCs) so as to protect the earth's atmospheric ozone layer. However, environmentalists and diplomats alike were very concerned that these efforts could be undercut if companies in the Global South initiated or increased indigenous production of CFCs. Alternatively, they feared that transnational corporations, after losing their primary market, might simply move polluting industries to developing countries, where the demand for relatively inexpensive refrigeration and air conditioning could eventually explode. To prevent either scenario from occurring, affluent states agreed to create a special multilateral fund to encourage states like China and India to follow their lead and limit CFC production and use. Funds provided by the North would buy more expensive new substitute chemicals that would allow poor states to avoid the ozone-depleting CFCs that affluent states had long used. In turn, the GEF was created partly because northern environmentalists feared that future agreements to limit greenhouse gases or other pollutants would be undermined if states of the South could not afford to abide by them.

Moreover, the influential World Commission on Environment and Development actively promoted the notion of green development funding. Most global environmental problems pose complex development dilemmas for the South. Indeed, the advocates of sustainable development recognize the inherent links between environmental goals and economic development. According to the Brundtland Commission (as the WCED was commonly known), sustainable development "meets the needs of the present without compromising the ability of future generations to meet their own needs."[2] Economic plans should avoid both pollution and resource exhaustion, even though such restrictions could significantly complicate development planning. States of the Global South would need to preserve their forests, for example, even though they might not have viable economic alternatives to cutting them down and selling the timber. As Ken Conca has noted, "the South appears to hold an effective veto over . . . international environmental protection—merely by staying on its current course."[3] Thus, in order to divert development in a more sustainable direction, the Brundtland Commission recommended that "serious consideration" be given "to the development of a special international banking programme or facility linked to the World Bank."[4] A new international institution could perhaps fund environmentally friendly development in the South.

Yet, even as states generally agreed that additional aid resources would have to be found, few wanted to create a large, new international bureaucracy to administer them. The Global Environment Facility (GEF) was therefore created as a three-year pilot project in 1991 by resolution of the World Bank's Executive Directors. France and Germany took the lead in establishing the GEF by making concrete proposals at an international financial ministry meeting, and even more importantly, by offering significant cash contributions. The GEF was not chartered as a new international organization per se, but rather as a cooperative project of the World Bank, United Nations Development Project (UNDP) and UN Environmental Program (UNEP). These organizations served as the GEF's "implementing agencies."

Though lacking formal organizational status, the GEF quickly became an important participant in global environmental policymaking. At the so-called Earth Summit in 1992, for example, the GEF was named the official funding instrument for Agenda 21, the conference's ambitious, forward-looking blueprint for achieving sustainable development.[5] More concretely, the GEF was also designated as the interim funding mechanism for the two major environmental agreements signed at the summit, the Framework Convention on Climate Change (FCCC) and the Convention on Biological Diversity (CBD). Over time, the once-experimental entity evolved into the principal source of environmental assistance for states of the Global South and Eastern Europe, serving by design as their financial backer as they attempt to meet global environmental goals. The GEF has authorized more than $4 billion worth of grants since its inception. As might have been expected, given the explicit linkage to the FCCC and CBD, between 30 percent and half of GEF project funds have typically been aimed at mitigating global warming. According to GEF calculations, it is now the largest financier of renewable energy in developing countries. Another 30 to 40 percent of its funds flow to projects protecting biological diversity, which has often meant funding parks or range management. Finally, almost 15 percent has gone to preserving international waters and nearly the same amount has gone to prevent and control land degradation, which are also official institutional objectives.[6] As of late summer 2002, 173 states were GEF members, including 145 different hosts to GEF-supported projects.

The GEF is additionally charged with "mainstreaming" global ecological considerations into the development planning of its partner organizations, namely the World Bank and UNDP.[7] By mandate, in fact, GEF funds are only added to ongoing development projects that would otherwise overlook possible global environmental objectives. The idea is to make ongoing development sustainable, not to finance new stand-alone green projects. In practice, the GEF employs a so-called "incremental cost" criterion to establish the additional funding needed to make projects greener, but recipient states view this as a backhanded way of imposing additional conditions on their receipt of development aid. The requirement has meant that the GEF can claim to have leveraged an additional $11 billion worth of development spending to date, by attaching funds to projects cofinanced by the World Bank and others.[8]

In any event, the GEF is a pivotal part of several of the most important international environment and development regimes and organizations. It is integral to the nascent agreements on climate change and biodiversity, since North-South cooperation is vital to addressing these problems, and is an important partner of the World Bank. A significant and growing portion of World Bank funds, in fact, are now distributed for new environmental projects—which arguably means that environmental goals have been somewhat successfully mainstreamed in development planning at the Bank. Yet, while these green purposes are interesting and notable, perhaps the most intriguing dimension of the GEF is its unusually open and inclusive decision-making procedures.

As shall be demonstrated in this chapter, the GEF has certainly embraced at least the language of participatory and transparent development. At the very top of the organization, GEF CEO Mohamed T. El-Ashry often boasts that his organization promotes democracy in development: "The Facility has put a premium on inclusiveness, consensus and transparency."[9] This chapter primarily explores the construction and meaning of these procedural norms at the GEF.

Before examining the democratization of this institution, however, a bit more should be said about the GEF's early history. When it was initially created in 1991, virtually no one considered the GEF an especially open or inclusive international institution. Instead, it was a fairly exclusive club. Only twenty-nine nations joined the original GEF, with merely a dozen from the developing world. Ordinarily, there is great temptation for impoverished states to accept almost any offers of international financial assistance, especially grants, regardless of the specific circumstances.[10] Their great poverty provides them with few realistic alternatives. Since the GEF was created principally to provide grants to these states, the failure of affluent nations to convince a wide array of potential patrons to enlist suggests that something must have been wrong with the original organization. In this case, the GEF was viewed as illegitimate.[11] Affluent states created a new development organization that was too much like the often-criticized World Bank and International Monetary Fund to satisfy its targeted constituency.

Structurally, the world's wealthiest states favor multilateral development institutions featuring weighted voting mechanisms common to the World Bank and IMF. These Bretton Woods institutions assign voting shares according to financial contributions—the so-called "one dollar, one vote" approach—and thereby assure a relatively small number of affluent states with the overwhelming balance of institutional power. States of the Global South, by contrast, typically support institutional arrangements featuring one-state, one-vote procedures, which are employed, perhaps most prominently, in the General Assembly of the United Nations. Designs that use such "equal" voting rights easily favor the Global South since a substantial majority of the world's states are poor. In the UN, poor states have constituted a two-thirds majority of voting members in the General Assembly since 1963. The South and some sympathetic NGOs typically label one-state, one-vote processes "democratic," but more heavily populated states might reasonably object to having only the same clout in international affairs as microstates. Both the North and South want to be able to have great influence over decisions regardless of the terminology.[12]

Because wealthy donor nations wrote the original guidelines and provided most of the budgetary resources, they viewed the GEF as a natural fit within the Bretton Woods network of development institutions. Moreover, they agreed that the World Bank should make virtually all of the most important decisions for the GEF. The Bank is the financial Trustee, the Facility's secretariat is physically located within the Bank, and daily operations occur on its premises.[13] As pilot-era GEF administrator Ian Johnson proclaimed, "In the GEF, the World Bank is judge, jury and executioner."[14] In turn, it should not have been surprising that the GEF inherited many of the harshest criticisms levied against Bretton Woods institutions. Just like the World Bank, the IMF, or virtually any other multilateral financial institution, the GEF was an instrument dominated by rich donor nations and largely reflective of their interests. Because of this dominance, the pilot-stage "GEF structure was resoundingly rejected by the majority of developing countries."[15]

The pilot stage GEF was also rejected by many NGOs. Some called it a "greenwash," for attempting to provide the veneer of environmentalism to neoliberal development-as-usual. For example, a project in the Congo allegedly designed to protect and manage the Nouabele rainforest was roundly criticized by NGOs since it seemed merely to serve as a distraction from a much larger World Bank forestry loan aimed at jump-starting serious logging.[16] Perhaps predictably, given the new institution's explicit link to the World Bank, NGOs were assigned a relatively modest role in the original GEF. In public documents, the institution claimed to value their input, but in practice NGOs were mostly excluded from playing an important part in the GEF's operations. Ian Rowlands points out, for example, that the GEF originally "adopted many of the [World] Bank's worst characteristics and habits," including lack of transparent, participatory and accountable governance.[17] This was not, however, merely the critical assessment of a single scholar. Prior to the Rio de Janeiro gathering, a group of forty influential NGOs from all over the world called for democratizing GEF governance for an upcoming Participants' Meeting in Geneva. In that document, NGOs made the familiar demands for greater "transparency, a participatory decision-making process and public accountability."[18] In fact, virtually the same environment and development groups that had long been campaigning against secrecy and exclusivity at the World Bank also targeted the GEF for change. They repeated the same arguments against a new target—and, as shall be explained below, were ultimately quite successful in fomenting some meaningful changes.

As briefly discussed in chapter 3, the World Bank itself has become increasingly transparent and participatory in the past decade. Thus, before looking at the construction of democratic governance norms in the GEF—achieved primarily in an ongoing international negotiation—it is worthwhile first to understand the process by which a global reform movement transformed World Bank operations. That movement's influence peaked at virtually the same time that states were negotiating GEF changes, and as noted, many of the most prominent NGOs and activists worked on both campaigns.

World Bank Reform

Although David Holloran Lumsdaine argues that Western-dominated development institutions have historically been "committed to public scrutiny and criticism," many activists and scholars claim that the World Bank has instead traditionally maintained very tight control over information.[19] These critics assert, in fact, that many of the Bank's operational procedures are quite undemocratic. In large part, secrecy is maintained via the conclusion of broad financial confidentiality agreements between borrowing states and the Bank.[20] World Bank managers are said to be aloof from the needs of ordinary people living in loan recipient states, most decisions are made in secret without the input of affected individuals or representative NGOs, and the Bank itself has been ultimately unaccountable for its actions. In all, NGO critics have maintained that the Bank's defective and undemocratic procedures call "into question the Bank's legitimacy to function as a governance institution."[21] Building up to the auspicious occasion of the institution's half-century anniversary in 1995, broad coalitions, including dozens of discomfited NGOs, argued to close, scale-back, or dramatically remake the Bank. They were claiming that "50 years is enough" of the same marred practices.[22] The campaign engaged in behind-the-scenes lobbying, public demonstrations, legal maneuvering, and numerous other techniques common to social movements, interest groups, or transnational advocacy networks.[23]

The transnational NGOs devoted great effort to changing both the operational policies and internal practices of the World Bank. Originally, beginning with earnest in the 1980s, the groups worked hardest to stop a large number of questionable loans for projects viewed as ecologically and developmentally unsound, such as the enormous Sardar Sarovar dam on the Narmada River in India, the Indonesian Transmigration project, and the Brazilian Polonoroeste infrastructure project, which was viewed as a direct threat to Amazon rainforests.[24] However, and most importantly for the present analysis, transnational groups soon mobilized resources to criticize standard Bank procedures, and provided compelling reasons why more democratic practices should be used by the World Bank and other development institutions. The campaigns interacted, of course, as procedural changes were sought in large part because of the exclusion NGOs experienced when they tried to have influence over specific projects. Groups were frustrated, for instance, when the Bank denied them access to information about the environmental impacts of development projects and refused to listen to their views on a range of policy issues.

In any case, the procedural reforms pursued by the NGOs—they sought greater participation, transparency and accountability—have obvious roots in basic principles of democratic governance and institutional legitimacy. Indeed, arguments about procedural legitimacy ultimately reflected democratic values broadly shared in advanced industrial states.[25] Claudio Grossman and Daniel Bradlow conclude that the promotion of these particular principles at the World Bank "merely represent[s] the extension of the principles of democracy from the domestic to the international realm."[26] They note that embracing these principles might well provide "a means to distinguish between legitimate international action" and "the unjustified use of power." Constructivist scholars have previously found that "democracies externalize their internal norms when cooperating with each other."[27]

Because the United States is by far the largest financial backer (or shareholder) of the World Bank, Washington-based NGOs, such as the Environmental Defense Fund and Natural Resources Defense Council, conducted an extensive publicity and lobbying campaign targeting the U.S. government.[28] For instance, these environmental groups and other NGOs hoped to convince the Congress to add a number of specific operational conditions on legislation authorizing U.S. funds for the Bank. Ideally, Congress would threaten to withhold American funding unless the Bank added a number of environmental provisions to its lending mandate and made its decision and operational procedures more open and accountable. NGO activists thought that congressional leverage might be sufficient to attain their Bank-reform goals, and their appeals to Congress quite directly and powerfully challenged the institution. Consider the testimony of Durwood Zaelke and David Hunter of the Center for International Environmental Law (CIEL). Their joint presentation summarized the deep-seated anti-Bank sentiments of the relevant NGO community: "Various CIEL attorneys have come to refer to the Bank as a 'lawless' institution." Zaelke and Hunter argued that the U.S. government must assure that the Bank's policies "fully reflect our concern with the standards of good governance: openness, transparency, objectivity and accountability."[29]

Ultimately, after holding numerous hearings featuring this kind of testimony, Congress imposed a variety of specific restrictions on U.S. payments to the Bank, contingent upon the institution's implementation of substantive and procedural reforms.[30] In 1993, some funds were actually withheld from the International Development Association (IDA), the part of the Bank that lends to the poorest states, until the Bank adopted transparency and accountability reforms.[31] Normally, Congress authorized IDA payments for three years, but in this case did so for only two years and sliced $200 million out of a $3.7 billion budgeted authorization. "In 1994, Congress continued to withhold the third year of IDA authorization and conditioned further support on the implementation of the new reforms."[32] NGOs recommended that monies targeted for IDA should be extended to alternative institutions that were more democratic.

At this point, it should be acknowledged that not all NGO efforts were aimed at Congress, as groups also formed transnational coalitions with like-minded NGOs in loan recipient countries (some leaders of those organizations ended up testifying before Congress), established relationships with sympathetic officials within the World Bank bureaucracy, and publicized case studies of several Bank-funded "ecological disasters" with the help of mass media.[33] Moreover, the World Bank-reform campaign was ultimately quite transnational in nature, as NGO advocates from other wealthy donor states advanced essentially the same sorts of arguments in a variety of public and private forums over a period of many years. The U.S. Congress held significant power, but the Bank was ultimately feeling pressure from all over the world and, to a lesser extent, from within.[34]

In all, because of the various NGO and national efforts, the World Bank has been dramatically transformed in the past decade or so. Quite a number of changes were made on substantive policy issues and are outside the scope of our analysis. Suffice it to note that the Bank now purports to embrace environmental impact assessment, provides significant direct environmental lending, and has taken some steps to mitigate the worst adverse consequences when Bank projects force mass resettlement of peoples.[35] More interesting for present purposes, an extensive literature describes how NGOs convinced—or perhaps more accurately, coerced—the World Bank to embrace procedural norms such as greater participation, transparency, and accountability.

Since 1982, the "NGO-World Bank Committee," which includes equal numbers of Bank employees and NGO representatives, has met regularly to discuss matters of mutual concern. Obviously, as NGO criticisms of the Bank sharpened over the years, this forum theoretically presented a great opportunity for NGOs to critique the most problematic projects. However, staff members who design projects were charged with filtering the results of these meetings into Bank operations, so NGOs did not view this mechanism as nearly adequate.[36] After years of criticism for failing to account for NGO views, the Bank supplemented this disappointing mechanism with specific staff guidelines for action. Operational Directive (O.D.) 14.70 "Involving Nongovernmental Organizations in Bank Supported Activities" was adopted in 1989 to provide guidance for Bank-NGO interactions. These measures, in conjunction with a few others, helped assure much greater NGO involvement in the analysis of sustainable development issues, as well as in the identification, design, financing, implementation, monitoring, and evaluation of World Bank projects.[37]

Hypothetically, every project is now open to various kinds of NGO inputs. However, activist-turned-scholar Paul Nelson contends that "direct" participation is mostly staged and limited to the implementation portion of projects, which obviously constrains real NGO input into development planning.[38] Nelson presents and evaluates the Bank's data to challenge their claims about NGO involvement. Still, over time, participation at the project-level has grown measurably and many analysts expect current trends to continue given the procedural changes adopted by the Bank in the recent past. Even Nelson now acknowledges that Bank President James Wolfensohn "has made common cause with the Bank's NGO critics on some issues, and sought their cooperation in funding discussions."[39] Though NGOs have a limited ability to influence structural adjustment policies, they have been consulted extensively in sector policy planning. Their greatest influence is on environment and social policy issues. As Seamus Cleary argues, NGOs "are increasingly closely involved in the project cycle and in sector work on which Bank policy-making is based. The influence of NGOs can be expected to increase in the short- and medium-term future."[40]

The Bank's Information Disclosure policy, which was instituted by its Executive Directors in 1989 and modified in 1993 and 1994, was designed to make public vast amounts of information about proposed development projects.[41] The new transparency requirement presumes that information should be disclosed and thereby potentially provides concerned parties with almost any important data they might want about planned projects. If fully implemented, affected peoples and other potential project critics would have access to internal reports that assess the viability and value of projects, or that consider their environmental and social implications. Officially, in fact, under Operational Directive 4.01, interested NGOs are supposed to be able to receive written statements describing every project, including their objectives and possible adverse consequences. The Bank is not to make loans unless borrowers, which prepare their own Environmental Assessments, agree to release relevant information. To facilitate information disclosure, the Bank even created a new Public Information Center, which opened in January 1994. Public Information Documents (PIDs) are intended to provide (including by electronic means) up-to-date and detailed information about Bank-sponsored ventures, though the value of the material in PIDs is in dispute. Critics charge that information in PIDs is too general, making detailed criticism quite difficult.[42]

Despite the formal disclosure requirements placed on states and the Bank, many NGO representatives claim that the Bretton Woods institution remains too secretive, in part because financial confidentiality agreements continue to countermand transparency goals. However, if the World Bank fails to live up to its new obligations, people directly adversely affected by projects can pursue relief by filing a claim with the Inspection Panel.[43] The Inspection Panel, which in its own right is a unique international organization designed to assure project accountability, opened in 1994 thanks largely to the pressures posed by transnational advocacy groups.[44] While early returns from the Panel were promising—one suit helped stop a questionable hydroelectric project in Nepal—critics point out that the Bank's Executive Directors wield arbitrary power to limit the scope of investigations and to deny information about cases even to claimants.[45] Moreover, after a few years of operation, the Bank's Executive Directors took several steps in 1999 to limit the authority of the Inspection Panel. Long-time NGO activist Lori Udall acknowledges that the Bank's Information Disclosure Policy and Inspection Panel are "important steps in moving toward public accountability and transparency," but notes that "it is too early to tell whether these reforms will have a long-term or profound impact."[46]

This section has demonstrated the power of NGO criticism against the World Bank, an institution long thought to suffer a deficit of democracy. Though far from ideal, the Bank is now a more inclusive and open institution. Indeed, the ongoing focus of NGO critics now seems to be on further reform of Bank practices, often at the country-level where projects are implemented, while the "50 years is enough" campaign to kill the World Bank has essentially run its course. We now turn our attention to the democratization of the GEF, a process that paralleled World Bank reform.

The Refurbished GEF

Even as the World Bank's practices were undergoing democratic transformation, the GEF received an extensive makeover that addressed many of the same shortcomings common to its pilot phase. The following pages concern whether the GEF, with deep roots in the aloof World Bank, can now actually be considered an "incipient discursive design." Since many critics continue to point out the inadequacies of some World Bank reforms, it should be noted up front that significant GEF grant monies continue to be attached to Bank projects. Many skeptics, especially from the world of NGOs, now consider the GEF to be a "friendly foe" at best.[47]

In its first three years of operation, the experimental GEF was "subjected to an extraordinary amount of international scrutiny and criticism," which culminated in a fairly negative finding by an Independent Evaluation of the Pilot Phase.[48] Though the Earth Summit impressively named the GEF the primary funding mechanism for the new climate and biodiversity conventions, this status was granted only on an interim basis and was explicitly conditioned on a major structural overhaul. As the GEF's Head of External Affairs explained, refurbishing the GEF specifically had to include new provisions for "universal participation" as well as "greater transparency and democracy in governance."[49] Institutional legitimacy and survival hinged on reconstructing GEF's internal workings to the satisfaction of many of its critics.[50] The Conferences of the Parties of the FCCC and CBD, for example, withheld support for the GEF until reforms were completed. Obviously, these entities are constituted by states and their position on these issues was significant for apparent reasons. However, it is also important to emphasize that developing state skeptics were essentially joining (if not echoing) NGO critics in demanding fundamental procedural reforms during the GEF restructuring negotiations.

In any case, majority support at the Earth Summit for greater transparency and universality in membership appear to reflect a new international shared understanding about the minimum requirements for the democratization of development.[51] The Brundtland Commission report included fairly strong language explaining the importance of open and inclusive decision-making in this policy realm. Moreover, even governments of important donor nations soon publicly embraced these ideals. For example, at a 1993 congressional hearing on GEF funding, a United States Treasury Department official stated that "a restructured GEF must be transparent and accountable, and must provide for the active participation of affected peoples and NGOs."[52] Obviously, these statements about the need for GEF restructuring occurred at roughly the same time as the U.S. Congress was coercing the World Bank into accepting greater democracy. Media accounts at the time indicated that British government officials also shared these views.[53] Democracy, virtually all the relevant actors seemed to agree, "implies equity, or balance between donors' and recipients' views."[54]

NGOs, however, worried about the sincerity of donor (and even recipient) state claims. Some pointed out during the renegotiation period that while "there is a certain consensus on these principles" it existed only on a "theoretical and rhetorical level."[55] The practical challenge was to institutionalize the apparently shared understandings into meaningful GEF policies. After a thorough external review and a contentious international negotiation, the initial democratic retooling of the pilot GEF was finally agreed in March 1994. Ultimately, NGOs "generally" supported the results of the GEF restructuring process, which implies that it provided genuine rather than merely symbolic changes.[56] The refurbished GEF Instrument includes new guidelines encouraging participation by nonstate actors, governance structures imparting unprecedented influence to grant recipient states, unusually open disclosure requirements, more onerous project approval procedures, and stipulations for independent monitoring and evaluation of performance.[57] Not all of these changes were implemented at once as the GEF has made some reforms through its operational practices. The following sections explore these fairly remarkable changes in more detail.

Participation at the GEF

Though not quite up to UN standards, GEF state membership is now nearly universal. Thus, the GEF instrument and many of its practices are legitimated by the fact of widespread voluntary participation by sovereign equals.[58]

Additionally, all member states are automatically granted full voting rights in the institution's Assembly, which is supposed to meet every three years to review general policies, membership issues, and broad operational concerns. Given the numerical dominance of developing countries, it is expected that the Global South will direct the body's meetings just as it typically controls the UN General Assembly.[59] This is difficult to ascertain empirically, since only one Assembly has been held to date (a second meeting was scheduled for Beijing in October 2002). In any case, the inclusive membership, while important in legitimating institutional practices, also reflects the fact that states consider the transformed GEF a proper authority. Membership grew from only 29 states in the pilot project to 173 nations by 2002.

Even though most of the organization's funds come from a small number of affluent states, all GEF member states are automatically granted representation, with full and equal voting rights, in the institution's Assembly. Thus, if this body were the most important internal decision-making entity, the GEF would be an extraordinary international development institution, potentially controlled by the great number of recipients and not the much smaller number of wealthy donors. Of course, the GEF's Assembly simply meets too infrequently to control project selection and oversight, which are the entity's most important regular functions. These functions, in fact, are explicitly granted to another body within the GEF organizational structure, which renders the Assembly relatively weak.

The real power within the GEF lies in its Governing Council, which meets twice annually in Washington, DC, sets general operational policies, selects projects for funding, and guides them through implementation. Interestingly, however, the institution's most radical democratic promise also resides in this Governing Council, which features an unprecedented participatory structure that is surprisingly open to external scrutiny. To begin, the GEF does not utilize the simple weighted voting mechanisms common to multilateral financial institutions, but has instead achieved a more equitable structural arrangement based on a balance of donor and recipient authority.[60] While a small number of affluent contributors effectively control similar Bretton Woods organizations, the GEF Council includes sixteen representatives from developing countries (six from Africa, six from the Asia/Pacific region, and four from Latin America and the Caribbean), two from economies-in-transition (essentially Eastern Europe) and fourteen from developed nations. In essence, the retooled GEF combines some features from the UN General Assembly and others from the World Bank. The voting members are mostly poor recipient countries, but the body is disproportionately affluent when compared to the wider membership. Potentially, this arrangement significantly limits the distorting influence of national wealth. It should be observed, however, that any affirmative Governing Council vote requires a double majority of members and contributors. Still, this structure provides unusual influence for recipient states in development decision-making.

Perhaps even more remarkably, transnational and local NGOs have also been awarded a participatory voice directly into GEF Council decision-making. In the early discussions and during the pilot phase of operations, NGOs were excluded from important sessions, meaning that their "participation was severely restricted."[61] However, the GEF can now credibly boast of a "spirit of partnership with NGOs and community groups around the world."[62] GEF documents catalog the benefits that various stakeholders and NGOs can bring to development debates, such as identifying and questioning dubious projects and involving affected peoples.[63] In practice, the day before every Governing Council meeting, accredited NGOs meet with this body in Washington, DC for a formal consultation. According to NGO analysts, accreditation "involves a very simple process," and therefore cannot be used by GEF management to control NGO participation.[64] Unfortunately, the fact that Governing Council meetings occur in Washington, DC does assure that so-called "beltway" NGOs are better positioned to dominate these consultations. Skeptics like Zoe Young and Sonja Boehmer-Christiansen indeed argue that "size and wealth remain major factors in the ability of NGOs to influence and access" the GEF. Worse, these Washington-based NGOs are "in no real sense democratic," since they represent a relatively narrow range of interests in global debates about environment and development.[65] While these "beltway based NGOs" have important interests in GEF proceedings, their views tend to tilt more to the global environmental agenda of the affluent rather than to the basic development needs of the world's poor.[66] Their influence magnifies the institutional bias already cemented in the GEF's substantive mandate, which focuses on ostensibly global concerns such as climate change and biodiversity rather than basic sanitation needs or clean urban air that are viewed as purely localized concerns.

For the purpose of deliberative democracy, participation by a full range of interested parties is vital for assuring meaningful external critique and institutional accountability. NGOs in the Global South, as noted, have extensive practical experience working on environment and development issues and can offer vital firsthand expertise on projects. Thus, perhaps the most important GEF procedure grants ten NGOs "observer status" at all meetings of the Governing Council. Five are physically in the meeting room and five view proceedings by watching a broadcast on closed-circuit television. The GEF is the only multilateral financial institution that creates these openings for NGOs. Since early 1995, the observing NGOs have been allowed to partake directly in Council meetings. The GEF grants them "an opportunity to intervene on every agenda item," though this role is apparently limited when budgets are discussed.[67] Based on interviews she conducted, Charlotte Streck points out that the NGO staff members on the Governing Council "can sometimes be more outspoken than people within the system," which is an important purpose of deliberative democracy.[68] NGO analysts report that they have been most successful when making short presentations, featuring "a few well chosen points, backed by good examples."[69] Seemingly, their influence is grounded in the power of a good argument.

Kal Raustiala notes that the GEF once selected Council observers based instrumentally on whether they had "something specific and valuable to offer," such as information.[70] However, to ensure that the NGOs genuinely represent diverse global interests, informal operational guidelines were established some years ago. Logistically, NGOs organized a network with thirteen contact points in five regions (Africa/Middle East, Asia, Latin America/ Caribbean, Europe, and North America). This network helps assure proper diversity in the NGO delegation to the Governing Council (potentially including the consultation) and also publishes and distributes a newsletter for worldwide consumption.[71] According to agreed procedures, eight of the ten NGO representatives originate from developing nations and only two are from developed nations.[72] The GEF Secretariat funds travel grants, which are awarded through a process controlled by NGOs, to assure that delegations from the Global South are able to attend both the Council Meetings and the precursor consultations. Thus, this participatory practice is not controlled by beltway NGOs and is genuinely noteworthy—though Washington-based organizations have sometimes taken the lead in coordinating related meetings and distributing information. Unfortunately, the discursive potential of NGO inclusion seems to be greater than the practice. The official NGO newsletter contains only a couple of pages of general information and does not discuss internal GEF debates, nor does it provide any critique of decisions.

An additional participatory role can be found in broader GEF operational procedures, which stipulate that NGOs are to be consulted about many basic policy and program issues. GEF management now claims, in fact, that NGOs are already "an important partner in the design and in the implementation of GEF projects."[73] In support of this assertion, the GEF-NGO Network notes that NGOs were greatly involved in the design and implementation of the Medium-Sized Grants program and have also been integrally involved in developing both operational strategies and monitoring and evaluation guidelines.[74] Though this sort of participation is difficult to document in any detail, NGOs would presumably have a strong incentive to complain publicly if they were excluded from this important function. While the GEF faces dissent, numerous NGOs seem to accept the restructured status quo.[75]

Recent figures released by NGOs indicate that nearly 300 groups are "involved" in over 200 GEF projects.[76] CEO El-Ashry claims that NGOs "are the source of about 20 percent of the actual projects proposed to the

Facility."[77] The GEF's Small Grants Program, which sponsors relatively inexpensive, and often experimental, initiatives, has awarded 1,200 NGO proposals. Numerous studies of grassroots involvement in development crucially recommend this kind of "stakeholder" participation, especially in the identification and design stages of projects. In these phases, projects can be tailored to community needs and substantially revised, if necessary, if specific problems or needs are identified along the way. In fact, the GEF's own study of "Project Lessons" concluded that agency staff and local community constituents must interact "especially at the outset" in order for projects to be successful.[78] Nonetheless, many NGOs convincingly charge that, in practice, affected peoples rarely participate extensively in projects.[79] Atherton Martin, an NGO representative for the Caribbean region has claimed that "the new emphasis on participation extends only as far as the paper work. The design teams and implementing agencies merely go through the motions in order to tick off the relevant boxes for donor approval."[80] Indeed, GEF projects, like World Bank projects, are viewed widely by NGOs as donor-driven, "with minimal input from institutions and groups in the country where they are being implemented."[81] These are serious shortcomings that must be overcome if the GEF is to be an authentically inclusive institution. In theory, the NGO presence at the Governing Council meetings could make for indirect stakeholder participation in development decisions, but it is not at all clear that adequate representation is occurring in these meetings. Nonetheless, substantial progress has been made within the GEF to institutionalize participatory norms, which is a vital first step to assuring public accountability and strengthening legitimacy.

Transparency at the GEF

When it was initially created, the GEF was "untransparent: acquisition of documentation was difficult." As previously mentioned, the organizational culture reflected secretive World Bank practices, so this was not especially surprising to external observers. The most recent operational procedures, however, remarkably designate that "all GEF-financed projects will 'provide for full disclosure of all non-confidential information.' "[82] According to Streck, the disclosure policy in effect since the agency was overhauled makes "almost all GEF documents publicly available and open for public scrutiny and feedback. Today the GEF is one of the most transparent international entities."[83] In practice, this means that documents are made widely available—including on the internet—even in advance of Governing Council meetings.[84] In contrast, and despite a similar new Information Policy, the World Bank continues to be criticized for its secrecy, which is often justified in terms of national financial confidentiality.

The unique NGO participant-observer status at GEF Council meetings obviously helps assure transparent decision processes. Put simply, NGOs are now relatively free to both monitor and report about the internal workings of this international institution. NGO participants in the Council typically document their experiences and then integrate them into "one summary report, which is then supposed to be distributed widely to the international NGO community."[85] As noted above, however, this report is apparently not widely available. The GEF-NGO Network's quarterly distributed newsletter is available in several languages (English, French, and Spanish) and can be obtained electronically. It reminds readers of important items on the environment and development agenda, including GEF-NGO consultation dates, up to a year in advance of these meetings. In all, analysts conclude that the mechanisms for implementing GEF transparency provisions are genuinely "ground-breaking," though the measures would be much more impressive if NGO notes of Governing Council meetings were freely accessible.[86]

GEF funding of greenhouse gas inventories and biodiversity assessments also facilitates transparent debate about global environmental issues. States eligible for GEF grants often lack specific information about even their own production of greenhouse gases. Moreover, such states frequently have not assessed the effects of their development policies on biological diversity—and may not even have attempted to catalog their biodiversity resources. Because GEF funds can be used for "enabling" the FCCC and the CBD, many states of the Global South can obtain grants to compile or assess inventories and needs.[87] Once armed with new information, global policy actors (including NGOs and scientists) can better debate priorities for future project funding. Essentially, this means that a relatively common dimension of the transparency norm, gathering information about regime-related activity, can also be viewed as an important precursor of public decision making. If GEF funds are widely used in future years for accumulation of environmental data from the Global South, this should make a substantial contribution to policy debates in various issue areas since data is notoriously lacking or of very poor quality.[88]

Some limits, of course, constrict GEF transparency. Most importantly, states continue to have latitude in preventing disclosure of some financial information that they view as confidential.[89] While there are valid reasons to worry that too much information might be considered confidential and therefore kept secret, the level of GEF transparency certainly seems to be very high as compared to other multilateral financial institutions, which do not have a similar presumption for information disclosure. The physical NGO presence in the decision-making body also provides an opportunity to challenge secrecy at virtually every turn. Yet, somewhat surprisingly, other than planning materials prepared by GEF staff in advance of meetings, Governing Council transcripts or meeting notes do not seem to be publicly available.[90]

Conceivably, this constraint could reflect the high level of transparency already within the GEF, rather than an entrenched practice of secrecy—though a publicly available record of meetings would help establish ongoing institutional accountability. After all, the NGO officials who serve on the Governing Council rotate and may have very little understanding about the details of prior meetings and agreements.

Discursive Democracy?

Interestingly, the GEF Council has so far functioned by consensus, having apparently not yet resorted to a vote.[91] Without direct access to the discussions or to meeting notes, however, it is difficult to know whether the NGO presence, coupled with the numerical advantage of recipient states, has made for decisions reflecting anything like communicative rationality. Still, the GEF procedures clearly represent a promising political step forward towards implementing discursive design features.[92] It is plausible that the consensual practices could reflect a practicing deliberative institution, though it is difficult to know whether powerful states or even beltway NGOs have undue influence. Streck argues that "the balance of power within the Council is still weighted in favor of OECD countries. The major donors underline their demands for influence with policy recommendations linked to the replenishment procedure."[93] Though they do not totally control the votes as they do in the World Bank, affluent states still provide most of the institution's funds. This potentially provides these states with a coercive lever to achieve their goals. If Streck's charge has merit, then the policy results attained to date cannot be viewed as genuinely consensual.

The Governing Council technically operates under a "double majority" voting system. As briefly noted above, all successful votes require both a 60 percent majority of members and the approval of donor countries representing at least 60 percent of contributions. On one hand, the wealthiest states share power and do not unilaterally call the shots in the organization, though their implicit threat of veto presumably looms over projects and procedures. This could mean that more radical proposals would never be seriously considered. On the other hand, the innovation might aptly be called a "double veto" because the South now also possesses a mechanism for blocking projects and procedures urged upon them by the North. This bestows unprecedented authority to the Global South since development officials from affluent nations have long been accused of dominating the development process. Any action of the GEF Council is logically going to reflect broad member agreement. Conceivably, however, failure to achieve deliberative consensus on a particular project or decision might convince parties that a formal vote would be futile.

Another important factor to consider is the comportment of NGOs, which apparently have so far behaved tentatively in meetings.[94] The GEF-NGO Network points out that NGO participation in formal decisions of the GEF Governing Council has so far been "very limited."[95] In fact, the very novelty of the NGO situation might invite them to act cautiously, perhaps out of fear that states could withdraw observer status should they prove too contentious. This would mean that the NGOs could never really serve as genuine peers to the state representatives sitting around the meeting room table. Habermasian deliberative democracy works only if the participants in an open discussion wield equal argumentative authority. Given the relatively active participation by NGOs in other multilateral forums, such as Conferences of the Parties to the FCCC and CBD, NGOs will presumably one day assume a more energetic presence at Governing Council meetings.

NGO analysts note that Governing Council participation norms constrain the freedom of all members to deliberate. "Council members are asked to limit their comments on proposed work programmes to GEF programming and associated policy issues that particular projects might raise. The intention is to avoid detailed discussions in Council meetings on the technical aspects of each project, leading to inefficient micro-management by the Council." This procedure is especially problematic from the NGO point of view since expertise on specific issues and regions is the greatest asset they bring to these sessions. Members of the Council "are invited and encouraged to submit comments of a technical nature directly to the Secretariat," but it is not clear what might result from this input. In practice, the Governing Council approves most proposals. However, "if serious problems with a project are raised by Council members, a project is typically removed from the work programme, at least temporarily."[96] Rather than deliberating toward resolution of difficult questions, it seems as if the Governing Council ducks these issues by avoiding discussion. Still, the current process does allow for a rare measure of accountability and responsiveness in international development and finance. Consultative meetings, which occur regularly between NGOs and Governing Council members, also provide an independent venue for third party critique of proposed projects.

The GEF, because of a major restructuring that occurred earlier in the 1990s, has generously been labeled an institution "open to learning from its mistakes."[97] Quite clearly, there remain important structural shortcomings to overcome. The GEF persists as an institution dominated by states, and especially the wealthy donor states of the North. The agency's agenda, for example, focuses on global environmental problems of primary current interest to environmentalists in the United States and Western Europe, such as climate change and biodiversity, not sanitation or other basic needs of the Global South.[98] However, the decisions about priorities and goals were originally made during the negotiations that established the GEF and could potentially be overturned or modified in practice by the Governing Council. As Gupta argues, GEF procedures now provide "a first step towards introducing norms and ideas that represent the views of the South . . . and as the GEF becomes universal and a little bit more democratic and transparent, change becomes inevitable."[99] Years from now, observers will know better whether this democratic course is actually followed.

Within the GEF, states of the Global South and other relatively powerless actors have achieved extraordinary access to an important area of global decision-making. NGOs, in particular, have attained a truly unique position in what might be called a "quasi-deliberative forum" to challenge state assertions about environment and development. Additionally, the GEF's deliberative potential could be enlarged since its innovative processes and practices seem likely to be copied by other institutions. The World Bank's Assistant General Counsel refers to the reformed GEF as a "state of the art" organization, and notes that it might serve as "a model for other" institutions addressing various global problems.[100] To date, some other development assistance entities have already been recast to reflect NGO calls for greater participation and openness. This includes the U.S. Agency for International Development, the European Union, and regional development banks.[101] These institutional structures were not typically reformed with the GEF in mind, but their new governance arrangements do seem to reflect a broadly shared global understanding about the value of participation and transparency in environment and development regimes.

Publicity and Global Deliberation

The GEF, unfortunately, is almost certainly a more impressive institution on paper than it is in practice. Many critics remain justifiably skeptical of its ability to implement fairly radical democratic procedures. Young and Boehmer-Christiansen, for example, claim that the GEF has merely mastered "the most up-to-date and ambitious jargon of development and environmental management."[102] Institutional documents and leaders may describe policies in a way consistent with the discourse of "emancipatory development," but GEF activities too often "cannot really be anything but politically and economically supportive of 'business-as-usual.' "[103]

The GEF could, of course, adopt a number of new measures that would go much further in democratizing and legitimizing the institution. For example, more than ten NGOs could readily be granted access to closed circuit broadcasts of Governing Council meetings. This would not cost very much, would increase the transparency of the process, and might discourage unhealthy competition among NGOs for this viewing role. Some groups should, without a doubt, then make sure to transcribe and widely distribute meeting notes to assure a far more transparent final decision process. Next, the five NGOs granted access inside the Governing Council meetings need not be excluded from budget discussions. After all, many NGOs are eventually involved directly in the implementation stage of GEF projects and should be able to provide useful input concerning questions about spending. It would be more difficult to convince states to grant NGOs voting rights in the Governing Council, but so long as decisions are made by consensus among members, this may not matter very much. NGOs and other participants in these meetings, however, should put far more emphasis on turning these sessions into genuine deliberations about development choices. Almost none of the potential benefits of public deliberation transpire in meetings that serve primarily to ratify decisions all-but-made prior to the event. While NGOs have an opportunity to contribute to policy discussions in the regular consultation meetings held in advance of Governing Council sessions, those meetings do not include key representatives of the member states.

In all, as we explored throughout this chapter, the GEF's apparent commitment to relatively inclusive participation and transparent decision-making provide unique deliberative possibilities. More broadly, environment and development regimes and institutions are being recast to reflect norms of participation and transparency. We have argued that these norms function as crucial "discourse norms," creating the possibility of genuinely inclusive and open deliberation at least in some issue regimes. Together, in fact, they perhaps constitute an important norm of publicity in global politics, potentially making the institutions and regimes democratically accountable. Ultimately, by promoting the inclusion of transnational civil society and the development of public reason and community, these norms may well provide tremendous opportunities for transformative and emancipatory politics in specific issue areas of global governance. Additional change is required, but the GEF has adopted and implemented democratic procedures virtually unmatched in global politics.

5

The Democratization of the World Trade Organization

Introduction

This chapter considers the deliberative potential of the World Trade Organization, the central new institution in the global trade regime. The WTO, of course, is much less participatory and open than the GEF. One knowledgeable observer, in fact, recently wrote that the relative openness of the GEF versus the secrecy of the WTO demonstrates that "multilateral negotiations on trade and on the environment have been following two largely incompatible paths."[1] However, as we document below, even this often-criticized institution seems to be undergoing a discursive transformation.

The WTO was formed in order to address a variety of challenges to world trade in a rapidly globalizing international economy. The restructuring of the trading system mandated by the WTO is profound, reflecting what Sylvia Ostry calls a "deepening integration of the world economy" based on a new degree of intrusiveness into the domestic regulatory sphere.[2] By contrast, the precursor General Agreement on Tariffs and Trade focused on the relatively more superficial problem of regulating borders.

This deepening, as it were, is occurring with an institutional infrastructure that, when compared to other specialized intergovernmental agencies, is rather weak. For example, the secretariat employs about 500 people and the operating budget is only about $80 million. Furthermore, decision-making within the WTO is by consensus, rather than by majority or even weighted voting. In theory, this means that small subsets of states can preclude WTO action.[3] On the other hand, the appearance of weakness is compensated for by growing support among major governments for an open trading system, which is just one element of what critics assert is an entrenched neoliberal ideological hegemony.[4]

The new trade consensus is seen by many as antidemocratic and exclusionary in the sense that the rules do not account for the world's poor, do not adequately address core labor standards, and do not sufficiently protect the environment. Moreover, given the nature of the WTO negotiating process and dispute resolution mechanism, the opportunities to articulate these interests in formal processes at the global level may be quite limited. Neoliberalism's excessive dependence on the market to promote wealth, too, often neglects crucial issues of equity and justice. At the international level, the IMF, World Bank, and WTO are merely the instruments through which this ideological transmission occurs. By excluding numerous affected groups, these Bretton Woods institutions and the policies they seek to implement are arguably illegitimate, merely reflecting the economic interests and power of dominant states and global corporate elites.

Such criticisms resonate powerfully with an emerging transnational social movement that drew worldwide attention in Seattle in November and December 1999 and later in Prague in September 2000. While critics of the WTO offered a variety of charges, many of the complaints revolved around the fundamental need for institutional transparency and participation.[5] Put simply, they argued that the world trading system itself lacks the necessary democratic procedures to account for concerns of labor, development, environment, and other social justice advocates. Failure to provide this kind of minimal democratic accountability suggests that the WTO lacks basic institutional legitimacy. Consider the words of former U.S. President Bill Clinton, who remarked at the time of the Seattle meetings that "if they don't want people like the protesters outside of every trade meeting until the end of time, they're going to have to open the process so that the voices of labor, the environment and the developing countries can be heard, and so that the decisions are transparent, the records are open, and the consequences are clear."[6] Ultimately, as one concerned NGO declared, if the WTO does not become more open and accountable, "it will suffer the same fate as other institutions and systems that are illegitimate and undemocratic."[7]

Before diving into a more detailed discussion of WTO procedures, we should note that the organization's formal and explicit rules represent a rigorous attempt to "legalize" trade practices. In large measure this process of codification facilitates the domestic adoption processes, but it also highlights the democratic deficit in the emerging trade regime. First, these rules arise from negotiations between states, a practice and operating principle that few members of the WTO are willing to abandon. Second, the dispute resolution mechanisms are closed and restricted, again, to states.[8] It is in these two fundamental procedures wherein claims for greater participation and transparency are lodged by nongovernmental organizations. Addressing the deficit of democracy requires a rethinking of these procedures and introducing norms of publicity at the global level. By doing so, though, the WTO and the resulting trade regime would undergo a fundamental transformation, redefining the postwar bargain of embedded liberalism.[9]

In this chapter, we seek to demonstrate that the WTO serves as an "incipient discursive design." The evidence shows that norms of transparency and participation in the global trading regime are developing, albeit gradually. The World Trade Organization, which is the centerpiece of the trade regime, is taking halting but significant steps towards the kind of global democratic model we postulate.

The GATT and the Emergence of the WTO

The WTO emerged from the Uruguay Round of negotiations under the General Agreement on Tariffs and Trade (GATT). The GATT itself was the product of negotiations to create an International Trade Organization as expressed in the Havana Charter. This Charter provided an extensive set of rules governing world trade of both a general and specific nature. Some of the topic areas included were tariffs, preferences, internal taxation and regulation (including quotas), labor and employment, economic development and reconstruction, antidumping and countervailing duty issues, and special provisions for free trade areas and customs unions. It was an exceptionally ambitious and wide-ranging treaty that failed after encountering significant opposition in the U.S. Senate. Consequently, the GATT, which was based on parts of the Havana Charter, emerged as the primary instrument to manage international trade. In fact, the GATT narrowly focused on tariff reduction; thus, it did not have, nor did it require, substantial institutional mechanisms. Responsibility for trade liberalization was to be assumed by the ITO. When plans for the ITO collapsed, the GATT became, by default, the framework for the postwar international trading regime.

The GATT functioned on the basis of four key principles: most-favored nation treatment (MFN), the principle of national treatment, reciprocity, and the elimination of nontariff barriers (NTBs). The MFN principle requires that any concession granted to one GATT member must be granted to all other members, with limited exceptions. National Treatment refers to Article III of the GATT and asserts that once goods enter into a domestic market, they must be regarded no less favorably than the equivalent domestically produced goods. The principle of Reciprocity means that all trade concessions granted to one party must be matched by equivalent concessions or value by another party or parties. Finally, the effort to eliminate Non-Tariff Barriers intends to direct all trade restrictions towards tariffs, which are a preferred form of protection because of their transparency and measurability relative to NTBs.

In order to promote regular tariff reductions GATT empowered members to initiate new rounds of negotiations. Ultimately, there were eight, including the Uruguay Round (1986–1994) that established the WTO. It is notable that the length of the negotiating rounds grew over time as the number of participating countries increased and as the issues became more complex. So, for instance, the first four rounds (Geneva, 1947; Annecy, France, 1949; Torquay, England, 1951; Geneva, 1956) were completed within one year and involved twenty-three primarily developed countries. The fifth (Dillon) Round began in 1960 and concluded in 1961, and involved forty-five member states. With the waiver of reciprocity requirements for developing countries in 1964, the GATT became far more attractive to many new states. As a consequence 99 countries participated in the Tokyo Round (1973–1979) and by the start of the Uruguay Round there were 125 member states.

The informal nature of the GATT led to negotiations involving mostly interested parties—the largest suppliers and markets for the products or sectors under consideration. Consequently, Southern states were not early participants in many of the negotiations, which were led generally by the United States, Japan, and Western Europe. The expansion of membership and the trade agenda beyond tariff reduction created new coalitions that transcended North-South and East-West divides. By the beginning of the Tokyo Round, then, the ambit of GATT negotiations centered upon nontariff trade barriers including, for example, subsidies and countervailing measures, technical barriers to trade, import licensing procedures and antidumping provisions.

The evolution of the international trade regime under GATT reflected a gradual shift from a decentralized and weak institution to one characterized by greater legalization and comprehensiveness.[10] In part this shift reflected changing patterns of trade, the ability of defending states in a dispute to block or delay the organization of dispute panels, and the growing unilateralism of major states, particularly the United States. Thus, despite the availability of the formal dispute resolution procedures, most differences were actually resolved through informal consultation processes. To help strengthen dispute settlement processes, the Tokyo Round Agreements of 1979 codified procedures that were subsequently strengthened during the Mid-term Review of the Uruguay Round of trade negotiations.

The new context for an expanded trade regime followed from the growth of services trade, the need to address intellectual property rights, the rise of NTBs, and the increasing diffusion of production and differentiated integration of developing countries into the global economy. After nearly eight years of negotiations, the Uruguay Round concluded in April 1994 with the formation of a new World Trade Organization, featuring a permanent Secretariat headquartered in Geneva. Perhaps the most crucial difference between the GATT and the WTO is their legal character. Whereas GATT was a provisional multilateral agreement that never required ratification by contracting parties, the WTO is a formal international institution ratified by member states. In addition, the WTO has fixed procedures to resolve disputes and appeals. Rulings from WTO dispute resolution bodies are presumptively adopted unless there is a consensus for rejection. Since the GATT essentially required a consensus for adoption of rulings, the threshold for reversals in the new regime is considerably higher.

In the new organization, all member states participate in both the biannual Ministerial Conferences and in the General Council, which oversees the daily operation of the WTO. The Ministerial Conference has three bodies that meet regularly and report back to it: the Committee on Trade and Development, the Committee on Balance of Payments, and the Committee on Budget. It is under the first Committee that the most important interests of the developing countries are voiced. Decisions reflect consensus, which typically means unanimity, though when that is unattainable voting provisions are triggered. This principle of consensus is crucial to some of the current divisions in the organization, especially those that have motivated protestors in Seattle and elsewhere. In particular, differences on labor and environmental standards as well as increasing calls for external transparency must overcome resistance among developing countries, who make up the majority of the membership.

The differences between rich and poor states are not as clear as they once were. Many of the so-called developing economies have a strong interest in liberalizing trade and are demanding greater access to the markets of advanced industrial states. Consequently, the nature and extent of Southern participation—the degree of "internal transparency," to employ the language of the WTO—varies considerably. While there are many substantive trade issues that remain at the core of trade disputes among the affluent, middle income and poor states, our focus is on the procedural norms and how they foster greater inclusiveness. In this regard, the challenge to enhance norms of publicity in the WTO is located in two different and frequently contradictory areas: so-called "internal" transparency, or internal decision processes, and "external" transparency, which means the inclusion of nonmember actors and interests, such as nongovernmental organizations (NGOs). It is our argument that the potential for greater democratic practice entails a commitment to publicity norms of participation and transparency in both internal and external processes.

Internal Processes

With the formation of the WTO, states of the Global South began promoting their trade interests in that forum rather than in the United Nations Conference on Trade and Development. Previously, their collective commitment to UNCTAD instead of the GATT was evident in the limited membership and participation by these states in the latter regime. For instance, in 1982 the number of developing country members of GATT was 58; by contrast, in 1997 there were nearly 100 developing country members of the WTO. One observer characterized developing state participation in the GATT as "passive" because they did not regularly partake in any significant way in the "mutual exchange of concessions on a reciprocal basis."[11]

The changing global political economy has altered considerably the structure of production and trade that informed the early design of the GATT. Thus, the Uruguay Round of negotiations, in contrast to the original GATT negotiations, was inclusive, with developing countries playing an important role. In large measure, this change in the level of participation reflected the increased integration of developing countries in a liberalizing world economy and their growing level of manufacturing with the changing structure of global production. Finally, many developing countries now recognize the benefits of a rule-governed trading regime as a means to promote their own economic interests. These trends are evident in a variety of measures. For instance, the share of developing nations in world exports increased from 4 percent in 1963 to more than 24 percent in 1997. This shift was accompanied by a substantial increase in the ratio of their foreign direct investment portfolio to GDP, growing from 5.9 percent to 16.6 percent between 1980 and 1997.[12]

This level of integration is not, of course, consistent across the developing world, but is in fact highly skewed. Much of the progress in trade and foreign direct investment has been located in the newly industrialized countries of East Asia, India, Mexico and the core South American economies. The poorest states of the Global South have experienced much slower trade growth: since 1980 export growth of the least-developed economies has grown only one-quarter as fast as the developing country average.[13] The consequence is that interests, roles and influence on trade issues vary across developing countries and, therefore, the level of "internal" transparency within the WTO likewise varies. This is evident not only in formal and informal procedures, but also in the inequitable distribution of resources for staffing and the domestic capacities of states.

This complexity of interests presents unique procedural challenges in an organization whose 142 members emphasize consensus through consultation. So even though the WTO's General Council includes all members, regular and informal consultation occurs rather frequently among a small subset of state members from major trading nations of the developed and developing world, and some selected other members whose views are considered representative of the general membership. As Constantine Michalopoulos describes it,

> The actual composition of this ["Green Room"] group . . . tends to vary by issue. But on issues of general importance to the organization it could consist of upwards of thirty members. Given that in such a meeting, the representative of the European Commission speaks on behalf of the fifteen members of the European Communities, developing countries, typically form the majority of "voices" in such consultations.[14]

He notes further that in the 1970s and early 1980s an attempt was made to formalize smaller consultative groups in GATT. For example, the "Consultative Group of Eighteen" included ten developing countries to represent the interests of the developing world in trade discussions. More recent attempts to reconstitute such a consultative group in the WTO have failed because the growing number of developing countries and the differentiation of their level of development make it difficult to represent adequately these diverse interests. Indeed, it is becoming harder to formulate common policies among countries whose economies, state capacities, and degree of integration into the global economy and participation in WTO varies considerably. For many of the more advanced economies of the developing world, interests and goals often overlap more with the wealthy industrial states rather than with low-income states. For example, Korea, Mexico and Turkey are also members of the OECD, while the "Carins Group" of agricultural states includes Australia and Hungary in addition to Thailand and Argentina. In effect, the increased complexity of the global economy is rendering traditional divisions in world politics less meaningful. Newly emerging coalitions are being constructed as much by transnational sectoral interests as they are by gross domestic product.

Consequently, the role of informal consultations and loose consultative groupings is growing significantly. Consider, for example, the so-called Invisible Group, comprised of trade ministers from major trading nations of both the developing and developed world, and the "Beau-Rivage Group" of developed and developing smaller countries with a strong commitment to trade multilateralism. Finally, groupings based on regionalism or sectoral patterns and organization also play a part. Here, for instance, ASEAN or the Africa Group of nations consult in association with a body such as the International Textiles and Clothing Bureau.[15]

For many developing countries the challenge of internal transparency and consensus formation in the context of a trading system characterized by diversity, complexity, and interdependence, is one of finding standardized mechanisms through which to forge a common position when negotiating with the largest industrialized trading states. The effect of transnational production processes, reduced transportation costs and increasing value-added trading patterns is to disaggregate interests, thereby undermining not only the search for common bargaining positions, but also the creation of a strong institutionalized process to defend those interests within the WTO. Thus, while the signatories of WTO agreements are primarily developing states, the initiative for these agreements typically comes from the industrialized states with the support of leading trading states of the Global South from East Asia and Latin America.

The other area where developing countries confront obstacles to improved internal transparency can be broadly described as institutional capacity. Membership in any organization is relatively meaningless unless a state possesses the capacity to defend its interests and participate effectively in the complexities and technicalities attendant to a growing number of issues. For the trade regime, this involves compensating for the small WTO secretariat with states' own technical and analytical expertise. Variances in state capacity have garnered recognition in terms of differential treatment of developing countries based on their ability to adapt to and implement accords on, for example, Sanitary and Physiosanitary Standards, and TRIPs (trade-related intellectual property rights). These agreements, following similar practices in other issues, provide for longer implementation periods and technical assistance to strengthen domestic capacity to meet provisions of the agreements. Nonetheless, developing countries often suffer from the inadequacies of their bureaucracies. Poor and weak states lack legislative and enforcement capabilities, and may be unable to pursue careful monitoring strategies. Not only do these conditions undermine the ability of these states to fulfil commitments, but their plight also means that they cannot fully enjoy the benefits that may arise should other states' unfair trade practices be revealed.[16]

Ademola Oyejide has identified these obstacles in Africa and elsewhere, noting that the reluctance of many developing countries to participate in a new round of trade negotiations with a comprehensive agenda stems from the challenges of adjustment from the previous Uruguay Round agreements. These challenges include administrative and financial obligations deriving from the agreements as well as formulating a set of negotiating interests that reflect an appropriate strategy for a new trade round.[17] Hence, the extent and quality of a country's participation in the WTO is dependent on several competencies. These competencies include the capacity to understand fully and internalize the WTO agreements, including not only fulfilling the obligations but also taking advantage of opportunities presented. Another set of competencies includes a country's capacity to articulate trade agendas, pursue them in multilateral negotiations, and to formulate economic development strategies consistent with the WTO agreements. A final set of competencies involves a country's ability to "assert and defend its acquired trade and trade related rights against potential and actual infringement and other challenges"[18]

Oyejide notes that these competencies are channeled through several mechanisms: A country's delegation in Geneva, key bureaucratic and policy personnel in the home capital to support the delegation, and finally a broader set of bureaucratic and personnel competencies across the legislative, political, technical and legal realms that can interact with various domestic actors to implement effectively the requirements of WTO agreements. In this regard, the challenges to establishing a strong domestic support system for multilateral trade negotiations include, for example, the diffused nature of the policy process and the lack of internal coordination of trade related institutions.[19] As a consequence, in many cases bureaucratic agencies are unable to institutionalize patterns of durable cooperation below the highest levels of government and to foster the effective involvement of the private sector in the international trading system.

In addition to the challenges posed by domestic capacity, the member-driven character of the WTO places a premium on strong representation in Geneva. This means that the consultative and often informal process of generating consensus demands technically skilled representation in the organization. Here again, the inability of many developing countries to staff their Geneva offices at all, or with representatives with minimal technical expertise or negotiating experience poses a severe obstacle to their effective participation.[20] For some states, outside consultants have been an option, though the lack of a presence in Geneva can lead to confusion and misunderstandings.[21]

Thus the obstacles to effective participation for many developing countries are significant and reflect, as Oyejide has suggested, an historic practice of subordinating particular interests to the more general interests of the developing world. The relative lack of differentiation rendered participation in every and all forums unnecessary and, consequently, the development of technical skills in trade issues was also unnecessary.[22] It is the underlying transformation in global trade that has challenged the capacity of many developing countries to adapt to new processes and rules.

In order to improve the operation of the WTO and enhance the sense of inclusion in discussions, the WTO's Sub-Committee on Least-Developed Countries proposed an Integrated Framework Pilot Scheme in February 2001. Drawing on the recommendations of the High Level Meeting on Integrated Initiatives for Least Developed Countries (LDC), the proposal seeks to mainstream trade into particular LDC development strategies and, equally important, to strengthen trade-related technical assistance and trade-related capacity building activities, both of which will enhance LDC ownership in the evolving trade regime.[23] The proposal also reflected a general and growing recognition of the need to reassess WTO procedures to ensure greater participation for developing countries. This goal was central to a submission by the United States to the General Council calling for improvements in external transparency. The American communication emphasized that greater external transparency would by default help internal transparency, especially for members with small delegations, by virtue of increasingly the accessibility and availability of information.[24] The discussion paper submitted by the European Community (EC) in October 2000, was more directly focused on internal transparency issues.[25] The EC submission sought to enhance the role of informal consultations to strengthen the process of consensus building. In part, the consultations should be "broadly representative of the WTO membership at different levels of development and reflect the substantive views on the issue being discussed. Noting that in the past a Consultative Group of 18 functioned under the GATT, the EC recommended the formation of a similar consultative group that might contribute to the greater involvement of senior level capital based officials in WTO matters. Additional recommended measures included improvements in transparency, greater outreach to non-resident representatives by the Director-General, and rationalizing the scheduling, number and duration of WTO meetings.[26]

As the Fourth WTO Ministerial Meeting approached in Doha, Qatar, in November 2001, internal transparency remained a primary concern of developing countries, particularly as plans for a new round of trade negotiations took shape. Hence, preparatory discussions emphasized the need for greater consideration of issues of concern to developing countries as well as ensuring their participation in the negotiating process.[27] The Ministerial Declaration adopted at the Doha meeting laid out a framework for negotiations on a variety of issues through a Trade Negotiations Committee.[28] The TNC is the supervisory body for negotiating groups on specific issues as called for in the Ministerial Declaration. Importantly, the negotiating procedures are based on a "best practices" approach that ensures transparency and the full participation of all members through informal consultations and the principle that no member or group of members shall be assumed to be representing the interests of other members.[29] The rapid circulation of reports, frequent reporting by informal groups to members, and advance notice of informal consultations are all new procedural elements intended to strengthen internal transparency. Indeed, the establishment of the TNC in February 2002 was noted by one NGO to "go some way towards ensuring greater transparency and inclusiveness in the negotiating process."[30]

The new TNC negotiating procedures extend the general trend since the initial signing of the Marrakesh Agreement to foster a greater sense of inclusion in the WTO through enhancements in internal transparency. The demands for reform in the global trading system are a consequence of the larger transformations in the structure of trade and production that incorporated and differentiated the interests of the developing countries. It is important to note, also, that these changes are occurring with a broad consensus of the membership of the WTO. From our perspective, these developments reflect a larger transformation taking place in the world trade regime suggestive of new modes of global democratic practice. The consideration of measures to broaden effective participation on the one hand, and greater openness on the other, are essential requirements for a strengthened regime built around consensual and inclusive principles. To the degree that previously excluded developing country interests are increasingly able to offer a meaningful voice to trade deliberations, the regime itself becomes regarded as a legitimate institution among its membership. We recognize that the state-centric nature of the WTO and the trade issue itself tends to emphasize the domestic arena as the site to effect particular interests. In this case, of course, the degree of domestic political openness can determine the extent to which sectoral economic interests or various other social interests are accounted for at the international level. Thus, while we believe that incorporating the diverse needs and interests of the countries of the developing world is crucial to our contention that global democratic norms are emerging in the world trade regime, we do not argue that it is nearly sufficient. To the contrary, the kind of political community that we argue emanates from certain international regimes requires broader inclusionary commitments than those represented by states alone. In effect, the deliberative practices that have the potential to foster real forms of global democracy are those that transcend the interests of states to account for the interests of people across national boundary lines. The progress realized in the accounting for the needs and objectives of developing countries represents only an incremental step towards a truly legitimate and accountable trade regime. Much of the rest of the distance can be overcome, we believe, by expanding channels of participation and enhancing transparency for global civil society.

"External" Participation and Transparency

The demand for greater NGO participation in a global trade regime is not new, though under the General Agreement on Tariffs and Trade, such pressures were limited. By contrast, the predecessor to GATT, the ill-fated International Trade Organization, recognized a role for nongovernmental organizational consultation similar to the emerging role of NGOs in the WTO. For instance, Article 87 paragraph 2 of the final ITO Charter reads: "the Organization may make suitable arrangements for consultation and co-operation with non-governmental organizations concerned with matters within the scope of this Charter."[31] In the case of the ITO, there was a desire for flexibility in relationships with NGOs, rather than a structured approach in which specific organizations *required* consultation as a matter of principle.[32] The underlying assumption, however, was that the knowledge and experience of specific NGOs were valuable to the development and implementation of a new global trade regime. With the demise of the ITO, the GATT emerged as the institutional mechanism to structure global trade, incorporating many of the procedures and norms of the ITO, but not those provisions relating to NGOs. Thus, the relationship between civil society groups and the GATT were informal and ad hoc in nature. The politics of trade were channeled to the national level rather than to negotiation rounds or dispute settlement at the global level.

Both the ITO and GATT experiences with global civil society have informed the WTO-NGO relationship since the Marrakesh Agreement established the new trade regime in 1994. The agreement formally recognized the role of NGOs in Article 5, paragraph 2, stating that "the General Council may make appropriate arrangements for consultation and cooperation with nongovernmental organizations concerned with matters related to those of the WTO."[33] It quickly moved beyond this initial statement and by July 1996, the General Council adopted expanded guidelines for arrangements with NGOs, and did so once again in July 1998, when then Director-General Renato Ruggiero outlined further steps to strengthen cooperation with NGOs.

Recalling provisions in the original ITO Charter, the 1996 guidelines acknowledge generally "the role NGOs can play to increase" public awareness of the WTO. To that end, the organization can broadly seek "to improve transparency and develop communication with NGOs."[34] Paragraph 3 notes that transparency would be improved through faster and more extensive document "derestriction" than in the past, while paragraph 4 emphasizes the central role of the Secretariat in facilitating NGO relationships. In particular, the Secretariat should promote interaction with NGOs "through various means such as" organizing ad hoc "symposia on specific WTO-related issues" and developing other "informal arrangements to receive the information NGOs may wish to make available," especially in consultations with interested delegations. The flexibility implied in the ITO provisions of 1948 is evident as well in the latitude given to particular committees and councils to pursue NGO discussions or meetings.[35] In contrast, the final paragraph (6) reasserts the state-centered nature of the WTO "which is both a legally binding intergovernmental treaty of rights and obligations among its members and a forum for negotiations."

In terms of establishing new norms of publicity, then, the guidelines outlined in 1996 represent progress for NGOs, while at the same time they clearly articulate the unique character of the WTO, which places inherent limits on NGO participation. Since 1996, NGOs regularly have been invited to attend ministerial meetings and have even been provided facilities so that they can disseminate and exchange information with conference participants. Moreover, the guidelines were augmented in July 1998 when the WTO announced still more plans for enhancing cooperation with NGOs. WTO Director Ruggiero outlined several steps including a program of regular briefings on the work of WTO committees and working groups by the External Relations Division, the monthly provision to WTO members of a list of documents, position papers and newsletters submitted by NGOs, and the creation of an NGO section on the WTO website.[36] The announcement also noted, however, that while the Secretariat has some discretion with respect to consulting with NGOs and providing information to them, other matters such as opening dispute resolution hearings or various WTO meetings to the public, and enhancing document derestriction, would require the consent of the membership.

Thus, despite the formal acknowledgement of global civil society's interest in WTO proceedings and some seemingly earnest attempts by the Secretariat to accommodate those interests, states remain reluctant to offer extensive access. In large measure, the remaining policy gap reflects North-South divisions in the global political economy. Industrialized states have been the primary advocates of open access to documents and of new labor and environmental clauses in the trade agreement. Developing countries have resisted such provisions. Although the NGO community and developing countries share many of the same substantive concerns, the latter have been far more concerned with issues relating to internal transparency than external transparency.[37] As we highlight below, interstate divisions have not completely prevented NGOs from achieving greater transparency and participation in various forms. In regard to document access, as well as participation in Ministerial conferences and the dispute resolution mechanism, some real progress has been made within formal WTO channels.

The WTO, NGOs, and Norms of Publicity

The NGO guidelines outlined in 1996 and 1998 clearly had an impact on the relationship between global civil society networks and the WTO. In particular, these changes are occurring in three principal areas: negotiations on rules and procedures, the dispute resolution mechanism, and in extraprocedural forums. Ultimately the changes are constrained by the lack of general consensus among the member states. As noted in the 1996 guidelines, the primary responsibility and place for NGO interface with trade policy currently rests at the national level.

The first indication of how the new guidelines might influence practice was signaled at the initial WTO Ministerial meeting at Singapore in December 1996. On the one hand, members were feeling great pressure at the domestic level to permit increased NGO participation and, in fact, the issue was prominent in the preparatory meetings prior to the conference. The Secretariat proposed inviting NGOs to the conference so long as their activities were "concerned with those of the WTO."[38] While members did not have to approve the list of NGOs to be invited, they were encouraged to consult informally with the Secretariat about the NGOs who submitted registration requests. State concerns that NGOs would have a right to participate in the event, as well as observe it, resulted in their replacing the phrase "observe" with "attend" in the official documents relating to the conference. Further, members were reluctant to allow the policy on NGOs employed at the Singapore Conference to serve as a precedent for future WTO meetings. Hence, state members emphasized that the relevant guidelines authorizing the NGO presence referred to interactions merely on an ad hoc basis, rather than through an institutionalized procedure.[39]

Of the 159 NGOs that submitted requests to attend the conference, 108 actually went to Singapore. The Secretariat established an NGO Centre one block away from the conference site and a taskforce that met daily was created which was comprised of representatives of the NGO community and a representative from the WTO Secretariat. As Gabrielle Marceau and Peter N. Pederson point out, the meetings served a practical purpose and proved to be an integral part of a confidence-building process between the WTO and the NGO community. This step reflected a concern with institutional legitimacy, as Ruggiero stated at the conference: "a world trading system which has the support of a knowledgeable and engaged global community will be in a far stronger position to manage forces of globalization for everyone's benefit."[40] As a first step in expanding participation and transparency, the Singapore Ministerial Conference far exceeded long-established practice under the GATT and signaled a willingness on the part of the WTO Secretariat to account for the concerns of civil society actors.

Following the Singapore meetings, the WTO Geneva Ministerial Conference met in May 1998. Three hundred sixty-two representatives from 128 NGOs attended the meeting and were provided similar facilities to those available in Singapore. Access to delegates was improved by locating the NGO center in the same hall as the Ministerial Conference itself, by allowing NGO document tables to be placed near the official documents desk, and by providing fifty seats in an NGO gallery for the plenary sessions of the conference. The WTO's relationship with civil society was the focus of considerable attention in the wake of the street protests by various groups at the 1999 Ministerial meeting in Seattle. Hence, in the preparations for the

Ministerial Meeting in Doha, Qatar, in November 2001, the Secretariat outlined a set of NGO outreach activities including a series of issue-driven discussions, regular briefings after WTO meetings of interest to NGOs (including General Council sessions on preparations for the Doha Ministerial Meeting), technical seminars and workshops organized by the Secretariat.[41]

For the meeting itself, the WTO notified 647 NGOs of their eligibility to attend and 388 registered. The Secretariat established the NGO Centre in Doha near the main conference facility. In a situation where security was a paramount concern just weeks after the September 11 terror attacks, access to the vicinity of the conference was limited to registered and accredited representatives. Similar to previous ministerial meetings, NGOs were allowed to attend only the plenary session of the conference as observers, but informal interactions with delegations were permitted. The Secretariat provided the NGO Centre with communication and office equipment, and allowed NGOs to engage with representatives and to distribute their documents near the negotiating area. Finally, daily briefings about the proceedings were held for NGOs.[42]

At first glance these accommodations appear symbolic and, indeed, given the resistance of many member states to NGO roles, they were to a considerable degree. Nonetheless, the Secretariat has expanded NGO access to the delegates and WTO officials, thereby fostering informal dialogue and exchange of information during the proceedings and, importantly, afterwards. Such consultation is an essential prerequisite to establishing the global accountability that historically is not evident in the formal procedures of the world trade regime. Furthermore, the use of formal channels of communication rather than protests outside of institutions offers opportunities for NGOs to participate in or contribute substantively to trade discussions. For example, some western governments include certain NGOs in their official delegations. The United States invites business lobbyists to trade negotiations, and the United Kingdom's delegation to Doha included Digby Jones, Director-General of the Confederation of British Industry, a trade union official, and an Oxfam representative.[43]

In other cases, NGOs are using their expertise and their access to resources to assist poorly staffed developing countries—helping them to overcome the capacity problems of internal transparency noted above. For example, in the debate on intellectual property rights and public health a good deal of the research was provided by groups such as Médecins sans Frontières, Oxfam, and the Consumer Project on Technology. According to one trade negotiator, "NGOs are offering to work very closely with developing countries to achieve their objectives. It's how they intend to get into the negotiating room."[44] At the same time, however, some NGOs have been criticized for encouraging developing countries to take difficult and unrealistic negotiating positions. Although NGOs do not take part in ministerial negotiations, their inclusion on delegations and substantive contributions to negotiating positions place them in a unique position to influence bargaining.[45] These advances in NGO participation thus go beyond transformations in procedural norms mandated by the WTO Secretariat alone, to increasing visibility on member delegations.

An additional arena where procedural norms are being redefined is in the WTO's dispute resolution mechanism. In contrast to the original GATT, the WTO is distinctive in that its dispute resolution feature strengthens the durability and obligatory character of the negotiated rules. The dispute panels and Appellate Body are not permitted to add further rights and obligations when settling disputes, though interpretation of the rules is an implicit part of the process. Where interpretation occurs, it necessarily involves rethinking the "rules of the game" as it were, with the consequence being that those rules may entail rights and obligations not originally acknowledged. Under these circumstances, NGOs have sought to participate in dispute resolution by providing evidence or their own interpretation of the rules. Yet the formal mechanisms of the dispute resolution procedure considerably limit the role of NGOs. For example only member states can initiate dispute settlement procedures, and only the members—including the complaining party or parties, can bring the process to a halt. Nonetheless, a potential role for NGOs in dispute resolution has been asserted by a provision of Article 13, paragraph 2 of the Dispute Settlement Understanding (DSU) which states:

> Panels may seek information from any relevant source and may consult experts to obtain their opinion on certain aspects of the matter. With respect to a factual issue concerning a scientific or other technical matter raised by a party to a dispute, a panel may request an advisory report in writing from an expert review group. Rules for the establishment of such a group and its procedures are set forth in Appendix 4.[46]

Arguably, Article 13 offers panels broad discretion to decide whether or not to seek outside information; yet, the Article may well apply only to panels and not to the Appellate Body. This means that the information and technical assistance provided by NGOs is merely evidence and the briefs they might file do not constitute legal arguments.[47] This became more than a hypothetical issue in an environmental dispute brought before a panel, *United States—Import Prohibition of Certain Shrimp Products*.[48] In this case, the panel received two amicus briefs submitted by NGOs, which also sent copies to the parties in the dispute. The complaining parties requested that the brief not be considered in the dispute, while the United States argued that, according to Article 13, the panel could seek relevant information from any source. The panel noted that it had not requested information under Article 13 and therefore did not intend to take the documents into consideration. At the same time, it indicated that parties to a dispute could put forward materials from the briefs as part of their own submission to the panel and other parties would have two weeks to respond to the additional material. The United States did this, designating Section III of the amicus brief from one of the NGOs as an exhibit in one of its panel submissions.

On July 13, 1998 the case went before the Appellate Body where the complainants objected to the United States' decision to attach as exhibits the amicus curiae briefs submitted by the group of NGOs.[49] The complainants argued that the views of NGOs, as opposed to the views of the appellant member are "not contemplated in or authorized by, the DSU or the *Working Procedures for Appellate Review*" (italics in original). The incorporation of the exhibits into the American submission, they claimed, gave rise to inconsistencies, raising "serious procedural and systemic problems." In particular, the distinction between the official position of the member state and NGOs was no longer clear. In August the Appellate Body issued a preliminary ruling on the matter, deciding "to accept for consideration, insofar as they may be pertinent, the legal arguments made by the various non-governmental organizations in the three briefs attached as exhibits to the appellant's submission of the United States."[50] In the same ruling the Appellate Body also asked the United States whether or not it accepted or agreed to the legal arguments set forth in the exhibits.

In response the U.S. argued that "these non-governmental organizations have a great interest, and specialized expertise, in sea-turtle conservation and related matters. It is appropriate therefore that the Appellate Body be informed of those organizations' views. . . . The United States agrees with the legal arguments in the submissions of the non-governmental organizations to the extent those arguments concur with the U.S. arguments set out in our main submission."[51] The American position, challenged by the complainant parties as beyond the scope of Appellate procedures, is notable because of the view that not only NGOs with expertise, but also those with interests, can offer arguments that the Appellate Body should hear through the Member's submission. Interest transcends expertise and widens, potentially, the breadth of non-state actors whose views might be accorded relevance as part of the dispute process.

The final report of the Appellate Body concluded that "the attaching of a brief or other material to the submission of either appellant or appellee, no matter how or where such material may have originated, renders that material at least prima facie an integral part of that participant's submission."[52] The decision was significant in two ways. First, the Appellate Body accepted material provided by NGOs as part of a disputant's submission in the dispute resolution process. The fact that this material can be considered so long as it is incorporated into a member's submission reinforces the prevailing sentiment that participation in WTO processes should remain confined to states themselves.

Second, the Appellate body also addressed the question of whether NGOs can submit materials directly to panels rather than merely including them as part of a member's submission. In its ruling, the Appellate Body reiterated the Panel's original finding and went even further. It made clear that procedures under the WTO Agreement currently preclude panels from accepting materials from individuals and intergovernmental and nongovernmental organizations. The report of the Appellate Body stressed, "only members who are parties to a dispute, or who have notified their interest in becoming third parties in such a dispute to the DSB, have a *legal right* to make submissions to, and have a *legal right* to have those submissions considered by a panel."[53] Nonetheless, a limited victory was attained. On the crucial issue of panel discretion to gather additional information, the Appellate Report established that this range under Article 13 is potentially quite broad. Citing earlier rulings in *EC Measures Affecting Meat and Meat Products (Hormones)* and *Argentina—Measures Affecting Imports of Footwear, Textiles, Apparel and Other Items*, it concluded that:

> It is particularly within the province and the authority of a panel to determine *the need for information and advice* in a specific case, to ascertain the *acceptability* and *relevancy* of information or advice received, and to decide *what weight to ascribe to that information or advice* or to conclude that no weight at all should be given to what has been received.[54]

In addition, according to Article 12.1 of the DSU, Panels are authorized to depart from or add to the working procedures—in effect to develop their own procedures, to resolve a dispute after consultation with both parties—in order to ensure high quality panel reports. At the same time, panels have the authority to accept or reject information and advice whether or not they request that information in the first instance. Hence, in a legal interpretation of the DSU, the Appellate Body asserted that "the Panel erred in its legal interpretation that accepting non-requested information from non-governmental sources is incompatible with the provisions of the DSU . . . the Panel acted within its authority under Articles 12 and 13 of the DSU in allowing any party to the dispute to attach briefs by non-governmental organizations, or any portion thereof, to its own submissions."[55]

The decision in the *Shrimp* case represents a fundamental shift in the potential role for nongovernmental organizations to participate in dispute resolution processes. This can occur in several forms—in conjunction with parties to a dispute who may submit material from NGOs that amplify a particular position, or in response to the requests of a Panel or Appellate Body as it reviews disputes or, alternatively, even on an NGO's initiative. While the panel ultimately decides whether or to what extent such material will be taken into account, the legal recognition of the opportunity for NGOs to offer arguments represents a significant advance in participation by nonstate actors.

Another venue for enhancing both participation and transparency is found in what we will call extraprocedural activities of the WTO. These are primarily symposia originally created through the Committee on Trade and Environment (CTE) which are intended to facilitate dialogue between the WTO and NGOs on environment, sustainable development and trade issues. Somewhat less formally, two dozen trade and environment ministers, representatives of intergovernmental organizations and directors of leading environmental NGOs met in Geneva in September 1999 to discuss trade and development issues.[56] And more recently the WTO sponsored a Symposium on Issues Confronting the World Trading System, bringing together member states, intergovernmental organizations and NGOs to discuss issues such as agriculture, intellectual property rights, services, the environment and the role of NGOs in the WTO.[57] Hence, what is now an institutionalization of symposia offers an attractive venue for civil society organizations to interact with representatives of the WTO, allowing them to explore issues and articulate concerns. The informal meetings reflect a growing acceptance among member countries that support for a global trade regime can be strengthened by accounting for interests expressed by NGOs.

While these symposia have been called mere "holding actions" to blunt further civil society pressure for greater access and accountability of the WTO, in fact these meetings provide an innovative and increasingly frequent means of strengthening the relationship between NGOs and the WTO. For instance, a September 1997 joint WTO-UNCTAD NGO Symposium on Trade-related Issues Affecting Least-Developed Countries held in Geneva broadened NGO representation to include increased Southern NGO participation. The meeting preceded by two weeks a High-Level Meeting for Least Developed Countries that would focus on capacity-building and investment issues. The NGO Symposium mirrored the agenda of the High-Level Meeting and its conclusions and recommendations were consequently submitted to the HLM as formal documents. Indeed, the two Chairpersons of the NGO Symposium were invited to present these conclusions to the HLM, a significant advance in participation within WTO forums.

The March 1999 High-Level Symposium on Trade and the Environment reflected a desire on the part of major states, especially the European Union and the United States, to seek stronger rules for environmental protection and enforcement and greater transparency and inclusion in the WTO.

The growing emphasis on environment and development issues has proved an important means by which NGO participation might increase at the global institutional level. Though divisions were evident among the aims of developed and developing countries and NGOs, the symposium offered yet another forum for NGO and member dialogue that not only included principles for incorporating environmental issues into trade negotiations, but also expanded the discussion to account for development concerns. This dialogue gathered momentum after the Doha Ministerial Meeting in a WTO sponsored symposium on the "Doha Development Agenda and Beyond" in which more than 800 academics, government, and NGO representatives gathered to assess the implications of the Doha Ministerial Conference.[58] These symposia, in providing a regular vehicle for the exchange of views between NGOs and WTO member states as well as other intergovernmental organizations, can thus be regarded as expanding participation in the evolution of the global trade regime. To the extent that the issues raised and recommendations expressed find their way onto High-Level Meeting agendas and, eventually, into the ministerial meetings, then these forums have served to broaden frameworks of authentic participation.

Certainly, these modes of inclusion are not as meaningful as direct participation in negotiations about the trade rules from the start. However, several points are worth making in this regard. First, as the discussion above notes, the WTO is gradually expanding channels for formal NGO input into the negotiating process by organizing symposia that include member states and interested nonmember parties, and by permitting NGO representatives to attend Ministerial meetings that also include regular briefings by WTO officials. These not insignificant steps allow nongovernmental actors to articulate positions, to initiate dialogue with members and the WTO secretariat and, importantly, to sustain that dialogue over time and through various forums. Indeed, participating in the formation of the global trading agenda and the rules of trade at the *international* level is, as WTO members never fail to note, the prerogative of states who are members. Yet, by fostering regular mechanisms for inclusion, the WTO has enhanced and institutionalized procedures whereby the concerns and interests of segments of global society unrelated to and transcending the particular interests of states can be expressed. In many ways, the extent of inclusion offered by the WTO in the formation of trading norms in preliminary and formal settings is not considerably different from NGO participation in other multilateral forums. For example, at the Seattle Ministerial Conference, the WTO recognized and accredited over 750 nongovernmental organizations before the session collapsed under pressure from protests.

Additionally, the WTO dispute settlement mechanism, the vehicle through which trade norms are becoming more clearly defined, is proving sufficiently flexible to recognize the potential contributions of nonmembers. In both the initial phases of a dispute and in the appeal, the rules permit solicited and unsolicited submissions by nongovernmental organizations. Moreover, the disputing parties can also attach NGO materials to their submissions. Though legal standing remains confined to states, the participation right granted to NGOs, which allows them to provide information, means that NGOs can influence the interpretation of rules. Thus, in an indirect though significant way, the World Trade Organization is adopting new procedural norms that widen opportunities for NGOs to contribute to the formation and clarification of the trading regime.

A third point is that in the arena of trade, domestic politics continues to play a dominant role in determining what sectors are regulated, the extent of the regulation, and the degree to which other social issues are included in new rules. In this regard, the WTO emphasizes that the primary locus of political activity should remain within national institutional contexts. This is because member states bring to the negotiating table positions that reflect the needs and interests of domestic actors in both the tradable and nontradable sectors. Of course, the dominant trading states, given their typically more open political systems, offer greater channels for participation than found at the global level. On the other hand, many member states are nondemocratic, and many developing countries oppose the growing influence of nongovernmental organizations in the WTO. Indeed, for these states, the demands that NGOs put forward for improving labor or environmental standards undermine one of their key competitive advantages in the global market place. Given these circumstances, the ability of poor states to block NGO participation in the WTO is a potential obstacle to expanding participation in the formal processes of the organization. The alternative is, therefore, to pursue agendas at the national level, particularly in the democratic and industrialized states.

The procedural transformations promoting greater NGO inclusion, subtle though they may be, coincide with equally important improvements in transparency. Without a doubt, greater transparency is achieved by the presence of NGOs at various meetings, in particular at the ministerial conferences and through regular interactions with the WTO membership and Secretariat at various symposia and informal meetings. Beyond those measures, transparency has improved considerably since 1994 with regard to the availability of internal WTO documents to nonmembers. A July 1996 decision on "derestriction" of documents in fact represented a substantial step forward in terms of WTO transparency that has since been expanded in a May 2002 decision by the General Council.[59]

Under consistent urging from the several industrialized states[60] the WTO General Council adopted procedures for derestricting documents on 18 July 1996, with a review period of two years.[61] The guiding principle of the new policy was to minimize the prior GATT practice of presumptively restricting document availability. In general, there is now a stated presumption of unrestricted circulation of documents unless limits are specifically identified in the appendix to the new procedures. Consequently, by 2001 approximately 65 percent of the more than 21,000 WTO documents were available to the public. However, the documents identified in the appendix generally pertained to pending policy decisions and cases, thereby rendering the new policy not much different in practice from the GATT procedure.[62] In addition, members had considerable discretion to restrict documents, which might indefinitely prevent material from becoming public. The arbitrary restriction periods clearly limited the capacity of citizens and nonmembers to contribute to decision-making processes both at the global level—within the institutional mechanisms of the WTO—and at the national level, through domestic political processes. As L. Brennan Van Dyke and John Barlow Weiner contend, "automatic *but after the fact* access to documents is of limited value. Any response the public might have would have to overcome what is likely to be a consensus position of the Membership."[63]

A review of the 1996 procedures began in 1998 as mandated. In particular, the United States, Canada and the European Union have been at the forefront of efforts to improve transparency and participation procedures in the WTO. For instance, in a memo circulated to the WTO General Council in July 1998, the European Communities stressed that the broader political remit of the organization—broader than that of the GATT—requires reflection on how this mandate could be better fulfilled by members. Focusing on ways to increase transparency, the EC suggested that rapid document derestriction and the fostering of a more systematic use of channels of interaction with civil society would aid the WTO in becoming "fully sensitive to its broader environment and contribute towards the fulfillment of its mandate on coherence in global policy making including cooperation with Bretton-Woods institutions."[64] The European Community took the position that civil society organizations are key stakeholders in domestic trade policy; hence, WTO members have a responsibility to develop sound procedures for consultation and cooperation at the domestic level. Yet, these measures should be complemented by "greater and more systematic use of opportunities for dialogue and consultations with organizations of civil society at the multilateral level."[65]

In October 2000 the United States submitted an opinion to the General Council on enhancing external transparency.[66] The United States, recalling the 1996 guidelines on improved relations with NGOs, noted that members have already agreed that participation and dialogue at the national level is crucial to fostering the sense of inclusiveness in trade negotiations sought by nongovernmental organizations. While a consensus had been emerging on enhancing transparency through a new document derestriction policy, some members argued that the new policy negatively effected WTO procedures. Bulgaria, in a position noted by India and several other developing countries, argued that a radical derestriction of WTO documents might encourage creation and use of informal rather than formal documents leading to a proliferation of unofficial material. This unofficial information would not be transparent. Furthermore, the immediate derestriction of documents might result in a reluctance to prepare and submit in advance official documents, but instead lead to the tabling of last minute proposals. Any last minute proposals, perhaps formulated in "green room" discussions by small or exclusive groups of Members are a form of both internal and external secrecy; thus, the procedural consequence would contradict the intent of the new rule.[67]

The Bulgarian position, while finding some sympathetic members, did not prevail as the General Council pressed for greater transparency through changes in the derestriction policy. The new procedures streamline the administrative process considerably while reducing the time to derestriction. The guiding principle was to balance demands for transparency with the interests of members. As a result, most documents are subject to automatic derestriction after an initial period while at the same time, Members' rights are protected regarding their own submissions. For example, a member's own submission is restricted until its first consideration by a relevant body, or sixty days after the date of circulation, whichever is earlier. If the member requests, the document may be restricted for additional periods of thirty days, subject to renewed requests. The previous rule restricted such submissions initially for a period of one to six months with sixty-day extensions. Background documents from the Secretariat, which were restricted six months plus sixty days after the date of circulation with the possibility of extensions, are now restricted if decided by the requesting body and derestricted sixty days after date of circulation. However, upon request by a member, a document can remain restricted for one additional thirty-day period, after which it is automatically derestricted. A third set of documents, minutes of meetings, are derestricted forty-five days after their date of circulation (except the minutes of the Trade Policy Review Body which are circulated as unrestricted).[68]

As a means of enhancing transparency, the new derestriction policy is a substantial improvement over earlier practices of the GATT and the WTO procedures adopted in 1996. The new policy limited member discretion to restrict documents to their own submissions and reduced the average time to derestriction from eight to nine months to approximately six to twelve weeks—still after the fact but closer to the deliberative process than ever before. It represents one more procedural change that facilitates political access by global civil society actors. To be sure, neither the WTO nor NGOs would describe this policy as perfect. It is, on the other hand, an advance over past practice that enhances public accountability, which is a significant development in itself.

Democracy, Publicity and Accountability in the WTO

Exploring mechanisms whereby participation and transparency in the World Trade Organization are strengthened goes beyond satisfying the demands of nonmembers and, in particular, nongovernmental organizational advocates. At stake, to be sure, is the legitimacy of the new global trading regime. As the authoritative legal and regulative institution for world trade, one that is often seen as deeply intrusive and challenging of state sovereignty, the perception of a lack of accountability in the WTO reflects a persistent democratic deficit. This, as Daniel Esty has noted, gets to the heart of the procedural fairness issue: those who have interests in specific disputes are unable to participate by offering their views or by observing the process.[69] Indeed, the problem of fairness is central to our larger concern with broadened participation and transparency norms and the unique role for NGOs to represent excluded sectors of global society. As Esty notes, the WTO has a special need for *connectedness* to people, particularly those often underrepresented by governments. A minority viewpoint held in multiple jurisdictions may add up to a plurality of silenced dissent. In this event, NGO participation may ensure a voice for those whose concerns would otherwise go unheard or underrepresented.[70] It may also be the case that an improved set of WTO institutional procedures would overcome weak democratic practices in many countries, practices that in fact inhibit representation of viewpoints that are inconsistent with those held by political and economic elites. Inclusion in the WTO, in other words, can be fostered through broadened roles for global civil society.

Indeed, because of the generally more open and participatory domestic processes that characterize political systems in the United States and Europe, the sharp division between the industrial and developing nations is reinforced. For example, in a November 2000 meeting of the Asia-Pacific Economic Cooperation (APEC), the United States, in an attempt to ignite a new round of WTO negotiations, insisted that new issues such as labor and environmental standards be included on the agenda. By contrast, states from the Global South wanted a clearly defined agenda that would prevent the inclusion of issues regarded as beyond the mandate of the WTO. Indeed, labor standards, they argued, were already and more properly addressed in the International Labor Organization.[71] The American position, however, reflected the growing influence of a variety of interest groups and labor unions—a unique coalition at points—whose voice was strengthened with the opportunities provided by domestic political structures. These same NGOs operating in many domestic contexts in the industrialized world are also pushing for a greater voice at the global level. Thus, the United States regards outreach programs already underway, such as symposia and web-site development, as necessary though not necessarily sufficient measures to secure WTO transparency and participation.

The result of these efforts include liberalization of the document derestriction policy, and greater systematic exchange between the WTO and NGOs in a variety of forums throughout the year and at General Council and ministerial meetings. The transformations in the procedures of the WTO are clearly not to the complete satisfaction of most nongovernmental organizations, and indeed, not even to some major trading states. Nonetheless, the gradual strengthening of transparency and participation norms in the organization reflect a general perception that an effective and *legitimate* trading regime of the scope envisioned by the members requires a greater sense of inclusion and accountability than was found in the earlier GATT regime or than was originally permitted in the Marrakesh Agreement. The notion of accountability is crucial to the formation of an effective public sphere within which the rules promulgated by the WTO will be regarded as responsive to the needs of the diverse interests in global society. There is an assumption in the procedures of the WTO that the primary public sphere for civil society resides not at the global level but at the domestic level where interest groups can participate in the formation of national policy positions, which are then carried to multilateral negotiations. In effect, the WTO trade regime is constituted by a multiplicity of public spheres whose integration at the global level has thus far been constrained by the commitment of WTO members to the exclusive intergovernmental character of the organization. There may be, in other words, limits to the degree of democratization within the institution itself, and any fundamental changes must integrate political activity at both the domestic and international levels to fully legitimize the trade regime.[72] Yet, and this is a crucial point about our survey of procedures within the WTO, there are continuous pressures emanating from major states as well as from substantial elements within global civil society to open up the WTO. Various actors seek enhanced access to meetings in order to foster dialogue among WTO officials, NGOs, and state representatives. These actors also argue for making information available in a more timely fashion and for including non-state voices in formal dispute resolution processes. So long as the WTO responds to these pressures with procedural reforms, those limits to democratization will expand and the boundaries between domestic and global activity will likewise blur.

Ultimately an international organization such as the WTO may be construed to be fully democratic and accountable only when the changes taken thus far are further carried out to their logical conclusion. For instance, new procedures might assure the formal participation of NGO representatives at WTO General Council and ministerial meetings to establish the trade agenda and negotiate new rules of international trade. Development of a formal advocacy role for NGOs in dispute resolution processes, or permanent representation on national delegations, singly or collectively, would likewise constitute a substantial advance from the current relationship between civil society and the WTO. And these changes would necessarily entail access to WTO documents circulated by the Secretariat or members themselves, thereby enhancing transparency. As for issues related to internal transparency, or the access of developing countries to decision-making, the establishment of the Trade Negotiating Committee at the Doha meeting sought to account for exclusionary practices. The need to balance efficiency and representation, however, demands a broader commitment among members to establishing negotiating groups based on interests, national development, and geography, for example. This would allow for many states to be represented in the "green room" process while providing a channel for broad consultation and information sharing among group members.

The collective meaning of these subtle, incremental, and, we believe, significant changes in participation and transparency practices is the gradual formation of a public sphere that institutionalizes modes of communication and inclusion essential to fostering accountability and legitimacy. The WTO regime, in other words, is becoming an "incipient discursive design" at the global level with complex and dense linkages to the public spheres that are found within domestic contexts. To the extent that these linkages solidify global civil society's position within the regime—which means that not only are opportunities to influence trade policy at the domestic level strengthened, but also channels for participation and access to information at the global level are expanded—then public accountability is institutionalized. This is no small achievement, for it is in the provision of a voice and accountability that institutions in a quickly and intensely pluralizing world acquire a democratic quality.

6

Conclusions

Introduction

The previous chapters have sought to challenge a prevailing conception of international regimes as mere artifacts of states. We have argued that the foundation for their transformative role in world politics is evident by virtue of the incorporation of certain procedural norms such as participation and transparency that can generate legitimate authority in world politics. We examined these norms in the environment, development, security and human rights regimes, and with greater detail in the Global Environment Facility and the World Trade Organization. The idea of legitimacy is significant in itself, but our argument goes beyond the assertion of some minimal conditions for the creation of legitimate international institutions (and the authority that would imply). We contend that certain international regimes feature the kinds of global democratic practices that are integral to building transnational political community. Indeed, this extension of our argument to account concretely for the potentialities of legitimate international institutions addresses what Andrew Linklater refers to as the "next stage" of a critical international theory.

In this concluding chapter, then, we bring together various themes of the book that inform the more explicit discussion of procedural norms: legitimacy, accountability, global democracy, citizenship, and community. First we briefly explore the concept of legitimacy in international relations as it relates to the development of procedural norms in international regimes. The next section places our argument in the context of recent explorations of global democratic practice by a number of other scholars. It is our contention that the incorporation of procedural norms into regimes goes far to satisfy the minimal conditions for their vision of a cosmopolitan democratic order in world politics. The last section then draws this argument to the critical theoretical project in international theory. In other words, having argued that certain procedural norms legitimate international institutions, then having argued that these institutions reflect forms of global democratic practice, we inquire as to the transformative implications of our study. Here, it is our position that many international institutions incorporating procedural norms fulfill important conditions for equating regimes to new forms of political community: universal ethical principles, activation of global civil society, and universal inclusion. Thus, global transformation is evident in the emergence of what we have called a global society, one in which state and nonstate actors converge on minimum principles that promote the ends of human security. The point is not to secure an absolute set of universal principles, as we have emphasized repeatedly in the text. Instead, we are concerned with finding a "thin universalism" in which authentic dialogue generates reconciliation in a global polity whose diversity need not be weakened by the attainment of emancipatory ends.

Legitimacy and International Regimes

We began this book by situating our argument in the context of debates about legitimacy in global politics. In an excellent recent essay on this topic, Ian Hurd explores the motivation for states to follow rules in an anarchic environment. The achievement of order in anarchy is posited to follow from two primary explanations found in traditional international relations theory. On the one hand, the exercise of material or coercive power will compel actors to follow rules while, on the other, actors will be guided by their perception of self-interest. Hurd argues that these explanations present only a "shallow reading" of international relations and he thus offers a third possibility: actors follow rules because they understand them to be legitimate.[1] For our purposes, the concept of legitimacy is crucial because, as we have argued in earlier chapters, the transformative potential of institutions is constrained by their inability to overcome the so-called democratic deficits that characterize many international regimes and organizations.

Hurd defines legitimacy as "the normative belief by an actor that a rule or institution ought to be obeyed. It is a subjective quality, relational between actor and institution, and defined by the actor's *perception* of the institution."[2] The perception of actors, as he notes, may come from the rule itself or "the procedure or source by which it was constituted."[3] Compliance is provided by an "internal reason" for an actor to follow a rule, rather than motivated by a recurring calculation of self-interest or the fear of retribution generated by coercion. In an important passage, Hurd asserts that

> The operative process in legitimation is the internalization by the actor of an external standard. Internalization takes place when the actor's sense of its own interests is *partly constituted* by a force outside itself, that is by the standards, laws, rules, and norms present in the community, existing at an intersubjective level.[4]

Once internalized there is no real conflict between an actor's perceived interest and the obligations that follow from the rules and norms of the institution. It is the case historically that certain rules and institutions are initiated through coercion or through the gradual effect of recurring self-interested calculation, but that does not mean these institutions forever lack legitimacy. Rather, relations between an actor and an institution and the forces that gave rise to it in the first place are susceptible to change. Hence, coercion can and indeed does give way to legitimacy as a motivating factor for following rules, as the rules and norms become internalized over time.

This shift in motivation may not be a "bad" thing, as it were, in the case of certain institutional goals, such as achieving or identifying human rights standards. In fact, we would argue that despite the initial motivations of certain regimes that ultimately reflect the promotion of human security—such as early human rights conventions, for example—the fact that these regimes have empowered a variety of nonstate actors and have evolved into new modes of international law thereby establishing standards of conduct for states, suggests precisely the process of internalization of which Hurd writes.

The consequence of actors internalizing legitimate institutional rules and norms is "authority." This peculiar and much studied concept implies the presence of power, but not in the coercive sense. Rather, as Peter Blau describes, its power rests in consensual understanding:

> Resort to either positive incentives or coercive measure by a person in order to influence others is *prima facie* evidence that he does not have authority over them. . . . We speak of authority, therefore, if the willing unconditional compliance of a group of people rests upon their shared beliefs that it is legitimate for the superior . . . to impose his will upon them and it is illegitimate for them to refuse obedience.[5]

Authority, then, reflects a transformation in the nature of power—from the material exercise of one actor over another to the internalization of rules and norms "within a structure of legitimate relations."[6] It vests power with a perception that fuses one's sense of interest with the rules and norms of the institution.

To the extent that legitimate authority is increasingly exercised in global politics through the rules, norms and principles of various international regimes, it is possible to argue that the space of anarchy is, too, increasingly displaced by a system of decentralized governance institutions.[7] This displacement occurs because global politics in general is experiencing dramatic changes in terms of the transnational challenges confronting the capacity of states. We believe many of these changes are mirrored in the procedural norms incorporated into international regimes. In particular, norms of transparency and participation in the regimes we examined in this book have contributed significantly to bridging accountability gaps in global governance, thereby strengthening the legitimacy of international institutions. They do this not only by ensuring access to relevant decision-making information and processes, but also by allowing interested *nonstate* actors to engage these processes. A commitment to these kinds of procedural norms facilitates the internalization by societies and states of regime rules, principles, and norms because various segments of the global polity and their representative agents (NGOs or social movements) contribute to the formation of the rules, principles and norms.[8]

To be sure, new procedural norms do not necessarily ensure a perfect process, and some regimes are perceived as remaining closed and therefore have been susceptible to popular protests—the World Trade Organization is, of course, a leading example. Yet an examination of the procedural changes in the operation of the WTO made either through the dispute resolution process or by the Secretariat itself suggests that even this regime is reaching a level of transparency and participation significantly exceeding the older GATT trade regime. This trend, we believe, is growing throughout the variety of issue areas subject to global governance institutions. Hence, the gradual development of procedural norms in international regimes facilitates the generation of legitimate authority in world politics that is a prerequisite to any vision of global democratic practice.

Global Democracy and Global Transformation

Increasing attention is being focused on the prospect and *need* for new mechanisms of global governance characterized by greater democratic participation. These arguments reflect a larger debate in normative international theory between communitarians and cosmopolitans—a debate that we noted in chapter 2. Aside from a short description of the two positions, this discussion need not detain us here.

Briefly, cosmopolitanism follows from the tradition of Kant and a vision of human progress that emanates from the project of modernity. According to cosmopolitan thinkers, the existence of universal moral law makes possible the creation of a single world society, even world government, whose foundation is this moral law. From this foundation, principles of justice are universal and include not only individual political and civil rights, but in some versions also assertions of equality of access to global resources. The emphasis on universalism and individualism implies a concept of world citizenship anchored in a feeling of mutual loyalty and obligation for others that transcends national identity or particular cultural affiliation. For cosmopolitans, then, the essential project is to create the kind of world society that recognizes and ensures individual rights and shared bonds of loyalty characteristic of world citizenship.[9]

Whereas cosmopolitanism embeds universal moral priority in the person and therefore seeks to construct a political order that prioritizes the universalized rights of the individual, the communitarian position emphasizes the value of the community in defining the meaning of justice. Here, individual identity is constituted by the shared values and ideals of the community, and notions of the good and ethical life reflect those values and ideals. A universal moral law thus confronts particular conceptions of right and justice whose legitimacy is derived from the individual's place in the community. This being the case, it will be impossible to realize some moral and ethical aspirations through transnational democratic practices and world political institutions because universal moral agreement is both unlikely and illegitimate in the absence of community.[10]

It is evident that much of the concern for global democratic practice emanates from the cosmopolitan perspective, and to the degree we seek to outline processes underway toward that end, we may be considered partial to the cosmopolitan position. In this regard, scholars such as David Held, Richard Falk, James Bohman, and Andrew Linklater have contributed to debates on the forms, rationales, and principles of global democracy, revealing and celebrating a commitment to cosmopolitan aspirations. For instance, Held's concern with cosmopolitan democracy derives from a recognition that "there are tendencies at work seeking to create new forms of public life and new ways of debating regional and global issues"[11] These conditions include the way various economic, cultural, social, and political processes are changing the nature, scope, and capacity of the regulatory authority of the state; the way chains of interconnectedness among states and their citizens are changing the nature and dynamics of political systems and outcomes; and the way a variety of local groups are challenging the nation-state as a representative and accountable power system.[12] The consequence, he argues, is a need for new mechanisms that guarantee democratic accountability at all levels of power.

This complex layering of accountability and authority informs Held's vision of cosmopolitan democracy and has three requirements. First, it is necessary to recast the boundary of systems of accountability so that transnational challenges and responses can be brought under democratic control. Second, the role of regional and global regulatory and functional organizations should be reevaluated in order to become a better focal point in global public affairs. Finally, the relationship at all levels between key groups and agencies of civil society and political institutions require redefinition so that the former becomes part of a democratic process. This entails, according to Held, "adopting a structure of rules and principles compatible with those of democracy."[13]

The failure of existing systems of geogovernance to maintain order, justice, and peace suggests for Held that the international community is at a crossroads. The United Nations presents an opportunity to redefine the purposes and mechanisms of global governance that foster greater democratic accountability, but this would entail an unlikely development: "actually living up to its Charter." Beyond this, other elements that contribute to a lack of justice and equity in world affairs would remain as the logic and asymmetries of political and economic power continue to be mirrored in the functioning of the organization. Ultimately, the challenge to instituting cosmopolitan democracy in the United Nations is presented by a structure and organization created to reflect the geopolitical realities of the post-World War II era, rather than the contemporary global system and its needs. Consequently, in the absence of structural reforms, Held does not envision the UN itself as being capable of integrating the wider interests of the world community into its agenda.[14]

By contrast, a cosmopolitan model of democracy entails a much greater degree of complexity and an interweaving of principles and practices at the local, national and global level, than ever envisioned in the United Nations system. As a starting point, the UN requires fundamental reforms that include a reformulation of the Security Council—eliminating the veto and reforming the representational system, compulsory jurisdiction of the World Court, a new International Human Rights Court with compulsory jurisdiction, an effective and accountable international military force to enforce the imperatives of the organization and, most significantly, a second (democratic) chamber. Held argues that the full implementation of a cosmopolitan democratic order requires the formation of an independent assembly of democratic peoples directly elected by them and accountable to them as "an unavoidable institutional requirement."[15] This vision of a cosmopolitan order utilizing the United Nations is remarkably similar to the outlines of a Kantian cosmopolitan order offered recently by Jürgen Habermas: direct elections of representatives to a world parliament, Security Council reform such that it acquires the character of an executive branch of government, and the creation of military forces to enforce the principles and imperatives of the world organization.[16]

For Held, however, the cosmopolitan project is realizable not only through the establishment of a representative body within the United Nations, but it must also account for the incorporation into national constitutions of democratic principles, the formation of global and regional legislative and executive institutions, the use of referenda and requirements for transparency, all of which provide mechanisms to promote and strengthen accountability and participation at the local, national, regional, and global levels. It is crucial that "a cosmopolitan democracy must always be an ensemble of organizations, associations and agencies pursuing their own projects, whether these be economic, social, or cultural; but these projects must always be subject to the constraints of democratic processes and a common structure of political action."[17] Hence, there is no requirement for universal consensus on the values, norms and beliefs of a cosmopolitan democratic community, only on the *procedures* through which outcomes are generated and decisions made.

Richard Falk's cosmopolitanism is equally committed to democratic procedures, but it also places great emphasis on the larger challenge to human security posed by neoliberal "globalization from above."[18] In part, this seems to respond to his skepticism regarding the possibilities of credible reform within the United Nations. Historically the UN, as an organization, designed for the interaction of *states*, was "reluctant to pass judgment on domestic public order issues," reflecting the dominant geopolitical tension that shaped the activities of the organization.[19] By contrast the post-Cold War era witnessed the emergence of a heretofore minor axis of tension—between economistic forces of transnational capital and those transnational social forces concerned with normative issues such as human rights, sustainable development, the environment, and poverty. Hence, for Falk, the possibilities for reform are present; indeed, as the global system continues its shift away from a statist society, these possibilities are necessary if the UN is to avoid marginalizing itself in world affairs.[20]

There are, according to Falk, two dueling tensions in the post-Cold War reformist movement. First, some reforms "reaffirm the statist character of the United Nations." Alternatively, reforms "can involve a grass-roots effort that exerts enough pressure to reassert transnational humanistic claims."[21] The former may reflect the imperatives of the economistic elements of global society seeking to facilitate and guard the penetration of global capital into domestic systems, whereas the latter emphasizes the emergence and influence of a global civil society. A crucial question is whether this global civil society is a durable force. The pattern of conference diplomacy during the 1980s and 1990s initiated by Secretary-General Boutros Boutros-Ghali encouraged an emerging sphere of world civic politics. Yet, Falk questions whether or not these global civil society forces had a lasting effect. To what degree, for example, are agendas articulated at various world conferences fully implemented? To what degree do economistic forces yield to the humanistic imperatives of transnational social movements?[22] As he argues in *On Humane Governance*, "Without appropriate democratization any transition to geogovernance is certain to remain subject to the manipulations of geopolitics and market forces of the sort characterized by the 'triple indictment,' that is, hegemonic in structure, exploitative in human effect, and wasteful of resources."[23] In other words, the attempt to come to terms with a rapidly changing global system, the erosion of state authority and the consequences of complex networks of economic, social and cultural exchange, by creating new mechanisms to regulate global life will only reproduce the patterns of insecurity, injustice and inequity that characterized geoeconomics and politics *unless* these mechanisms account for democracy.

In the domestic realm, this does not entail some universal conception of what democracy is, for "the specific reality of democracy and democratization is a matter for contextual interpretation by social forces variously situated and dedicated to the promotion of dignity and decency."[24] The enlargement of democracy beyond the state/society nexus, however, will only occur through pressure and struggle against the forces of globalization-from-above. These forces have, in fact, created their own forms of geogovernance—the International Monetary Fund, the World Bank, the World Trade Organization—that privilege in an undemocratic fashion the interests of global market forces. Overcoming globalization from above requires an alternative mode of geogovernance "through the agency of transnationalizing democratic forces operating within the forms provided by an emergent global civil society."[25] This is the essence of Falk's globalization-from-below imperative, in which global civil society forces are able to realize the aspiration of humane governance—the effective realization of a broad array of human rights, the extension of participatory mechanisms and accountability procedures to those institutions in which geopolitical and geo-economic forces operate—by civil initiatives, including "the energetic influence of citizen pilgrims of widely different ethnic, cultural, religious and geographical backgrounds."[26]

The challenge of democracy, then, is to open channels to "reinstrumentalize" the state away from the ideologies and influences of forces of neoliberal globalization-from-above toward the redefinition of its role as a mediator between the logic of capital and the needs of its people.[27] There is a strong parallel here with Held's vision of cosmopolitan democracy in which accountability and participation are operative on a variety of social levels. A key distinguishing feature of Falk's analysis, perhaps, is the commitment to global civil society forces as agents to promote humane governance and challenge the exclusions and symmetries of power reinforced by institutions of the neoliberal order. And while the existence and functioning of this civil society is not sufficient for the establishment of cosmopolitan democracy—success hinges on the widening and deepening of democratic structures within the UN and beyond—the rise of a humanistic agenda and the increasing readiness to intervene for humanitarian reasons suggest an opening for cosmopolitan aspirations on the one hand, while reinforcing global civil society on the other.

It is in the complex of international institutions and their associated processes of transformation where we see the potential for global democratic practices to emerge. The breadth of levels of governance outlined by Held and Falk are surely necessary to promote wider cosmopolitan ends, but the expanding network of international regimes and the growing influence of nongovernmental organizations in them creates a new and concrete potential to construct global democracy. Our argument, in this regard, offers specificity to the aspirations of Held and Falk in terms of the practical norms that are necessary to realize a form of global democracy on the one hand and, on the other, empirical cases that suggest the ongoing incorporation of procedural norms that can facilitate the kind of public accountability necessary to authentic democracy. We emphasize, again, that this is a process that is by no means complete nor, we acknowledge, is it occurring in nearly all international regimes. Nonetheless, international regimes in the areas of human rights and the environment, and the progress evinced in the WTO, suggest that public accountability can be strengthened at the global and national levels by norms of participation and transparency.

By making this argument, we also address one of the primary concerns of James Bohman, concerning the challenge of accountability in a social context characterized by decentralized governance. The international regime, according to Bohman, "not only creates new norms, but it is also a process of institutionalization, the creation of practices of decision-making, rule change and enforcement."[28] In chapter 2 we applied the concept of the public sphere to international regimes in order to highlight the potential for these decision-making practices to acquire a specific democratic character. Indeed, viewing the regime as a public sphere within which actors engage in deliberation opens the possibility of accountability and accessibility for those effected by the issues at hand even if, as Bohman notes, they are not members of the same political community, as that term is ordinarily understood.[29] To return to the point made in the first section of this chapter and which informs the argument of this book, public accountability and accessibility enhance the legitimacy and staying power of the regime, while also generating authority. Actor compliance thereby reflects not only their acceptance of the norms and rules, but also their capacity to engage in the decision-making process—the *procedures*. The conscious and intentional design of the requisite procedures—described by Bohman as providing "equal access to institutionalization"—reflects a commitment to a basic standard for constructing legitimate authority in international regimes.[30]

By incorporating the procedural norms of participation and transparency we have been discussing in this book, the international regime significantly widens the potential group of actors and interests in the deliberation of relevant issues, principles, and rules. This has more clearly been the case in human rights, environment and development regimes. The matter of the security and trade regimes are considerably more problematic. However, we outlined the evolving procedural changes within the WTO that seek to account for a greater range of interests and to provide a measure of public scrutiny. Thus, the problem of decentralization is addressed not by replicating at the global level the practice of democracy found at the state level. Rather, decentralized governance is overcome by segmenting global democratic practices into institutionalized transnational public spheres, such as the international regime. In this manner, it is possible to provide voice for those whose interests are at question, not in a direct participatory way, but through representative agents in global civil society.[31]

Regimes, Democracy and Political Community

The growing density, intensity and extensity of global interactions have compelled interest in techniques of global governance and its implications.[32] Indeed, the increasing scholarly attention to cosmopolitan governance addresses the "next stage" in critical international theory by directing inquiry to the transformative potential of international regimes in world politics. In particular, the next stage is about reflecting on modes of community, questioning boundary lines, and exploring ways to shed constraints on the realization of human freedom. While these concerns constitute the very essence of the critical theoretical project in international politics, they obviously depart substantially from the typical constructivist set of concerns, such as explaining how various international norms are developed and how these norms come to shape international behavior. At the same time, critical theorists have essentially ignored these empirical endeavors. Our project, by contrast, attempts to bridge the critical-constructivist divide by both exploring the construction of participation and transparency norms in world politics and evaluating the larger transformative potential of those developments.

Clearly, even though we have not attempted to build and test a specific theoretical model by examining detailed empirical case studies, we have been quite interested in ongoing, observable changes in world politics. Our study of "incipient discursive designs" perhaps sets us apart from most critical international relations theorists. At the same time, however, our study has been overtly committed to the critical mode of inquiry. Our stance is theoretically reflexive, accords primacy to human consciousness, and contains normative purpose. Critical theory offers opportunities to assess international regimes as more than mere artifacts of state interests. Rather, they can be places of genuine progressive change in global politics. This progress is revealed in the gradual discovery, through dialogue amongst interested and relevant actors, state and non-state, of what Molly Cochran calls "weak foundations" on which to realize the emancipatory ends of the critical theoretical project—these are ends, too, we emphasize, that are entirely consistent with the project of modernity.[33]

Ultimately this progress can only occur with the incorporation of procedures into political processes that allow for contending visions of freedom to be expressed, deliberated, and reconciled. This is our fundamental point: *norms of participation and transparency in international regimes offer great potential for a politics whose ultimate aim is emancipation because regimes constituted by these norms reflect a transformation of political community.* They do this by satisfying the various criteria we explored in chapter 2 that suggest the emergence of new boundaries of political community. Regimes of this type articulate a "thin universalism" and legitimize and strengthen the role of global civil society, thereby reflecting an aspiration for universal inclusion.

In contrast to the idea of a "thick universalism" in which substantive universal principles are vulnerable to pointed critique because of the threat they might pose to cultural diversity, the concept of a "thin universalism" reflects the a commitment to the "ideal of a universal communication community which enlarges the range of differences which can be publicly expressed."[34] Habermasian discourse ethics provides the basis for a universalism that "takes the form of a responsibility to engage others, irrespective of their radical, national and other characteristics, in open dialogue about matters which impinge on their welfare."[35] Reflecting on the regime as a site for global political community has informed our discussion of procedural norms, which we see as vital to ensuring that all relevant voices are heard, to providing a measure of accountability, and to fostering dialogical encounters within the globalized public sphere and thereby expressing some collective conception of the good. The arrival at universal ethical principles, then, is not about imposing some absolute moral standard, for to do so would merely reproduce the kinds of exclusionary practices that are core concerns of critical international theory. To the contrary, these principles and their validity follow from the use of appropriately public procedures in the formulation and reconciliation of those principles in the first instance. Thus, participation and transparency, we believe, are minimal necessary conditions to realize the "thin universalism" so essential to the transformative potential of international regimes.

A second element of a transformation of political community is broadly the activation of global civil society networks in world politics. By activation, we mean that these networks engage norm formation processes through formal and informal procedures and their activities and input become regarded as legitimate and credible in global forums. The ideal of universal communication communities requires that the voice of all those affected by a decision will be heard and accounted for equally within a global public sphere. Even with procedural guarantees assured by norms of participation and transparency, this kind of equal and universal access to political processes is, of course, very difficult to attain in world politics. Indeed, it would be quite difficult to attain in domestic democratic polities, as well. Yet, the growth of nongovernmental organizations and transnational social movements through extensive and dense networks of global civil society provides a means for participation and voice for wide segments of the global polity heretofore marginalized in world politics. We would certainly acknowledge the many instrumental and strategic practices of these entities, but we also believe that their ability to represent relevant interests and peoples that are not historically seen or heard is a crucial development in a politics of emancipation.[36]

The complexity of global governance mechanisms, on the one hand, and the substantial power of transnational forces of globalization can and do suppress the weak. This is, of course, a central concern of critical theorists—Falk, in particular, has emphasized the need to strengthen forces of "globalization-from-below" both within state institutions as well as international institutions. It has also been an important concern of practitioners active in world politics, including "anarchical" antiglobalization protesters and centrally organized members of various nongovernmental groups. Where it is not possible for individuals to participate directly in world politics, representative organizations found in global civil society can fill the void, effectively expanding the range of interests and arguments expressed in the dialogue. The resulting agreed principles should thereby more closely proximate a legitimate social purpose that would otherwise be lacking if outcomes were formulated exclusively by states, corporate elites, or both.

The thin universalism and NGO activity that is a consequence of procedural norms implies the satisfaction of a third element that we believe is necessary to an emerging transnational political community, the principle of universal inclusion. A global emancipatory politics is without substance if it fails to account for all. Here, NGOs and universal principles, activated and formulated by virtue of the incorporation of participation and transparency norms in various international regimes, are meant to expand the range of voice, of dialogue, to all those affected persons regardless of nationality, culture, language or religion.[37] Likewise, the growing role of states of the Global South in international institutions, whether based on "sovereign equality" or some other more inclusive principle, increases the diversity of voices active in worldwide debates about politics.

This requirement is intended to expand meaningfully the boundaries of community by ensuring that the principles expressed have application not only in a conceptual sense, but also in a substantive sense. In other words, there must be a real connection between global principles and their local implementation. Human rights conventions that do not enhance the security of individuals are meaningless; sustainable development principles that fail to address the needs of present and future generations are mere rhetoric. Thus, inclusion, not only by reference in the language and speeches of texts and meetings, but also in the concrete application of these principles, is necessary to move beyond a theoretical and philosophical study to real and purposeful change in world politics. It is fair to ask, of course, if inclusion is absolutely satisfied across issue areas. Unfortunately, it is not. But has there been significant progress toward these ends? Absolutely. Representative elements of global civil society stand in and account for many in the formulation of thin universalist principles—refugees, indigenous peoples, political prisoners, women, children, the poor—all of whom ordinarily have very little access to global processes. NGO representatives, social movements, transnational networks, and coalitions of intergovernmental leaders from the Global South connect principles to practice.

While we have focused rather narrowly on specific normative developments within an array of institutions and regimes, some scholars might suggest that the European Union could provide a broader, legitimate institutional context for achieving the critical ideal. After all, it constitutes a new supranational community, and because of the common passport, substantially reduces the significance of state boundaries. Moreover, since the EU apparently reflects a broader community's shared ideas about human rights and other values, then it also potentially helps realize human freedom. Some scholarly work on the EU even embraces Habermasian ideas about communicative rationality and deliberative democracy, which potentially situates the EU as a legitimate institution.[38] Our discussion of the Åurhus convention in chapter 3 additionally demonstrates that norms of participation and transparency are being taken seriously in the EU, especially on environmental questions. However, we conclude that the EU merely reproduces many of the problems seen in traditional international politics, albeit on a different scale. Political community is being redefined geographically—which makes for a broader concept of citizenship than any single nation can provide—but it is not nearly universal, and continues to draw boundaries against "outsiders" both inside as well as outside the boundaries of the EU. Turkish immigrants and external trade competitors, for example, are stymied by the region's territorial limits. Indeed, the EU's regional success has arguably motivated other states to regionalize their trade patterns and organizations as well. In effect, this ongoing redefinition of political community serves only to create fewer and larger political units and does not foster the cosmopolitanism that informs our project. Regional governance simply redefines and reproduces boundaries of exclusion and is therefore a false cosmopolitanism.

In the institutions and regimes we examine, global democratic practices are advanced because procedural norms facilitate the realization of a thin universalism, the activation of global civil society networks, and universal inclusion. The consequence is a redefinition of the boundaries of political community that correspond with the international regime. In other words, the public sphere created by the scope of the international regime provides a deliberative space within which global democratic practice can occur. The institutionalization of these practices and the realization of principles expressed through these practices is an essential step toward the redefinition of the boundaries of political community. Our argument here thus connects with the critical international theoretical project that is central to the work of Andrew Linklater.[39] Linklater envisions a post-Westphalian international order that overcomes the role that sovereignty, territoriality and national citizenship have played in obstructing progress towards the alleviation of transnational harm.[40] Of particular concern is the nature of the relationship between community and citizenship—the historical configuration of political order in the Westphalian international system. Transcending the exclusionary practices central to the maintenance of national citizenship is a necessary first step to a post-Westphalian order in which states willingly relinquish many of their sovereign powers entirely.

The extension of citizenship rights requires a decoupling of the historic nexus between the individual, the state, and territory, in favor of a "thicker conception of citizenship in which societal potentials for increasing human autonomy prevail over competing logics of social control."[41] For Linklater, this potential cannot be realized as long as national identity remains the constituent element of political community. Rather, it is necessary to identify those areas of global life that will encourage individuals to transcend their local bonds and foster a sense of identity with and obligation to others on the basis of universally shared principles. It is doubtful that this can be achieved in and by states themselves since, for many philosophical and theoretical perspectives, the state is a reflection of the highest form of legitimate community. Therefore, clashing ethical perspectives will be hard pressed to reconcile particular and universalistic claims in search of a higher synthesis.

The standard for a redefinition of political community is quite high, and we do not see the realization of a post-Westphalian order and a radical transformation of notions of citizenship, at this point, as a practicable alternative to organizing world politics. By contrast, the arguments presented in this book better reflect the idea of what Linklater calls a solidarist international society, defined as one in which there is "some consensus about the substantive moral purposes which the whole society of states has a duty to uphold."[42] While we agree with the definition, we prefer the phrase "global society" because it avoids the reference to inter*national*, a reference that suggests a limited shift in the character of world politics. The idea of *global* is a crucial and necessary departure when reflecting on the emerging *polis* that provides the historical context for our argument. In this version, the states-system is experiencing a reconfiguration, though we are not able to argue that it is in the midst of decline. And in this version, too, we believe that arguments about global democracy, political community, and weak forms of transnational citizenship as expressed by Held, Falk, Bohman, and Linklater, can be accommodated by a critical theoretical assessment of international regimes.

The transformation of political community immanent within the international regime can only be achieved through the enabling of political practices that both express principles that enhance human security and empower actors to translate those principles into concrete experiences for persons. In this manner citizenship could potentially expand beyond the territorial state to encompass a form of world citizenship, with the attendant formation of identities and loyalties that solidify community.[43] This is a vision that recognizes the place of the state in world politics but also anticipates the creation of modes of global governance which ensures that opportunities for human freedom can be secured. By arguing that existing international regimes have the capacity to promote these fundamental changes in world politics through the incorporation of procedural norms of participation and transparency, we believe that this vision can and must be realized.

Notes

Introduction

1. Barnett, 1997, 540.
2. See, for example, R. Hall, 285–93.
3. Koslowski and Kratochwil, 215–47.
4. Hurd, 383.
5. Hurd, 384–5.
6. Hurd, 387.
7. Morgenthau and Thompson, 1985.
8. Keohane, 1984.
9. Franck, 77.
10. Kingsbury, 1994.
11. Gamble, 325–38; Lodge, 343–68.
12. Caldeira and Gibson, 356.
13. Spiro, 46, 51; and Barnett, 1997, 538–9. NGOs often claim "a certain legitimacy" because of their representation of popular concerns. See Clark, 508. However, it is often noted that NGOs may be unaccountable and unrepresentative. See Raustiala, "Participatory Revolution," 573.
14. Commission on Global Governance, 65–7.
15. See Price and Reus-Smit, 1998.
16. Though we "bracket" the empirical questions, chapter 2 considers some of the latest scholarship that does examine the relationship between discursive procedures and outcomes.

Chapter 1. Critical Theory, Habermas, and International Relations

1. Much more is said about these actors in chapter 3. For a thorough discussion of ongoing turbulent change in world politics, see Rosenau, 1997.
2. Linklater, *Transformation of Political Community,* 17, 43.
3. See Sassen, 1998.
4. Scholte, 1996, 53. See also, Scholte, 2000.

5. See Annis, 1991. See also the relevant discussion in Payne, 2003.

6. See Held, McGrew, Goldblatt, and Perraton, Introduction and Conclusion.

7. Held, McGrew, Goldblatt, and Perraton, 1999.

8. These points are emphasized in Keohane and Nye, 1989; and Mueller, 1989.

9. Neufeld, 10.

10. Neufeld, 11.

11. Warkentin, 2001. See also, Payne, "Information Revolution."

12. Keck and Sikkink, 1998; and Slaughter, 1997.

13. On the idea of the social bond, see Devetak and Higgott, 1999. See also Lipschutz, 1992.

14. Wendt, 1995, 71–2.

15. Brown, 217; Bernstein, 11. Wendt argues that constructivists are "modernists who fully endorse the scientific project of falsifying theories against evidence." Wendt, 1995, 75.

16. Habermas, 1996, xli.

17. Brown, 1994, 217. Crawford, 1998, 123.

18. See Lapid, 247–49. For Keyman, 92, this debate merely carried on the "empirico-analytical" conception of theory grounded in the discourse of traditional international relations theory.

19. Walker, 5.

20. Dombrowski and Rice, 2000.

21. Hoffman, 233.

22. The now classic constructivist account is Wendt, 1992. See also Cox, 1981.

23. Keyman, 93.

24. Neufeld, 68.

25. For example, Cox, 1981; Ashley, 1987; Ruggie, 1993; Linklater, *Beyond Realism*; Walker, 1993; Der Derian, 1987; Gill, 1993.

26. Linklater, *Transformation of Political Community*, 21.

27. See note 26.

28. See, for example, Devetak, 1995; Rengger, 2000; Neufeld, 1995; Linklater, *Men and Citizens* and *Transformation of Political Community,* Crawford, 1998; Walker, 1993; Keyman, 1997; Brown, 1992; Dyer, 1997.

29. Here we emphasize the roots of critical theory in the Kantian tradition, thus anchoring our argument in the core critical theoretical principle that embraces, rather than rejects, the project of modernity as the pathway to realizing human freedom. It is important to note, however, that the critical project itself draws on the Hegelian and Marxian traditions of political thought to fully articulate, in the first instance, the relationship of human consciousness to community and, in the second, the connections between critique, human agency, and the transformation of oppressive material social and economic structures. For a comprehensive explanation of Hegel and Marx in the formulation of a critical international theory, see Neufeld, 1995, and Linklater, *Transformation of Political Community*. Of course, the critical approach is characterized by diversity and richness whose survey is beyond the scope and purpose of this work. See note 25 above for representative literature in critical and normative international theory.

30. Devetak, 31; Neufeld, chapter 1.

31. Gallie, 14 (italics in original).

32. Gallie, 15

33. Gallie, 15.

34. Gallie, 15–6. Brown, 1992, 30.

35. This evolution reflects the movement towards a political order that parallels, but is not identical to, the moral order. See Riley, 14, and on the conditions for peace see chapter 6.

36. See Brown, 1992, 28–33.

37. Devetak, 31. On the application of the Kantian project to peace see Gallie, 8–36. See also the discussion between Laberge, 1998, and Tesón, 1998.

38. Devetak, 27.

39. Keyman, 97.

40. Devetak, 29.

41. Rengger, 151.

42. Devetak, 1995.

43. Linklater, 1996, 281.

44. Linklater, 1999.

45. Linklater, 1999, 477.

46. Linklater, *Transformation of Political Community*, chapter 4.

47. Crawford, 1993, 52.

48. Linklater, *Transformation of Political Community,* 8.

49. Crawford, 1998, 129

50. Schweller, 147–50.

51. Dryzek, 1990, 40.

52. Risse, 2000. By contrast, instrumental rationality is utilitarian and strategic.

53. Dryzek, 1990.

54. Linklater, *Transformation of Political Community,* 219.

55. Mitzen, 2000, 15.

56. See Waltz, 1979.

57. Bohman, "International Regimes," 507.

58. Checkel, "Why Comply?"; see Haacke, 285.

59. See Calhoun, 1992; Lynch, 1999.

60. Lynch, 2000, 315.

61. Risse, 1999, 535.

62. See Lynch, 1999, 2000, 2002.

63. Risse, 1999, 551–2.

64. Lynch, 2000.

65. Ruggie, 1983, 96. For a critique of this argument, see Payne, "Persuasion."

66. Risse, 2000, 18

67. See Risse, 2000; Mitzen, 1999 (cited by permission of the author).

68. Lynch, 2000, 329.

69. See Risse, 2000, 21.

70. Morgenthau and Thompson, 579. See also chapter 7.

71. See OMB Watch, 2002.

72. German IR scholars conducted an extensive theoretical debate about Habermasian notions of argumentative rationality and its compatibility with rational-

choice theory. Much of this literature is cited in Risse, 1999; see also Dryzek, 1992.

73. Müller, 2001; and Checkel, 2001.
74. Dryzek, 1990, 43
75. Dryzek, 1990, 89.

CHAPTER 2. INTERNATIONAL REGIMES AND POLITICAL COMMUNITY

1. Krasner, 1983, 2.
2. Linklater, 1992.
3. Linklater, 1992, 83–4; and Gong, 1984.
4. Linklater, 1992, 84.
5. Ruggie, 1993, 163. Also see Tilly, 1975.
6. Burch, 1994; Spruyt, 527–9; and Anderson, 1996.
7. Rapaczynski, 255–6.
8. Rapaczynski, 258; and Viroli, 156.
9. See Carr, 9.
10. Cochran, 1995, 47; Brown, 1992, especially chapter 3.
11. Thompson, 1992, 177, cited in Cochran, 1995, 47. See also Frost, 1986.
12. Cochran, 1995, 48. This "social tradition" approximates the Hegalian view of the state as the third element of ethical life whose role is to "provide the context within which the external rules needful for relations between individuals can be internalized, no longer experienced as constraints." See Brown, 1992, 63.
13. Walzer, 70–83.
14. Walzer, 83.
15. Mitrany, 1966; E. Haas, 1958; Deutsch et al., 1957.
16. Carr, 63–4.
17. Carr, 43
18. Carr, 44.
19. Carr, 70.
20. Deutsch et al., 5, and see 36.
21. Puchala, 266.
22. Puchala, 264.
23. Adler and Barnett, eds., 1998.
24. Adler and Barnett, 37.
25. Bull, 66–74.
26. See Gong, 1984; and Bull and Watson, 1984.
27. Linklater, 1992, 85.
28. Nardin, 1983, cited in Brown, 1992, 124. See also Brown, 1995.
29. Brown, 1992, 125.
30. Bull, 67–8.
31. Vincent, 142.
32. Myers, 1997; Lewis, 1997; Myers, 1996.

33. Linklater, *Transformation of Political Community*, 167.

34. Adler (1997) argues that constructivism fills the middle ground between neoutilitarian and interpretive approaches (he includes critical theory in this category). Our argument, by contrast, is closer to the one offered by Price and Reus-Smit (262) who point out that modern critical theory serves "to distinguish plausible from implausible interpretations of social life . . . minimal consensually-based ethical principles are required for meaningful emancipatory political action."

35. Linklater (*Transformation of Political Community*, 167) refers to this form as a "solidarist international society." We prefer the term global society as it better reflects the implied transformation in world politics, a transformation that deemphasizes—but does not do away with—the sovereign state.

36. Linklater, 1995, 193.

37. Mearsheimer, 1994. But see Jervis, 1999.

38. This behavioral pattern parallels the distinction between a transformational ontology that accounts for fundamental reordering in global relations through intentional rule making and a positional ontology grounded in neorealism in which such reorderings reflect only changes in power capabilities. See Dessler, 1989.

39. Keohane and Nye, 1977.

40. Keohane and Nye, 1987; the quote is from 738.

41. Keohane and Nye, 1987, 740.

42. Keohane, 1984.

43. Zacher, 1992.

44. On epistemic communities see P. Haas, 1990, and P. Haas, ed., 1992. On transnational advocacy networks, see Keck and Sikkink, 1998. On learning and ideas, see Goldstein and Keohane, eds., 1993; P. Hall, ed., 1989; Levy, 1994; and Stein, 1994.

45. Adler and Haas, 338.

46. Keck and Sikkink, 1998, chapters 1 and 6. See also Sikkink, 1993. For a discussion of the reconfiguration of sovereignty see Camilleri and Falk, 1992.

47. Wendt, 1994.

48. Waltz, 1979.

49. Hansenclever, Mayer, and Rittberger, 1996; the quote is from 206. Finnemore (5) explicitly asks, "Where do preferences come from?" in her influential study, *National Interests and International Society*.

50. P. Haas, 1992, 30.

51. Paterson, 150.

52. Lipschutz, 389–420.

53. Keck and Sikkink, 34.

54. See Payne, "Persuasion."

55. See Finnemore and Sikkink, 1998.

56. Wendt, 1996, see especially, 61. See also, Wendt, 1995. In the latter piece, Wendt embraces "a commitment to states as units of analysis."

57. On the fairness-practices gap, see Keohane, 1989. See also Wendt, 1994.

58. Ruggie, 1993, 143.

59. Wendt, 1994, 393.

60. See, for example, Gill, 1995.

61. Thompson, 1998, 191.

62. Thompson, 1998, 190.

63. Thompson, 1998, 193.

64. Hurd, 379–408.

65. Of importance but beyond the scope of this book, is Hurd's argument that a legitimate international institution in a position of authority over actors exercises power. The nature of this power "runs deep and sometimes orders our lives in ways that are rarely recognized and difficult to democratize" (Hurd, 403). An example of a Foucaldian approach to regimes that explores networks of power relations is Keeley, 1990.

66. Thompson, 1998, 193.

67. See Linklater, "Citizenship and Sovereignty," 124–9. Linklater argues toward a "post-Westphalian state" although this book makes no such claim, remaining tied to a democratic global society.

68. Lynch, 1999, 11.

69. Lynch, 1999, 11, and see Calhoun, 1992.

70. Bohman, "Citizenship and Norms," 5.

71. Lynch, 1999, 37.

72. Lynch, 1999, 40.

73. Mitzen, 1999, 8. Cited by permission of the author.

74. Mitzen, 1999, 22.

75. Linklater, *Transformation of Political Community*, 18–22; Cox, 1981.

76. Linklater, *Transformation of Political Community*, 106.

77. See note 76 above.

78. Linklater, *Transformation of Political Community,* 107.

79. Note here Keeley's (1990) "Foucauldian" interpretation of international regimes. The relationship of regimes to community has been explored in detail elsewhere; see Samhat, 1997 (© *Millennium: Journal of International Studies*. This article first appeared in *Millennium* 26, no. 2 of 1997 and these excerpts are reproduced with the permission of the publisher).

80. Dryzek, 1990, 107. This argument is consistent with Wendt's (1992) famous proclamation that "anarchy is what we make of it."

81. Bohman, "International Regimes," 506.

82. While particular interpretation and application of these principles may vary, many theorists argue that there are certain "foundation-level moral values shared across cultures because they share the same objective property." See Harbour, 1995, 156.

83. Linklater, *Transformation of Political Community*, 106.

84. Linklater, "Citizenship and Sovereignty," 122.

85. Rustin, 1999.

86. Habermas, 1992, 83, quoted in Rustin, 1999, 170.

87. Crawford, 1998, 130.

88. Beitz, 19.

89. Linklater, *Transformation of Political Community*, chapter 3. Habermas requires that deliberators share a common lifeworld. See Risse, 2000, 14–6.

90. See note 89 above.

91. Habermas, 1992, 178, quoted in Rustin, 1999, 182. Note that Habermas distinguishes between a naively habituated life world characterized by the fusion of

moral and evaluative issues, and a rationalized life world in which moral issues become independent of issues of the good life.

92. Wapner, 4.

93. Lipschutz, 393.

94. Görg and Hirsch, 602.

95. Roe, 1995; Pasha and Blaney, 1998.

96. Pasha and Blaney, 437.

97. At the Global Forum during the UNCED in Rio de Janeiro, one component of the NGO Alternative Treaties was a proposed code of conduct. See NGO Alternative Treaties, 1992. For examples of codes of conduct and other initiatives to enhance NGO effectiveness, see Canadian Council for International Co-Operation, 1995; British Overseas NGOs for Development 2001; South African National NGO Coalition, c. 1995; United States Agency for International Development, 1995.

98. Görg and Hirsch, 602. For a discussion of NGOs and the limits of international economic liberalization see Walter, 2001.

99. Sell, 2000; the quote is from 181.

100. Varney and Martin, 2000. Note also that multinational corporations and other NGOs may share common interests, for instance, in the case of corruption. See Wang and Rosenau, 2001.

101. Görg and Hirsch, 603.

102. Görg and Hirsch, 608–9.

103. Pasha and Blaney, 437.

104. It is not our intent to offer a normative judgment on the character of existing global governance institutions; rather, our concern is the procedural norms that offer opportunities for inclusion, dialogue, and therefore outcomes that can be viewed as having greater legitimacy.

105. Bohman, "International Regimes," 510. See also Beetham, 67.

106. Samhat, 1997, 366.

107. Magnusson, 55.

108. Risse, 1999.

109. Risse, 1999, 534.

110. Risse, 1999, 534.

111. Risse, 1999, 549–50. For examples of the transformative role of NGOs see Boli and Thomas, eds., 1999; and Weiss and Gordenker, eds., 1996.

112. Risse, 1999, 551. See also Elster, 1998; the quote is from 12.

113. Boli and Thomas, 1999.

114. Boli and Thomas, 1999, 18

115. Boli and Thomas, 1999, 40.

116. See note 115 above.

117. Rosenau, 1998, 38, 40, 41–3.

CHAPTER 3. PARTICIPATION AND TRANSPARENCY NORMS

1. Mitzen, 1999, 3.
2. Bohman, "Citizenship and Norms," 198.
3. Bohman, "International Regimes," 506–7.

4. Linklater, *Transformation of Political Community*, 175.

5. Risse, 2000, 22.

6. Bohman, "International Regimes," 507.

7. Waltz, 72.

8. Keohane and Nye, 1977.

9. Keohane and Nye, 1989, 26.

10. Many neoliberals would embrace Charles Lindblom's argument that corporations have a privileged political position within states, which enables them to pursue and achieve favorable political outcomes with regularity. See Lindblom, 1977.

11. Linklater, *Transformation of Political Community*, 109

12. See, for example, Weiss and Gordenker, 1996; and Willetts, 1996.

13. Keohane and Nye, 1972.

14. Even though they are technically NGOs, scholars now frequently exclude profit-making corporations or banks, criminal or terrorist organizations, churches, political parties, and mass communications media. See Gordenker and Weiss, 19.

15. See Charnovitz, 1997; and Finnemore and Sikkink, 1998.

16. Fisher, 1998; and Livernash, 1992.

17. See Payne, "Information Revolution."

18. Wiseberg, 1995.

19. Sikkink, 1993. The latter figure is from Smith and Pagnucco, with Lopez, 1998.

20. Quoted in Wiseberg, 1994.

21. J. Fisher, 1993, 5.

22. Keohane and Nye, "Globalization," 116.

23. Dryzek, 1990, 100–1. See also, Mansbridge, 1992.

24. Habermas, 1996, 305.

25. Bohman, 1998, 205, 215n.

26. P. Simmons, 1998, 86; and Payne, "Legitimacy." For a skeptical view, see Zürn, 1998.

27. Florini, 1998, 50.

28. See Chayes and Chayes, 1995, chapters 6–8; and various chapters in Vig and Axelrod, eds., 1999.

29. Mitchell, 110.

30. Lynch, 2002.

31. Florini, 1996, 381. Haas asserts that international-level proposals for democratic decision making, notably including transparency and participation, do not have broad global support. He points to U.S. nonsupport for UN Security Council expansion as evidence. See P. Haas, 1996, 243–4.

32. Florini, 1998, 50, 51.

33. Florini, 1998, 50.

34. Florini, 1998, 63.

35. Consider IMF and World Bank structural adjustment programs, or the Missile Technology Control Regime. These institutions and regimes feature domination by great powers pursuing policies of their mutual interest that nonetheless hurt others affected by the agreed practices. The MTCR, for example, arguably constrains legitimate peaceful uses of rocket science.

36. See Risse and Ropp, 254.

37. See World Commission on Environment and Development, 1987; Keck and Sikkink, 1998; Wapner, 1996; and Princen and Finger, 1994.

38. Paul G. Harris additionally argues that increasing global attention to North-South inequality, a condition that he sees developing in various international institutions, makes for an emerging equity norm that provides for more meaningful participation by poor countries in global environmental governance. Harris, 1996.

39. Raustiala, "States and NGOs."

40. Raustiala, "States and NGOs," 724.

41. Zürn, 644.

42. Clark, Friedman, and Hochstetler, 33.

43. Rahman and Roncerel, 251.

44. Rowlands, 240.

45. Princen, 1994.

46. Humphreys, 110.

47. International Tropical Timber Agreement, 1994.

48. S. Carr and Mpande, 1996.

49. P. Langley, 2001.

50. Stairs and Taylor, 117.

51. Christensen, 4.

52. Cahn, 161, 192.

53. See Ghai and Vivian, 1992; and Fox and Brown, eds., 1998.

54. Shihata, 1995. See especially chapter 6, "The World Bank and Non-Governmental Organizations," 237–74.

55. Bradlow and Grossman, 428.

56. Nelson, "Whose Civil Society?", 422.

57. Udall, 1994.

58. Nelson, "Whose Civil Society?"

59. Nelson, "Whose Civil Society?", 422–3.

60. See Covey, 107.

61. See Grieco, 1988. Also see Powell, 1991; and Snidal, 1991.

62. Mearsheimer, 1994/1995.

63. See Walt, 1987.

64. Mearsheimer, 1990.

65. See Finel and Lord, 1999.

66. Risse-Kappen, 1994.

67. Rutherford, 2000; Price, 1998; and Thakur and Maley, 1999.

68. Barnett, 1995, 48.

69. Price, 639.

70. "Convention on the Prohibition of the Use, Stockpiling, Production and Transfer of Anti-Personnel Mines and on Their Destruction," 1997.

71. Crowley, 2001.

72. Florini, 1996, 382.

73. Florini, 1998, 54.

74. Short, 1999.

75. Burroughs and Cabasso, 476.

76. For a discussion of the relationship between human rights and political community see Samhat, 1999; Boyle and Anderson, 1996; and W. Langley, 1997.

77. Steiner, 10.

78. Wiseberg, 1995.

79. UN, ECOSOC Res. 1296, 1996, Para. 50.

80. The original provisions are found in UN ECOSOC Res. 296, 1968, Para. 17. The revised text is in UN ECOSOC Res. 1296, 1996, Para. 25.

81. Flood, 1999, chapter 3.

82. See for example, UN Office of the High Commissioner for Human Rights, c. 2002; and UN Office of HCHR, 1999.

83. Van Ness, 309; Drinan, 1995; A. Simmons, 1997; De La Garza, 1997; Lafranchi, 1991; and Christiansen and Dowding, 1994.

84. Gaer, 1996.

85. UN, Vienna Declaration and Program of Action, 1993.

86. International Helsinki Federation for Human Rights, 1996.

87. Wasserstrom and Reider, 1997; Cushman, 1998; and Branigin, 1998.

88. See Flood, 1998, 124.

89. Risse, Ropp, and Sikkink, 1999.

90. Vienna Plus Five Global NGO Forum on Human Rights, 1998.

91. See, for example, Gallarotti and Preis, 1999; and Rubin, 1999.

92. UN Office of HCHR, 1993.

93. See UN HCHR, c. 2002.

94. Bohman, "International Regimes," 507.

95. Checkel, "Norms and Institutions," 88; and Checkel, 1997, 476–7.

96. Keck and Sikkink, 201.

97. See Payne, "Persuasion."

98. Dryzek, 1990, 87.

99. Habermas, 1996, 304–6.

100. See Williams and Matheny, 1995; Dukes, 1996; and Gundersen, 1995. However, note Alford, 1996.

101. D. Thompson and Gutmann, 352.

102. See Gilbert, 189.

103. Identifying and documenting the important role of NGOs as "norm entrepreneurs" has been a major research achievement of constructivist scholars. See Finnemore and Sikkink, 1998.

104. Wendt, 1992.

105. While this argument has similarities to functionalist explanations, our emphasis is on civil society networks comprised of a diverse group of actors and interests, rather than the technical experts that characterized early functionalism.

CHAPTER 4. THE DEMOCRATIZATION OF THE GLOBAL ENVIRONMENT FACILITY

1. Tolba, 76–7.

2. World Commission on Environment and Development, 8.

3. Conca, 1993, 319.
4. WCED, 338.
5. Susskind calls the expansion and modification of the GEF "probably the greatest accomplishment" of the Earth Summit. By contrast, Jordan argues that the GEF is a "relatively minor player on the international stage." The latter view is supported by the fact that the GEF budget is minuscule when compared to all global spending devoted to development. See Susskind, 94; and Jordan, 35.
6. Funding allocations reported here are based on GEF figures, 1991–1999. Additionally, ozone-related projects have received some funds, but are supposed to be phased out altogether because that regime has its own multilateral fund.
7. Many external observers argue that GEF mainstreaming efforts have failed. See Horta, 2; and Bichsel and Horta, 1998.
8. El-Ashry, 2000. See also, El-Ashry, 1998.
9. El-Ashry, c. 1997.
10. Gupta, 1995. All member states of the original GEF were expected to make a modest, but significant, financial contribution ($4 million). This was not a requirement for receiving funds, but it obviously discouraged states from formally joining and partaking in the agency's decision-making. See Stone, 226.
11. Payne, "Legitimacy."
12. See Krasner, 1985.
13. See Gupta, 30.
14. Quoted in Tickell and Hildyard, 82.
15. Werksman, 51.
16. Bell, 1996.
17. Rowlands, 203. See also, Rich, 178–81.
18. NGO Statement to the Participants Meeting in Geneva, 261.
19. Lumsdaine, 276.
20. Rich, 193–4; and Udall, 1995.
21. Cahn, 161.
22. Greene, 1994.
23. Keck and Sikkink, 1998.
24. See Rich, 1994. See also, Payne, 1995; and W. Fisher, 1995.
25. Shihata, 1994, 28–9.
26. Grossman and Bradlow, 24.
27. Risse-Kappen, "Collective Identity," 368; and Sikkink, 437.
28. The Environmental Defense Fund is now Environmental Defense.
29. Zaelke and Hunter, 155, 158.
30. Bowles and Kormos, 1995. See also, Bowles and Kormos, 1999.
31. Bridgeman, 1021.
32. Wade, 728.
33. Ruttan, 34.
34. See Daly, 1994.
35. See Wade, 1997.
36. Bradlow, 562n.
37. Shihata, 1992.
38. Nelson, 1995.

39. Nelson, "Heroism and Ambiguity," 487.

40. Cleary, 94.

41. See Nelson, 1996.

42. Bradlow, 570. For a work skeptical of the value of Public Information Documents (PIDs), see Udall, 1998, 406.

43. Shihata, 1994. The inspection panel thus also serves a participatory function. It is "the first forum in which private actors can hold an international organization directly accountable for the consequences of its actions." Bradlow and Schlemmer-Schulte, 395; Zaelke and Hunter, 155. Note also that following the Bank's lead, regional development banks are now establishing inspection panels.

44. Fox, 2000.

45. These arguments are briefly summarized in Payne, 1996.

46. Udall, 1998, 426; Hunter and Udall, 3; Bradlow and Schlemmer-Schulte, 415.

47. See Young, 1999.

48. Fairman, 39.

49. Van Praag, 1994.

50. Jordan, 32; and Mertens, 108.

51. Gupta, 28.

52. Summers, 73.

53. Tickell, 309.

54. Mertens, 106.

55. NGO Statement, 261.

56. Burgiel and Cohen, 7.

57. Bowles, 1996.

58. See Barnett, 1997.

59. Jordan, 19.

60. Harris, 1996.

61. Jordon, 32; and Rowlands, 204.

62. Global Environment Facility, n.d.

63. For example, see GEF, 1996.

64. Burgiel and Cohen, 49.

65. Young and Boehmer-Christiansen, 47.

66. Streck, 1999, 42.

67. El-Ashry, 1997; and Streck, 1999, 38. See also, Streck, 2001.

68. Streck, 1999, 38.

69. Burgiel and Cohen, 49.

70. Raustiala, "States and NGOs," 736.

71. Young, however, claims that the NGO network in the GEF is a "self-selecting clique" that does not utilize democratic practices to make decisions about representation. Young, 253.

72. Burgiel and Cohen, 48.

73. El-Ashry, 1997.

74. GEF-NGO Network, 1998.

75. Some NGOs have complained that they were not involved in relatively secretive monitoring and evaluation studies conducted by the GEF. See Walsh, 1997.

76. GEF Digest, 1999. The same source indicates that funding to NGOs increased over 60 percent between 1996 and 1999.

77. El-Ashry, c. 1997.

78. GEF, 1998.

79. GEF-NGO Network, 1998.

80. Quoted in Bell, 1996.

81. Horta, 3.

82. Rowlands, 203–4.

83. Streck, 1999.

84. El-Ashry, c. 1997.

85. Burgiel and Cohen, 49.

86. Bowles, 40; and Mertens, 106.

87. Burgiel and Cohen, 14, 16; and El-Ashry, c. 1997.

88. For example, very little data exists on the world's remaining wild grasslands. Data on urban air quality is not uniform, sectoral water use data is based on relatively weak estimates, and greenhouse gas emission data is "modeled rather than measured directly." See World Resources Institute, 1998, 233–4.

89. Mertens, 108.

90. Young, 253.

91. El-Ashry, 1997.

92. See Gupta, 42.

93. Streck, 1999, 36–7.

94. Young, 1999.

95. GEF-NGO Network, 1998.

96. Burgiel and Cohen, 1997, 33–4.

97. David Okali quoted in Bagla, 374.

98. See Payne, 1998.

99. Gupta, 42.

100. Silard, 653; and Streck, 2001.

101. Other scholars have outlined these changes in organizations like the U.S. Agency for International Development and the European Union. See Auer, 1998; Putzel, 1998; Udall, 1998; and Nelson, 1996.

102. Young and Boehmer-Christiansen, 40, 50.

103. Young, 246; and Young and Boehmer-Christiansen, 50.

CHAPTER 5. THE DEMOCRATIZATION OF THE WORLD TRADE ORGANIZATION

1. Young, 264n.

2. Ostry, 8.

3. Keohane and Nye, Jr., "Club Model," 21.

4. On the "Washington Consensus," see Rodrik, 54–63; Naim, 2000. This has the character of what Robert Cox calls an "historic social bloc." See Cox, 1981.

5. Nye, Jr., 2001; Krajewski, 2001.

6. Paulson, 1999.

7. Third World Network Statement, 1999.

8. See World Trade Organization, "Guidelines for Arrangements," especially paragraph VI. See also the controversy surrounding the Appellate Body's decision on amicus briefs summarized in International Council on Trade and Sustainable Development, 2000.

9. Ruggie, 1984.

10. Goldstein and Martin, 2000.

11. Whalley, 1987. Quoted in Michalopoulos, 2000.

12. Sutherland, Sewell, and Weiner, 2000.

13. Sutherland, Sewell, and Weiner, 2000, 3.

14. Michalopoulos, 17. The Group tends to meet in the Director-General's green conference room.

15. Michalopoulos, 18.

16. See UNCTAD and WTO, 1996.

17. Oyejide, 1999, vii.

18. Oyejide, 1999, 22–3.

19. Oyejide, 1999, 23. See also Michalopoulos, 19; Blackhurst, 1999; Ohiorhenuan, 1998; and Blackhurst, Lyakurwa, and Oyejide, 1999.

20. Blackhurst, Lyakurwa, and Oyejide, 1999. Note that the Geneva staffs of many developing countries are responsible for diplomatic representation for the entire range of international organizations in the city. They also note that a small staff does not necessarily reflect a lack of resources, as many have significantly larger staffs in New York. See 16–9.

21. See, for example, Chaytor and Hindley, 1997.

22. See Oyejide, 1990.

23. World Trade Organization, Sub-committee on Least-Developed Countries, "Integrated Proposal."

24. World Trade Organization, "General Council Informal Consultations."

25. World Trade Organization, "Improving the Functioning."

26. See note 25 above.

27. At the "Meeting of the Ministers Responsible for Trade of the Least Developed Countries" held in Zanzibar in July 2001, forty-nine trade ministers committed themselves to the collective pursuit of a developing country agenda for the Doha conference, while the topic of internal transparency was raised at the January and July General Council meetings. World Trade Organization, "Zanzibar Declaration;" World Trade Organization, "Minutes, 30 January and 8 February, 2001;" World Trade Organization, "Minutes, 18 and 19 July, 2001."

28. World Trade Organization, "Ministerial Declaration," paragraph 46.

29. World Trade Organization, "Minutes, 17 and 20 July 2000," section 12(134).

30. Raghavan, 2002.

31. ITO Charter, Article 87(2), cited in Marceau and Pedersen, 8.

32. For an extended discussion of the ITO's intended relationship with NGOs, see International Centre for Trade and Sustainable Development, 6–7.

33. World Trade Organization, "Agreement," Article 5, paragraph 2.

34. World Trade Organization, "Guidelines for Arrangements," paragraph 2.

35. World Trade Organization, "Guidelines for Arrangements," paragraphs 3, 4, and 5.

36. World Trade Organization, "Ruggiero."

37. See for example, Leary, 1997; Trade Knowledge Network, 2000; World Trade Organization, "Minutes, 17 and 20 July, 2000." On the LDC position regarding labor standards, see World Trade Organization, 1999, sec. VIII (45); World Trade Organization, "Eleventh Summit," paragraph 4.

38. Marceau and Pederson, 13.

39. Marceau and Pederson, 13.

40. Cited in Scholte with O'Brian and Williams, 116.

41. World Trade Organization, "WTO Secretariat."

42. International Council on Trade and Sustainable Development, "Last-minute Arrangements."

43. Jonquieres and Williams, 2001.

44. Jonquieres and Williams, 2001; International Council on Trade and Sustainable Development, "NGOs Pursue New Avenues."

45. Jonquieres and Williams, 2001.

46. World Trade Organization, "Understanding Rules and Procedures," Article 13, paragraph 2.

47. See Marceau and Pedersen, 34

48. World Trade Organization, "Import Prohibition," 281–2.

49. The following is drawn from World Trade Organization, "Report of the Appellate Body," 28–9.

50. World Trade Organization, "Report of the Appellate Body," 29.

51. World Trade Organization, "Report of the Appellate Body," 30.

52. World Trade Organization, "Report of the Appellate Body," 31.

53. World Trade Organization, "Report of the Appellate Body," 35. Italics in original.

54. World Trade Organization, "Report of the Appellate Body," 37. Italics in original.

55. World Trade Organization, "Report of the Appellate Body," 39. This broad discretion was a central element of the decision by the Appellate Body to the Chairman of the Dispute Settlement Body in *European Communities—Measures Affecting Asbestos and Asbestos-Containing Products*. In this November 2000 decision, a unique procedure for this particular case was adopted which allowed written briefs to be submitted to the Appellate Body from persons other than a party or third party to a dispute. Here the Appellate Body, in a manner similar to the discretion available to the Panel hearing the original dispute and with the consent of the relevant parties, altered a specific procedure to allow material from nongovernmental actors to be submitted for consideration. The change generated considerable alarm among many WTO members, sufficient to call an extraordinary session of the General Council to review the Appellate Body's action.

56. Sampson, 2.

57. World Trade Organization, "Symposium on Issues."

58. World Trade Organization, "Doha Developments."

59. World Trade Organization, "Procedures for Circulation."

60. See, for example, World Trade Organization, "Improving Transparency"; World Trade Organization, "Transparency in WTO Work: Proposal"; World Trade Organization, "Transparency in WTO Work: Procedures."

61. World Trade Organization, "Procedures for Derestriction."

62. Van Dyke and Weiner, 2.

63. Van Dyke and Weiner, 10.

64. World Trade Organization, "Improving Transparency," 3.

65. World Trade Organization, "Improving Transparency," 5.

66. World Trade Organization, "General Council Informal Consultations."

67. World Trade Organization, "Minutes, 18 and 19 July, 2001," section 11(98).

68. World Trade Organization, "Procedures for Circulation."

69. Esty, 1998. On this point see 127.

70. Esty, 131.

71. On this point see Chada, Hoekman, Martin, Oyejide, Pangestu, Tussie, and Zarrouk, 2000; Khor, 2000; Hiebert, 1999; Rollo and Winters, 2000; Mead, Zedillo, Yeo, Samuelson, Rosencrance, and Van Wolferen, 2000.

72. See, for example, Walter, 2001. Walter suggests that because the collusion of government and business is strongest at the national level, NGO participation in national trade policy committees and debates may be the most effective means to generate greater accountability and transparency.

Chapter 6. Conclusions

1. Hurd, 1999.

2. Hurd, 381.

3. Hurd, 1999. See also Franck, 64.

4. Hurd, 388 (italics added).

5. Blau, 307, quoted in Hurd, 401.

6. Hurd, 401.

7. This is Hurd's assessment, and we are in agreement. The displacement of anarchy by a system of governance is attracting great attention among scholars that transcends the Grotian tradition of international society outlined by Hedley Bull. See, for example, Prakesh and Hart, 1999; Higgott, Underhill, and Bieler, 2000; Michie and Smith, 1999.

8. Jonathan Charney (1993) argues that because the global forums in which these norms are generated encompass all states and an increasingly large number of NGOs, the resulting principles are acquiring the character of universal international law.

9. See, for example, J. Thompson, 1992; Held, 1995; Beitz, 1979.

10. See J. Thompson, 1998. For overviews of this debate see Cochran, 1999, particularly part I; and Brown, 1992.

11. Held, 1998, 24.

12. Held, 1995, 267.

13. Held, 1995, 268.
14. Held, 1997.
15. Held, 1995, 273.
16. Habermas, 1998, 186.
17. Held, 1995, 278.
18. See Falk, 1995; and Falk, 2000.
19. Falk, 1998, 317.
20. Falk, 1998, 321.
21. Falk, 1998, 321.
22. Falk, 1998, 323.
23. Falk, 1995, 110.
24. Falk, 1995, 112.
25. Falk, 1995, 125.
26. Falk, 1995, 230.
27. Falk, 2000, 150.
28. Bohman, "International Regimes," 500.
29. Bohman, "International Regimes," 505.
30. Bohman, "International Regimes," 506.
31. See, for example, the essays in Boli and Thomas, eds., 1999.
32. See, for example, Annan, 2000; and the Commission on Global Governance, 1995.
33. Cochran, 1999.
34. Linklater, *Transformation of Political Community,* 107.
35. Linklater, *Transformation of Political Community,* 101.
36. Bohman, "Citizenship and Norms," 183.
37. For a compatible perspective, see Lynch, 2000.
38. See Risse-Kappen, "Nature of the Beast"; and J. Lewis, 1998. See also, Habermas, 1998, 150–61.
39. See Linklater, *Transformation of Political Community,* for his most recent and comprehensive treatment.
40. Linklater, *Transformation of Political Community,* 168.
41. Linklater, *Transformation of Political Community,* 200.
42. Linklater, *Transformation of Political Community,* 167.
43. On the relationship of NGOs and the creation of world citizenship, see Boli and Thomas, 1999, 13–49.

Bibliography

Adler, Emanuel. "Seizing the Middle Ground: Constructivism in World Politics." *European Journal of International Relations* 3 (September 1997): 319–63.

Adler, Emanuel, and Michael Barnett. "A Framework for the Study of Security Communities." In *Security Communities,* edited by Emanuel Adler and Michael Barnett, 29–65. Cambridge: Cambridge University Press, 1998.

Adler, Emanuel, and Michael Barnett, eds. *Security Communities*. Cambridge: Cambridge University Press, 1998.

Adler, Emanuel, and Peter M. Haas. "Conclusion: Epistemic Communities, World Order, and the Creation of a Reflective Research Program." *International Organization* 46 (winter 1992): 367–90.

Alford, C. Fred. "Comment." *Journal of Politics* 58 (August 1996): 753–6.

Anderson, Perry. *Lineages of the Absolutist State*. London: Verso Press, 1996.

Annan, Kofi. *The Millennium Report of the Secretary-General of the United Nations*, 2000. Available at http://www.un.org/millennium/sg/report/index.html.

Annis, Sheldon. "Giving Voice to the Poor." *Foreign Policy* 84 (1991): 93–106.

Archibugi, Daniele, David Held, and Martin Köhler, eds. *Re-imagining Political Community: Studies in Cosmopolitan Democracy*. Stanford, CA: Stanford University Press, 1998.

Ashley, Richard K. "The Geopolitics of Geopolitical Space: Towards a Critical Social Theory of International Politics."*Alternatives* 12 (October 1987): 403–34.

Auer, Matt. "Agency Reform as Decision Process: The Reengineering of the Agency for International Development." *Policy Sciences* 31 (June 1998): 81–105.

Bagla, Pallava. "Science Moves up Ladder in Push for Sustainable Growth." *Science* 280 (April 1998): 374–5.

Barnett, Michael N. "The United Nations and Global Security: The Norm is Mightier Than the Sword." *Ethics & International Affairs* 9 (1995): 37–54.

———. "Bringing in the New World Order: Liberalism, Legitimacy, and the United Nations." *World Politics* 49 (July 1997): 526–51.

Beetham, David. "Human Rights as a Model for Cosmopolitan Democracy." In *Re-imagining Political Community: Studies in Cosmopolitan Democracy,* edited by Daniele Archibugi, David Held, and Martin Köhler, Stanford, CA: Stanford University Press, 58–71.

Beitz, Charles. *Political Theory and International Relations*. Princeton, NJ: Princeton University Press, 1979.

Bell, Janet. "GEF—An Unsuitable Vehicle for Biodiversity Conservation." Genetic Resources Action International. *Biobriefing* no. 7 (November 1996). Available at www.ecoethics.net.

Bernstein, Jay. *Recovering Ethical Life: Jürgen Habermas and the Future of Critical Theory*. London: Routledge, 1995.

Bichsel, Anne, and Korinna Horta. "Leapfrog into Mainstreaming and Jump-Start the Learning Process: Critical Steps for the Future of the GEF." Presented at GEF Assembly and Council Meetings, New Delhi 29 March–3 April 1998. Available at www.forests.org.

Blackhurst, Richard. "Capacity Building in Africa for Enhanced Participation in the WTO." Paper presented at Dissemination Conference of the AERC Collaborative Research Project on Africa and the World Trading System, Yaounde, Cameroon, 17—18 April 1999.

Blackhurst, Richard, Bill Lyakurwa, and Ademola Oyejide. "Improving African Participation in the WTO." Paper Commissioned by the World Bank for a WTO Conference (20—21 September 1999). Available at http://www1.worldbank.org/wbiep/trade/papers/Sept99confp.pdf.

Blau, Peter. "Critical Remarks on Weber's Theory of Authority." *American Political Science Review* 57 (June 1963): 305–16.

Bohman, James. "The Globalization of the Public Sphere; Cosmopolitan Publicity and the Problem of Cultural Pluralism." *Philosophy and Social Criticism* 24 (April 1998): 199–216.

———. "Citizenship and Norms of Publicity." *Political Theory* 27 (April 1999): 176–202.

———. "International Regimes and Democratic Governance: Political Equality and Influence in Global Institutions." *International Affairs* 75 (July 1999): 499–513.

Boli, John, and George M. Thomas. "INGOs and the Organization of World Culture." In *Constructing World Culture: International Nongovernmental Organizations Since 1875*, edited by John Boli and George M. Thomas, 13–49. Stanford, CA: Stanford University Press, 1999.

Boli, John, and George M. Thomas, eds. *Constructing World Culture: International Nongovernmental Organizations Since 1875*. Stanford, CA: Stanford University Press, 1999.

Bowles, Ian A. "The Global Environment Facility: New Progress on Development Bank Governance." *Environment* 38 (April 1996): 38–40.

Bowles, Ian A., and Cyril F. Kormos. "Environmental Reform at the World Bank: The Role of the U.S. Congress." *Virginia Journal of International Law* 35 (summer 1995): 777–839.

———. "The American Campaign For Environmental Reforms at the World Bank." *Fletcher Forum of World Affairs* 23 (winter/spring 1999): 211–25.

Boyle, Alan E., and Michael R. Anderson. *Human Rights Approaches to Environmental Protection*. Oxford: Clarendon Press, 1996.

Bradlow, Daniel D. "International Organizations and Private Complaints: The Case of the World Bank Inspection Panel." *Virginia Journal of International Law* 34 (1994): 553–613.

Bradlow, Daniel D., and Claudio Grossman. "Limited Mandates and Intertwined Problems: A New Challenge for the World Bank and the IMF." *Human Rights Quarterly* 17 (August 1995): 411–42.

Bradlow, Daniel D., and Sabine Schlemmer-Schulte. "The World Bank's New Inspection Panel: A Constructive Step in the Transformation of the International Legal Order." *Zaörv Heidelberg Journal of International Law* 54, no. 2 (1994): 392–415.

Branigin, William. "Chinese Sweatshops Labor for U.S. Retailers, Report Says." *Washington Post,* 19 May 1998, C4.

Bridgeman, Natalie Laura. "World Bank Reform in the 'Post-Policy' Era." *Georgetown International Environmental Law Review* 13 (summer 2001): 1013–46.

British Overseas NGOs for Development. "BOND's Statement of Principles," 2001. Available at http://www.bond.org.uk/aboutus/principles.html .

Brown, Chris. *International Relations Theory: New Normative Approaches.* New York: Columbia University Press, 1992.

———. "Turtles All the Way Down": Anti-Foundationalism, Critical Theory and International Relations. *Millennium: Journal of International Studies* 23, no. 2 (1994): 213–36.

———. "International Political Theory and the Idea of World Community." In *International Relations Theory Today,* edited by Ken Booth and Steve Smith, 90–109. University Park, PA: Pennsylvania State University Press, 1995.

Bull, Hedley. *The Anarchical Society: A Study of Order in World Politics.* New York: Columbia University Press, 1977.

Bull, Hedley, and Adam Watson. *The Expansion of International Society.* Oxford: Clarendon Press, 1984.

Burch, Kurt. "The 'Properties' of the State System and Global Capitalism." In *The Global Political Economy as Political Space,* edited by Stephen J. Rosow, Naeem Inayatullah, and Mark Rupert, 37–60. Boulder, CO: Lynne Rienner, 1994.

Burgiel, Stanley W., and Sheldon Cohen. *The Global Environment Facility from Rio to New Delhi: A Guide for NGOs.* Washington, DC: World Conservation Union, 1997.

Burroughs, John, and Jacqueline Cabasso. "Confronting the Nuclear-Armed States in International Negotiating Forums: Lessons for NGOs." *International Negotiation* 4, no. 3 (1999): 457–80.

Cahn, Jonathan. "Challenging the New Imperial Authority: The World Bank and the Democratization of Development." *Harvard Human Rights Journal* 6 (spring 1993): 159–94.

Caldeira, Gregory A., and James L. Gibson. "The Legitimacy of the Court of Justice in the European Union: Models of Institutional Support." *American Political Science Review* 89 (June 1995): 356–76.

Calhoun, Craig, ed. *Habermas and the Public Sphere.* Cambridge: MIT Press, 1992.

Camilleri, Joseph A., and Jim Falk. *The End of Sovereignty?* Aldershot, England: Edward Elgar Publishing, 1992.

Canadian Council for International Co-Operation. "Code of Ethics" Approved at the Annual General Meeting, 25–27 May 1995. Available at http://www.ccic.ca/volsect/codeofethics/ce1-codofethics.htm.

Carr, E. H. *Nationalism and After.* London: Macmillian, 1945.

Carr, Susan, and Roger Mpande. "Does the Definition of the Issue Matter? NGO Influence and the International Convention to Combat Desertification in Africa." In *NGOs and Environmental Policies: Asia and Africa,* edited by David Potter, 143–66. London: Frank Cass, 1996.

Chada, Rajesh, Bernard Hoekman, Will Martin, Ademola Oyejide, Mari Pangestu, Diana Tussie, and Jamel Zarrouk. "Developing Countries and the Next Round of WTO Negotiations." *World Economy* 23 (April 2000): 431–37.

Charney, Jonathan I. "Universal International Law." *American Journal of International Law* 87 (October 1993): 529–51.

Charnovitz, Steve. "Two Centuries of Participation: NGOs and International Governance." *Michigan Journal of International Law* 18 (winter 1997): 183–286.

Chayes, Abram, and Antonia Chayes. *The New Sovereignty, Compliance with International Regulatory Agreements.* Cambridge: Harvard University Press, 1995.

Chaytor, Beatrice, and Michael Hindley. *A Case Study of Sierra Leone's Participation in the World Trade Organization.* London: Cameron May, Ltd., 1997.

Checkel, Jeffrey T. "International Norms and Domestic Politics: Bridging Rationalist-Constructivist Divide." *European Journal of International Relations* 3 (December 1997): 473–95.

———. "Norms, Institutions, and National Identity in Contemporary Europe," *International Studies Quarterly* 43 (March 1999): 83–114.

———. "Why Comply? Constructivism, Social Norms and the Study of International Institutions." *ARENA Working Papers* WP 99/24, 1999. Available at http://www.sv.uio.no/arena/publications/.

———. "Taking Deliberation Seriously." *ARENA Working Papers* WP 01/14, 2001. Available at www.arena.uio.no/publications/wp01_14.htm.

Christensen, Eric. "Green Appeal, A Proposal for an Environmental Commission of Enquiry at the World Bank." Washington, DC: Natural Resources Defense Council. Unpublished Manuscript.

Christiansen, Lars, and Keith Dowding. "Pluralism or State Autonomy? The Case of Amnesty International: The Insider/Outside Group." *Political Studies* 42 (March 1994): 15–24.

Clark, Ann Marie. "Non-Governmental Organizations and Their Influence on International Society." *Journal of International Affairs* 48 (winter 1995): 507–25.

Clark, Ann Marie, Elisabeth J. Friedman, and Kathryn Hochstetler. "The Sovereign Limits of Global Civil Society; A Comparison of NGO Participation in UN World Conferences on the Environment, Human Rights, and Women." *World Politics* 51 (October 1998): 1–35.

Cleary, Seamus. "The World Bank and NGO." In *The Conscience of the World: The Influence of Non-Governmental Organisations in the U.N. System,* edited by Peter Willetts, 63–97. Washington, DC: Brookings Institution, 1996.

Cochran, Molly. "Cosmopolitanism and Communitarianism in a Post-Cold War World." In *Boundaries in Question: New Directions in International Relations,* edited by John MacMillan and Andrew Linklater, 40–53. London: Pinter, 1995.

———. *Normative Theory in International Relations: A Pragmatic Approach.* Cambridge: Cambridge University Press, 1999.

Commission on Global Governance. *Our Global Neighborhood.* New York: Oxford University Press, 1995. Available at http://www.cgg.ch/contents.htm.

Conca, Ken. "Environmental Change and the Deep Structure of World Politics." In *The State and Social Power in Global Environmental Politics,* edited by Ronnie D. Lipschutz and Ken Conca, 306–26. New York: Columbia University Press, 1993.

Convention on the Prohibition of the Use, Stockpiling, Production and Transfer of Anti-Personnel Mines and on Their Destruction, (18 September 1977). Available at untreaty.un.org.

Covey, Jane G. "Is Critical Cooperation Possible? Influencing the World Bank through Operational Collaboration and Policy Dialogue." In *The Struggle for Accountability: The World Bank, NGOs, and Grassroots Movements,* edited by Jonathan A. Fox and L. David Brown, 81–119. Cambridge: MIT Press, 1998.

Cox, Robert. "Social Forces, States, and World Orders: Beyond International Relations Theory." *Millennium, Journal of International Studies* 10, no. 2 (1981): 126–55.

Crawford, Neta. "Decolonization as an International Norm: The Evolution of Practices, Arguments and Beliefs." In *Emerging Norms of Justified Intervention,* edited by Laura Reed and Carl Kaysen, 37–61. Cambridge, MA: American Academy of Arts and Sciences, 1993.

———. "Postmodern Ethical Conditions and a Critical Response." *Ethics & International Affairs* 12 (1998): 121–40.

Crowley, Michael. "U.N. Still Lacks Mandate for Small Arms Conference." *Basic Reports Newsletter on International Security Policy*, no. 77 (10 March 2001). Available at http://www.basicint.org/br77.htm.

Cushman, John H., Jr. "Nike Pledges to End Child Labor and Apply U.S. Rules Abroad." *New York Times*, 13 May 1998, sec. A1.

Daly, Herman E. "Farewell Lecture to the World Bank." In *Beyond Bretton Woods, Alternatives to the Global Economic Order,* edited by John Cavanagh, Daphne Wysham, and Marcos Arruda, 109–17. London: Pluto Press, 1994.

De La Garza, Paul. "Despite Reforms, Mexico's Human Rights Record Described as Dismal," *Chicago Tribune*, 9 November 1997, sec. 4, p. 1.

Der Derian, James. *On Diplomacy: A Genealogy of Western Estrangement.* Oxford: Blackwell Publishers, 1987.

Dessler, David. "What's at Stake in the Agent-Structure Debate" *International Organization* 43 (summer 1989): 441–73.

Deutsch, Karl W. et al. *Political Community and the North Atlantic Area: International Organization in the Light of Historical Experience.* Princeton, NJ: Princeton University Press, 1957.

Devetak, Richard. "The Project of Modernity and International Relations Theory." *Millennium: Journal of International Studies* 24, no. 1 (1995): 27–51.

Devetak, Richard, and Richard Higgott. "Justice Unbound? Globalization, States and the Transformation of the Social Bond." *International Affairs* 75 (July 1999): 483–98.

Dombrowski, Peter, and Tom Rice. "Changing Identities and International Relations Theory: A Cautionary Note." *Nationalism & Ethnic Politics* 6 (winter 2000): 83–105.

Drinan, Robert F. "NGOs—Not U.S.—Keep Eye on Human Rights in China," *National Catholic Reporter* 31 (5 May 1995), 16.

Dryzek, John S. *Discursive Democracy: Politics, Policy, and Political Science.* New York: Cambridge University Press, 1990.

———. "How Far Is It from Virginia and Rochester to Frankfurt? Public Choice as Critical Theory." *British Journal of Political Science* 22 (October 1992): 397–417.

Dukes, E. Franklin. *Resolving Public Conflict: Transforming Community and Governance.* New York: Manchester University Press, 1996.

Dyer, Hugh C. *Moral Order/World Order: The Role of Normative Theory in the Study of International Relations.* London: Macmillan Press, 1997.

El-Ashry, Mohamed T. "Remarks." Speech delivered at NGO Consultation, Washington, DC (29 April 1997). Available at gefweb.org.

———. "The Global Environment Facility: A Self-Assessment." c. 1997. Available at http://www.ecouncil.ac.cr/rio/focus/report/english/Gef.htm.

———. "Remarks." Speech delivered at National Press Club, Washington, DC 27 May 1998. Available at gefweb.org.

———. "Financing Sustainable Development: GEF and the 'Northern Dimension.' " Remarks for the Fourth Conference of Parliamentarians of the Arctic Region, Rovaniemi, Finland, 29 August 2000. Available at gefweb.org.

Elster, Jon. "Introduction." In Jon Elster ed. *Deliberative Democracy* (1–18). Cambridge: Cambridge University Press, 1998.

Esty, Daniel C. "Non-governmental Organizations at the World Trade Organization: Cooperation, Competition, or Exclusion." *Journal of International Economic Law* 1, no. 1 (1998): 123–48.

Fairman, David. "Commentary: The New GEF." *Environment* 36 (July–August 1994): 37–9.

Falk, Richard. *On Humane Governance: Toward a New Global Politics.* University Park, PA: Pennsylvania State University Press, 1995.

———. "The United Nations and Cosmopolitan Democracy: Bad Dream, Utopian Fantasy, Political Project." In *Re-imagining Political Community: Studies in Cosmopolitan Democracy,* edited by Daniele Archibugi, David Held, and Martin Köhler, 309–31. Stanford, CA: Stanford University Press, 1998.

———. *Predatory Globalization: A Critique.* Cambridge, UK: Polity Press, 2000.

Finel, Bernard I., and Kristin M. Lord. "The Surprising Logic of Transparency." *International Studies Quarterly* 43 (June 1999): 315–39.

Finnemore, Martha. *National Interests and International Society.* Ithaca, NY: Cornell University Press, 1996.

Finnemore, Martha, and Kathryn Sikkink. "International Norm Dynamics and Political Change." *International Organization* 52 (autumn 1998): 887–917.

Fisher, Julie. *The Road from Rio: Sustainable Development and the Nongovernmental Movement in the Third World.* Westport, CT: Praeger, 1993.

———. *Nongovernments: NGOs and the Political Development of the Third World.* West Hartford, CT: Kumarian, 1998.

Fisher, William F., ed. *Toward Sustainable Development? Struggling over India's Narmada River.* Armonk, NY: M.E. Sharpe, 1995.

Flood, Patrick James. *The Effectiveness of UN Human Rights Institutions*. Westport, CT: Praeger Press, 1998.

Florini, Ann. "The Evolution of International Norms." *International Studies Quarterly* 40 (September 1996): 363–89.

———. "The End of Secrecy." *Foreign Policy,* no. 111 (summer 1998): 50–63.

Fox, Jonathan A. "The World Bank Inspection Panel: Lessons from the First Five Years." *Global Governance* 6 (July–September 2000): 279–318.

Fox, Jonathan A., and L. David Brown, eds. *The Struggle for Accountability: The World Bank, NGOs, and Grassroots Movements*. Cambridge, MA: MIT Press, 1998.

Franck, Thomas M. *The Power of Legitimacy among Nations*. New York: Oxford University Press, 1990.

Frost, Mervyn. *Towards a Normative Theory of International Relations*. Cambridge: Cambridge University Press, 1986.

Gaer, Felice D. "Reality Check: Human Rights NGOs Confront Governments at the UN." In *NGOs, the United Nations, and Global Governance,* edited by Thomas G. Weiss and Leon Gordenker, 51–66. Boulder, CO: Lynne Rienner, 1996.

Gallarotti, Giulo M., and Arik Y. Preis. "Toward Universal Human Rights and the Rule of Law: The Permanent International Criminal Court." *Australian Journal of International Affairs* 53 (April 1999): 95–112.

Gallie, W. B. *Philosophers of Peace and War*. London: Cambridge University Press, 1978.

Gamble, Andrew. "Shaping a New World Order: Political Capacities and Policy Challenges." *Government and Opposition* 28 (summer 1993): 325–38.

Ghai, Dharam, and Jessica M. Vivian. *Grassroots Environmental Action: People's Participation in Sustainable Development*. New York: Routledge, 1992.

Gilbert, Alan. *Must Global Politics Constrain Democracy? Great-Power Realism, Democratic Peace, and Democratic Internationalism.* Princeton, NJ: Princeton University Press, 1999.

Gill, Stephen. "Globalization, Market Civilization, and Disciplinary Neoliberalism." *Millennium: Journal of International Studies* 24, no. 3 (1995): 399–423.

Gill, Stephen, ed. *Gramsci, Historical Materialism and International Relations* Cambridge: Cambridge University Press, 1993.

Global Environment Facility. "Public Involvement in GEF-Financed Projects," June 1996. Available at www.gefweb.org.

Global Environment Facility. "Summary Report of the Study of GEF Project Lessions," January 1998. Available at www.gefweb.org.

———. "Questions and Answers," n.d. Available at gefweb.org.

Global Environment Facility Digest. *Quarterly NGO Newsletter of the Global Environment Facility*, no. 1 (fall 1999).

Global Environment Facility—NGO Network. *The GEF in the 21st Century: A Vision for Strengthening the Global Environment Facility* 26 (February 1998). Available from IUCN—The World Conservation Union.

Goldstein, Judith, and Lisa L. Martin. "Legalization, Trade Liberalization, and Domestic Politics: A Cautionary Note." *International Organization* 54 (summer 2000): 603–32.

Goldstein, Judith, and Robert O. Keohane, eds. *Ideas and Foreign Policy: Belief, Institutions, and Political Change*. Ithaca, NY: Cornell University Press, 1993.

Gong, Gerrit W. *The Standard of "Civilization" in International Society*. Oxford: Clarendon Press, 1984.

Gordenker, Leon, and Thomas G. Weiss. "Pluralizing Global Governance: Analytical Approaches and Dimensions." In *NGOs, the United Nations, and Global Governance,* edited by Thomas G. Weiss and Leon Gordenker, 17–47. Boulder, CO: Lynne Rienner, 1996.

Görg, Christoff, and Joachim Hirsch. "Is International Democracy Possible?" *Review of International Political Economy* 5 (winter 1998): 585–615.

Greene, Stephen G. "Reforming Global Institutions." *Chronicle of Philanthropy* 7 (13 December 1994): 1, 7–10.

Grieco, Joseph M. "Anarchy and the Limits of Cooperation: A Realist Critique of the Newest Liberal Internationalism." *International Organization.* 42 (summer 1988): 485–507.

Grossman, Claudio, and Daniel D. Bradlow. "Are We Being Propelled towards a People-Centered Transnational Legal Order?" *American University Journal of International Law and Politics* 9 (fall 1993): 1–25.

Gundersen, Adolf G. *The Environmental Promise of Democratic Deliberation*. Madison, WI: University of Wisconsin Press, 1995.

Gupta, Joyeeta. "The Global Environment Facility in Its North-South Context." *Environmental Politics* 4 (spring 1995): 19–43.

Haacke, Jürgen. "Theory and Praxis in International Relations: Habermas, Self-Reflection, Rational Argumentation." *Millennium: Journal of International Studies* 25, no. 2 (1996): 255–89.

Haas, Ernst B. *The Uniting of Europe: Political, Social and Economic Forces, 1950–1957*. Stanford, CA: Stanford University Press, 1958.

Haas, Peter M. *Saving the Mediterranean.* New York: Columbia University Press, 1990.

———. "Introduction: Epistemic Communities and International Policy Coordination." *International Organization* 46 (winter 1992): 1– 35.

———. "Is 'Sustainable Development' Politically Sustainable?" *Brown Journal of World Affairs* 3 (summer–fall 1996): 239–47.

———, ed. "Knowledge, Power and International Policy Coordination." A special issue of *International Organization* 46 (winter 1992).

Habermas, Jürgen. *Moral Consciousness and Communicative Action,* trans. C. Lenhardt and S. Weber Nicholson. Cambridge Polity Press, 1992.

———. *Between Facts and Norms: Contributions to a Discourse Theory of Law and Democracy*, trans. W. Rehg. Cambridge, MA: MIT Press, 1996.

———. *The Inclusion of the Other: Studies in Political Theory.* Cambridge: MIT Press, 1998.

Hall, Peter A., ed. *The Political Power of Economic Ideas: Keynesianism Across Nations.* Princeton, NJ: Princeton University Press, 1989.

Hall, Rodney Bruce. *National Collective Identity, Social Constructs and International Systems.* New York: Columbia University, 1999.

Hansenclever, Andreas, Peter Mayer, and Volker Rittberger. "Interests, Power, Knowledge: The Study of International Regimes." *Mershon International Studies Review* 40 (October 1996): 177–228.

Harbour, Frances V. "Basic Moral Values: A Shared Core." *Ethics & International Affairs* 9 (1995): 155–70.

Harris, Paul G. "Considerations of Equity and International Environmental Institutions." *Environmental Politics* 5 (summer 1996): 274–301.

Held, David. *Democracy and the Global Order.* Cambridge, UK: Polity Press, 1995.

———. "Globalization and Cosmopolitan Democracy." *Peace Review* 9 (September 1997): 309–15.

———. "Democracy and Globalization." In *Re-imagining Political Community: Studies in Cosmopolitan Democracy,* edited by Daniele Archibugi, David Held, and Martin Köhler, 11–27. Stanford, CA: Stanford University Press, 1998.

Held, David, Andrew McGrew, David Goldblatt, and Jonathan Perraton. *Global Transformations: Concepts, Evidence and Arguments.* Stanford, CA: Stanford University Press, 1999.

Hiebert, Murray. "Hollow Victory: Asia Kept Labor Out of the WTO in Seattle, But Will It Suffer if Trade Talks Stall?" *Far Eastern Economic Review* 162, no. 50 (16 December 1999): 54.

Higgott, Richard A., Geoffrey R.D. Underhill, and Andreas Bieler, eds. *Non-state Actors and Authority in the Global System.* New York: Routledge, 2000.

Hoffman, Mark. "Critical Theory and the Inter-Paradigm Debate." *Millennium: Journal of International Studies* 16, no. 2 (1987): 231–49.

Horta, Korinna. "Global Environment Facility." *Foreign Policy in Focus* 3 (December 1998).

Humphreys, David. "Regime Theory and Non-Governmental Organisations: The Case of Forest Conservation." In *NGOs and Environmental Policies: Asia and Africa,* edited by David Potter, 91–115. London: Frank Cass, 1996.

Hunter, David B., and Lori Udall. "The World Bank's New Inspection Panel." *Environment* 36 (November 1994): 2–3, 44–5.

Hurd, Ian. "Legitimacy and Authority in International Politics." *International Organization* 53, no. 2 (spring 1999): 379–408.

International Centre for Trade and Sustainable Development. "Public Participation in the International Trading System: Accreditation Schemes and Other Arrangements for Public Participation in International Fora." BRIDGES Series on Public Participation in the International Trading System (November 1999).

———. "WTO General Council Slaps Appellate Body on Amicus Briefs." *ICTSD Bridges* 4 (28 November 2000). Available at http://www.ictsd.org/weekly/index.htm.

———. "Last-minuteArrangements for NGOs." *Bridges Weekly Trade News Digest* 5 (6 November 2001). Available at http://www.ictsd.org/weekly/index.htm.

———. "NGOs Pursue New Avenues to Get Their Voice to the Table." *Bridges Weekly Trade News Digest* 5 (15 November 2001). Available at http://www.ictsd.org/weekly/index.htm.

International Helsinki Federation for Human Rights. "Human Rights Monitoring and Assistance Program for Local NGOs in Bosnia and Herzegovina," 1996. Available at http://www.ihf-hr.org/projects/bosnia.htm.

International Tropical Timber Agreement. Available from Center for International Earth Science Information Network (CIESIN). 1996–2001. *Environmental Treaties and Resource Indicators (ENTRI).* Palisades, NY: CIESIN, 1994. Available at http://sedac.ciesin.org/entri/texts/ITTA.1994.txt.html.

Jervis, Robert. "Realism, Neoliberalism, and Cooperation: Understanding the Debate." *International Security* 24 (summer 1999): 42–63.

Jonquieres, Guy de, and Frances Williams. "Global Activists Adopt New Tactics: Switch to Behind-the-Scenes Influence," *Financial Times,* 12 November 2001.

Jordan, Andrew. "Paying the Incremental Costs of Global Environmental Protection: The Evolving Role of GEF." *Environment* 36 (July–August 1994): 12–20, 31–36.

Keck, Margaret E., and Sikkink, Kathryn. *Activists Beyond Borders: Advocacy Networks in International Politics.* Ithaca: Cornell University Press, 1998.

Keeley, James. "Toward a Foucauldian Analysis of International Regimes." *International Organization* 44 (winter 1990): 83–105.

Keohane, Robert O. *After Hegemony: Cooperation and Discord in the World Political Economy.* Princeton, NJ: Princeton University Press, 1984.

———. "Closing the Fairness-Practices Gap." *Ethics & International Affairs* 3: 101–16.

Keohane, Robert O. and Joseph S. Nye, Jr., eds. *Transnational Relations and World Politics.* Cambridge: Harvard University Press, 1972.

———. *Power and Interdependence: World Politics in Transition.* Boston: Little, Brown, 1977.

Keohane, Robert O., and Joseph S. Nye Jr. "Power and Interdependence Revisited." *International Organization* 41 (autumn 1987): 725–53.

———. *Power and Interdependence.* 2nd ed., Boston: Scott, Foresman, 1989.

———. "Globalization: What's New? What's Not? (And So What?)." *Foreign Policy,* no. 118 (spring 2000): 104–19.

———. "The Club Model of Multilateral Cooperation and Problems of Democratic Legitimacy." American Political Science Association Annual Meeting, Washington, DC, 31 August–3 September, 2000.

Keyman, E. Fuat. *Globalization, State, Identity/Difference: Toward a Critical Social Theory of International Relations.* Atlantic Highlands, NJ: Humanities Press, 1997.

Khor, Martin. "The APEC Debate: Launch a New WTO Round or Fix an Agenda First?: Why It Makes All the Difference." *Asia Pacific Research Network,* 2000. Available at http://www.aprnet.org/apecanal.htm).

Kingsbury, Benedict. "The Tuna-Dolphin Controversy: The World Trade Organization, and the Liberal Project to Reconceptualize International Law." *Yearbook of International Environmental Law,* vol. 5, 1–40. Norwell, MA: Kluwer, 1994.

Koslowski, Rey, and Friedrich V. Kratochwil. "Understanding Change in International Politics: The Soviet Empire's Demise and the International System." *International Organization* 48 (spring 1994): 215–47.

Krajewski, Markus. "Democratic Legitimacy and Constitutional Perspectives of WTO Law." *Journal of World Trade*, 35 (February 2001): 167–86.

Krasner, Stephen D. "Structural Cause and Regime Consequences: Regimes as Intervening Variables." In *International Regimes,* edited by Stephen D. Krasner, 1–21. Ithaca, NY: Cornell University Press, 1983.

———. *Structural Conflict: The Third World Against Global Liberalism.* Berkeley: University of California Press, 1985.

Laberge, Pierre. "Kant on Justice and the Law of Nations." In *International Society: Diverse Ethical Perspectives,* edited by David R. Mapel and Terry Nardin, 82–102. Princeton, NJ: Princeton University Press, 1998.

Lafranchi, Howard. "Morocco Spruces Up Human Rights Record," *Christian Science Monitor*, 26 September 1991, 4.

Langley, Paul. "Transparency in the Making of Global Environmental Governance." *Global Society* 15 (January 2001): 73–92.

Langley, Winston E. "Socio-Cultural Rights and Development." *Journal of Third World Studies* 14 (fall 1997): 133–60.

Lapid, Yosef. "The Third Debate: On the Prospects of International Theory in a Post-Positivist Era." *International Studies Quarterly* 33 (September 1989): 235–54.

Leary, Virginia A. "The WTO and the Social Clause: Post Singapore." *European Journal of International Law* 8, no. 1 (1997): 118–22.

Levy, Jack S. "Learning and Foreign Policy: Sweeping a Conceptual Minefield." *International Organization* 48 (spring 1994): 279–312.

Lewis, Jeffrey. "Is the 'Hard Bargaining' Image of the Council Misleading? The Committee of Permanent Representatives and the Local Elections Directive." *Journal of Common Market Studies* 36 (December 1998): 479–504.

Lewis, Paul. "U.N. and U.S. Pressed on Rights Stance," *New York Times* 2 February 1997, sec. 1, p. 8.

Lindblom, Charles. *Politics and Markets: The World's Political-Economic Systems.* New York: Basic Books, 1977.

Linklater, Andrew. *Men and Citizens in the Theory of International Relations.* London: Macmillan, 1990.

———. *Beyond Realism and Marxism: Critical Theory and International Relations.* New York: St. Martin's Press, 1990.

———. "The Question of the Next Stage in International Relations Theory: A Critical-Theoretical Point of View." *Millennium: Journal of International Studies* 21, no. 1 (1992): 77–98.

———. "Community." In *Fin de Siecle: The Meaning of the Twentieth Century,* edited by Alex Danchev, 177–97. London: I.B. Tauris Publishers, 1995.

———. "Achievements of Critical Theory." In *International Theory: Positivism and Beyond,* edited by Steve Smith, Ken Booth, and Marysia Zalewski, 279–98. Cambridge: Cambridge University Press, 1996.

———. "Citizenship and Sovereignty in the Post-Westphalian European State." In *Re-imagining Political Community: Studies in Cosmopolitan Democracy*, edited by Daniele Archibugi, David Held, and Martin Köhler, 113–37. Stanford, CA: Stanford University Press, 1998.

———. *Transformation of Political Community*. London: Polity Press, 1998.

———. "The Evolving Spheres of International Justice." *International Affairs* 75 (July 1999): 473–82.

Lipschutz, Ronnie D. "Reconstructing World Politics: The Emergence of Global Civil Society." *Millennium: Journal of International Studies* 21 (winter 1992): 389–420.

Livernash, Robert. "The Growing Influence of NGOs in the Developing World." *Environment* 34 (June 1992): 12–20, 41–3.

Lodge, Juliet. "Transparency and Democratic Legitimacy." *Journal of Common Market Studies* 32 (September 1994): 343–68.

Lumsdaine, David Halloran. *Moral Vision in International Politics: The Foreign Aid Regime 1949–1989*. Princeton, NJ: Princeton University Press, 1993.

Lynch, Marc. *State Interests and the Public Sphere: The International Politics of Jordan's Identity*. New York: Columbia University Press, 1999.

———. "The Dialogue of Civilisations and International Public Spheres." *Millennium: Journal of International Studies* 29 (summer 2000): 307–30.

———. "Why Engage? China and the Logic of Communicative Engagement." *European Journal of International Relations* 8 (June 2002): 187–230.

Magnusson, Warren. "The Reification of Political Community." In *Contending Sovereignties: Redefining Political Community,* edited by R. B. J. Walker and Saul H. Mendlovitz, 45–60. Boulder, CO: Lynne Rienner, 1990.

Mansbridge, Jane J. "A Deliberative Theory of Interest Representation." In *The Politics of Interest: Interest Groups Transformed,* edited by Mark P. Petracca, 32–57. Boulder, CO: Westview, 1992.

Marceau, Gabrielle, and Peter N. Pedersen. "Is the WTO Open and Transparent?" *Journal of World Trade* 33, no. 1 (1999): 5–49.

Mead, Walter Russell, Ernesto Zedillo, George Yeo, Robert Samuelson, Richard Rosencrance, and Karel Van Wolferen. "The Second Globalization." *New Perspectives Quarterly*, Special Issue 17 (spring 2000).

Mearsheimer, John J. "Back to the Future: Instability in Europe after the Cold War." *International Security* 15 (summer 1990): 5–56.

———. "The False Promise of International Institutions." *International Security* 19 (winter 1994/1995): 5–49.

Mertens, Shoshana K. "Towards Accountability in the Restructured Global Environment Facility." *Review of the European Community and International Environmental Law* 3, no. 2/3 (1994): 105–10.

Michalopoulos, Constantine. "The Participation of the Developing Countries in the WTO." WTO 2000 Capacity Building Project, Background Paper, 2000. Available at http://www1.worldbank.org/wbiep/trade/papers_2000/BPpart.pdf.

Michie, Jonathan, and John Grieve Smith, eds. *Global Instability: The Political Economy of World Economic Governance*. New York: Routledge, 1999.

Mitchell, Ronald B. "Sources of Transparency: Information Systems in International Regimes." *International Studies Quarterly* 42 (March 1998): 109–30.

Mitrany, David. *A Working Peace System*. Chicago: Quadrangle Books, 1966.

Mitzen, Jennifer. "Deliberation and Publicity in the Inter-State Context." Paper presented at the Annual Meeting of the American Political Science Association, Atlanta, GA.

———. *From Anarchy to Authority? The Globalization of Publicity and International Politics*. University of Chicago, unpublished doctoral dissertation (October 2000 draft).

Morgenthau, Hans J., and Kenneth Thompson. *Politics among Nations: The Struggle for Power and Peace*. 6th ed. New York: Knopf, 1985.

Mueller, John. *Retreat from Doomsday: The Obsolescence of Major War*. New York: Basic Books, 1989.

Müller, Harold. "Arguing and Persuasion in Multilateral Negotiations." Grant Proposal to the Volkswagen Foundation (6 August 2001). Available at www.fu-berlin.de/atasp/pub/vwneuantrag.pdf).

Myers, Steven Lee. "Business Interests Overshadow Human Rights, Survey Reports," *New York Times*, 5 December 1996, A8.

———. "Trade vs. Rights: A U.S. Debate with a Burmese Focus," *New York Times* 5 March 1997, A8.

Naim, Moises. "Fads and Fashion in Economic Reforms: Washington Consensus or Washington Confusion?" *Third World Quarterly* 21 (June 2000): 505–28.

Nardin, Terry. *Law, Morality and the Relations of States*. Princeton, NJ: Princeton University Press, 1992.

Nelson, Paul J. *The World Bank and Non-Governmental Organizations: The Limits of Apolitical Development*. New York: St. Martin's, 1995.

———. "Internationalising Economic and Environmental Policy: Transnational NGO Networks and The World Bank's Expanding Influence." *Millennium: Journal of International Studies* 25, no. 3 (1996): 605–33.

———. "Heroism and Ambiguity: NGO Advocacy in International Policy." *Development in Practice* 10, nos. 3–4 (August 2000): 478–90.

———. "Whose Civil Society? Whose Governance? Decisionmaking and Practice in the New Agenda at the Inter-American Development Bank and the World Bank." *Global Governance* 6 (October–December 2000): 405–31.

Neufeld, Mark A. *The Restructuring of International Relations Theory*. Cambridge: Cambridge University Press, 1995.

NGO Alternative Treaties. Global Forum at Rio de Janeiro, 1–15 June 1992. Available at http://www.igc.org/habitat/treaties/index.htm.

NGO Statement to the Participants Meeting in Geneva, 14 February 1992. "GEF Governance." *Authorizing Contributions to IDA, GEF, and ADF*. 103rd U.S. Congress, first session, House of Representatives, Subcommittee Hearing of the Committee on Banking, Finance and Urban Affairs (5 May). Washington, DC: U.S. Government Printing Office, 1993.

Nye, Joseph S., Jr. "Globalization's Democratic Deficit." *Foreign Affairs* 80 (July-August 2001): 2–7.

Ohiorhenuan, J. F. E. "Capacity Building Implications of Enhanced African Participation in Global Trade Rules-Making and Arrangements." African Economic Research Consortium Collaborative Research Project on Africa and the World Trading System, mimeo, AERC, Nairobi, 1998. Available at http://www.aercafrica.org/documents/AWTS/cbuilding.doc.

OMB Watch. "Access to Government Information Post September 11th," February 1, 2002 (last updated May 3, 2002). http://www.ombwatch.org/article/archive/104/.

Ostry, Sylvia. "WTO: Institutional Design for Better Governance." Unpublished paper, 2000. Available at http://www.utoronto.ca/cis/WTOID.pdf.

Oyejide, Ademola T. "Africa and the Uruguay Round." *World Economy* 13 (September 1990): 427–44.

———. "Interests and Options of Developing and Least-Developed Countries in a New Round of Multilateral Trade Negotiations." G-24 Discussion Paper Series. Research Papers for the Intergovernmental Group of Twenty-Four on International Monetary Affairs. No. 2 (May 1999). Available at http://www.g24.org/g24-dp2.pdf.

Pasha, Mustapha Kamal, and David L. Blaney. "Elusive Paradise: The Promise and Peril of Global Civil Society." *Alternatives: Social Transformation and Humane Governance* 23 (October–December 1998): 417–51.

Paterson, Matthew. *Global Warming and Global Politics*. London: Routledge, 1996.

Paulson, Michael. "Clinton Says He Will Support Trade Sanctions for Worker Abuse," *Seattle Post Intelligencer*, 1 December 1999, A1.

Payne, Rodger A. "Nonprofit Environmental Organizations in World Politics: Domestic Structure and Transnational Relations." *Policy Studies Review* 14 (spring–summer, 1995): 171–82.

———. "Deliberating Global Environmental Politics." *Journal of Peace Research* 33 (May 1996): 129–36.

———. "The Limits and Promise of Environmental Conflict Prevention: The Case of the GEF." *Journal of Peace Research* 35 (May 1998): 363–80.

———. "Persuasion, Frames, and Norm Construction." *European Journal of International Relations* 7 (March 2001): 37–61.

———. "The Legitimacy of the Global Environment Facility." In *Global Environmental Politics: Institutions and Procedures,* edited by Ho-won Jeong, 161–89. New York: Palgrave, 2001.

———. "The Information Revolution, Transnational Relations, and Sustainable Development in the Global South." In *Cyberimperialism? Global Relations in the New Electronic Frontier,* edited by Bosah Ebo, 153–67. Westport, CT: Praeger, 2001.

———. "Can New Information Technologies Promote Democratic Deliberation?" In *Media, Profit and Politics: Competing Priorities in an Open Society,* edited by Joseph Harper and Thom Yantek. (215–31). Kent, OH: Kent State University Press, 2003.

Powell, Robert. "Absolute and Relative Gains in International Relations Theory." *American Political Science Review*. 85 (December 1991): 1303–20.

Prakesh, Aseem, and Jeffrey A. Hart, eds. *Globalization and Governance*. New York: Routledge, 1999.

Price, Richard. "Reversing the Gun Sights: Transnational Civil Society Targets Land Mines." *International Organization* 52 (summer 1998): 613–44.

Price, Richard, and Christian Reus-Smit. "Dangerous Liaisons? Critical International Theory and Constructivism." *European Journal of International Relations* 4 (September 1998): 259–94.

Princen, Thomas. "The Ivory Trade Ban: NGOs and International Conservation." In *Environmental NGOs in World Politics: Linking the Local and the Global,* edited by Thomas Princen and Matthias Finger, 121–59. New York: Routledge, 1994.

Princen, Thomas, and Matthias Finger, eds. *Environmental NGOs in World Politics: Linking the Local and the Global.* New York: Routledge, 1994.

Puchala, Donald J. "The Integration Theorists and the Study of International Relations." In *Classic Readings of International Relations,* edited by Phil Williams, Donald Goldstein, and Jay M. Shafritz, 314–30. Belmont, CA: Wadsworth Publishing, 1994.

Putzel, James. "The Business of Aid: Transparency and Accountability in European Union Development Assistance." *Journal of Development Studies* 34 (February 1998): 71–96.

Raghavan, Chakravarthi. "WTO Endorses TNC Principles and Practices and Negotiating Structures." Third World Network, 2002. Available at http://www.twnside.org.sg/title/twe272a.htm.

Rahman, Atiq, and Annie Roncerel. "A View from the Ground Up." In *Negotiating Climate Change: The Inside Story of the Rio Convention,* edited by Irving M. Mintzer and J. A. Leonard, 239–73. New York: Cambridge University Press, 1994.

Rapaczynski, Andrzej. *Nature and Politics: Liberalism in the Philosophies of Hobbes, Locke and Rousseau.* Ithaca: Cornell University Press, 1987.

Raustiala, Kal. "States, NGOs and International Environmental Institutions." *International Studies Quarterly* 41 (December 1997): 719–40.

———. "The 'Participatory Revolution' in International Environmental Law." *Harvard Environmental Law Review* 21 (1997): 537–86.

Rengger, N.J. *International Relations, Political Theory and the Problem of Order: Beyond International Relations Theory?* London: Routledge, 2000.

Rich, Bruce. *Mortgaging the Earth: The World Bank, Environmental Impoverishment, and the Crisis of Development.* Boston: Beacon, 1994.

Riley, Patrick. *Kant's Political Philosophy*. Totowa, NJ: Rowman and Littlefield,1983.

Risse, Thomas. "International Norms and Domestic Change: Arguing and Communicative Behavior in the Human Rights Area." *Politics & Society* 27 (December 1999): 529–59.

———. "Let's Argue!: Communicative Action in World Politics." *International Organization* 54 (winter 2000): 1–39.

Risse, Thomas, and Stephen C. Ropp. "International Human Rights Norms and Domestic Change: Conclusions." In *The Power of Human Rights: International Norms and Domestic Change,* edited by Thomas Risse, Stephen C. Ropp and Kathryn Sikkink, 234–78. Cambridge: Cambridge University Press, 1999.

Risse, Thomas, Stephen C. Ropp, and Kathryn Sikkink, eds. *The Power of Human Rights: International Norms and Domestic Change.* Cambridge: Cambridge University Press, 1999.

Risse-Kappen, Thomas. "Ideas Do Not Float Freely: Transnational Coalitions, Domestic Structures, and the End of the Cold War." *International Organization* 48 (spring 1994): 185–214.

———. "Exploring the Nature of the Beast: International Relations Theory and Comparative Policy Analysis Meet the European Union." *Journal of Common Market Studies* 34 (March 1996): 53–80.

———. "Collective Identity in a Democratic Community: The Case of NATO." In *The Culture of National Security: Norms and Identity in World Politics,* edited by Peter J. Katzenstein, 357–99. New York: Columbia University Press, 1996.

Rodrik, Dani. "Trading in Illusions." *Foreign Policy* 123 (March–April 2001): 54–63.

Roe, Emery M. "Critical Theory, Sustainable Development and Populism." *Telos* 103 (spring 1995): 149–64.

Rollo, Jimm, and Alan L. Winters. "Subsidiarity and Governance Challenges for the WTO: Environmental and Labor Standards." *World Economy* 23 (April 2000): 561–76.

Rosenau, James N. *Along the Domestic-Foreign Frontier: Exploring Governance in a Turbulent World.* New York: Cambridge University Press, 1997.

———. "Governance and Democracy in a Globalizing World." In *Re-imagining Political Community: Studies in Cosmopolitan Democracy,* edited by Daniele Archibugi, David Held, and Martin Köhler, 28–57. Stanford, CA: Stanford University Press, 1998.

Rowlands, Ian H. *The Politics of Global Atmospheric Change.* New York: Manchester University Press, 1995.

Rubin, Alfred P. "Challenging the Conventional Wisdom: Another View of the International Criminal Court." *Journal of International Affairs* 52 (spring 1999): 783–95.

Ruggie, John G. "Human Rights and the Future International Community." *Daedalus* 112 (fall 1983): 93–110.

———. "International Regimes, Transactions, and Change: Embedded Liberalism in the Postwar Economic Order." In *International Regimes,* edited by Stephen D. Krasner, 195–232. Ithaca, NY: Cornell University Press, 1984.

———. "Territoriality and Beyond: Problematizing Modernity in International Relations." *International Organization* 47 (winter 1993): 139–74.

Rustin, Charles. "Habermas, Discourse Ethics, and International Justice." *Alternatives: Social Transformation and Humane Governance* 24 (April 1999): 167–93.

Rutherford, Kenneth R. "The Evolving Arms Control Agenda, Implications of the Role of NGOs in Banning Antipersonnel Landmines." *World Politics* 53 (October 2000): 74–114.

Ruttan, Vernon W. "United States Policy Toward the Multilateral Development Banks." *Policy Studies Journal* 23 (spring 1995): 26–40.

Samhat, Nayef H. "International Regimes as Political Community." *Millennium: Journal of International Studies* 26, no. 2 (1997): 349–78.

———. "Human Rights Regimes and the Emergence of International Political Community." *International Politics* 36 (December 1999): 503–27.

Sampson, Gary P. *Trade, Environment, and the WTO: The Post-Seattle Agenda.* Policy Essay No. 27. Baltimore, MD: Johns Hopkins University Press for the Overseas Development Council.

Sassen, Saskia. *Globalization and Its Discontents.* New York: New Press, 1998.

Scholte, Jan Aart. "Beyond the Buzzword: Towards a Critical Theory of Globalization." In *Globalization: Theory and Practice,* edited by Eleonore Kofman and Gillian Youngs, 43–57. London: Pinter, 1996.

———. *Globalization: A Critical Introduction.* New York: St. Martin's, 2000.

Scholte, Jan Aart, with Robert O'Brian and Marc Williams. "The WTO and Civil Society." *Journal of World Trade* 33, no. 3 (1999): 107–23.

Schweller, Randall L. "Fantasy Theory." *Review of International Studies* 25 (January 1999): 147–50.

Sell, Susan K. "Big Business and the New Trade Agreements: The Future of the WTO?" In *Political Economy and the Changing Global Order,* edited by Richard Stubbs and Geoffrey R.D. Underhill, 174–83. Don Mills, Ontario: Oxford University Press, 2000.

Shihata, Ibrahim F. I. "The World Bank and Non-Governmental Organizations." *Cornell International Law Journal* 25 (1992): 623–41.

———. *The World Bank Inspection Panel.* New York: Oxford University Press, 1994.

———. *The World Bank in a Changing World, Selected Essays and Lectures*, vol. 2. Cambridge: Kluwer Law International.

Short, Nicola. "The Role of NGOs in the Ottawa Process to Ban Landmines." *International Negotiation* 4, no. 3 (1999): 481–500.

Sikkink, Kathryn. "Human Rights, Principled Issue-Networks, and Sovereignty in Latin America." *International Organization* 47 (summer 1993): 411–41.

Silard, Stephen A. "The Global Environment Facility: A New Development in International Law and Organization." *George Washington Journal of International Law and Economics* 28, no. 3 (1995): 607–54.

Simmons, Ann M. "Kenya's Human Rights Record Draws Criticism; Africa: Amnesty International Cites Increasing Abuses by Moi Regime," *Los Angeles Times,* 11 September 1997, A12.

Simmons, P. J. "Learning to Live with NGOs." *Foreign Policy* 111 (fall 1998): 82–96.

Slaughter, Anne Marie. "The Real New World Order." *Foreign Affairs* 76 (September–October 1997): 183–97.

Smith, Jackie, and Ron Pagnucco, with George A. Lopez. "Globalizing Human Rights: The Work of Transnational Human Rights NGOs in the 1990s." *Human Rights Quarterly* 20 (May 1998): 379–412.

Snidal, Duncan. "International Cooperation among Relative-Gains Maximizers." *International Studies Quarterly* 35 (December 1991): 1–16.

South African National NGO Coalition. "SANGOCO Code of Ethics for NGOs," c. 1995. Available at http://www.sangoco.org.za/progs/consol_sector/code.html.

Spar, Debora L. "The Spotlight and the Bottom Line." *Foreign Affairs* 77 (March–April 1998): 7–12.

Spiro, Peter J. "New Global Communities: Nongovernmental Organizations in International Decision-Making Institutions." *Washington Quarterly* 18 (winter 1995): 45–56.

Spruyt, Hendrik. "Institutional Selection in International Relations: State Anarchy as Order." *International Organization* 48 (autumn 1994): 527–59.

Stairs, Kevin, and Peter Taylor. "Non-Governmental Organizations and the Legal Protection of the Oceans: A Case Study." In *The International Politics of the Environment,* edited by Andrew Hurrell and Benedict Kingsbury, 110–41. Oxford: Clarendon, 1992.

Stein, Janet Gross. "Political Learning by Doing: Gorbachev as Uncommitted Thinker and Motivated Learner." *International Organization* 48 (spring 1994): 155–84.

Steiner, Henry J. *Diverse Partners: Non-Governmental Organizations in the Human Rights Movement.* Cambridge: Harvard Law School/Human Rights Internet, 1991.

Stone, Christopher D. *The Gnat Is Older Than Man: Global Environment and Human Agenda.* Princeton: Princeton University Press, 1993.

Streck, Charlotte. "The Network Structure of the Global Environment Facility." Case Study for the UN Vision Project on Global Public Policy Networks, c. November 1999. Available at www.globalpublicpolicy.net.

———. "The Global Environment Facility—a Role Model for International Governance?" *Global Environmental Politics* 1 (May 2001): 71–94.

Summers, Lawrence. "Prepared Statement." *Authorizing Contributions to IDA, GEF, and ADF*, 103rd U.S. Congress, first session, House of Representatives, Subcommittee Hearing of the Committee on Banking, Finance and Urban Affairs (5 May 1993): 63–81.

Susskind, Lawrence E. *Environmental Diplomacy, Negotiating More Effective Global Agreements.* New York: Oxford University Press, 1994.

Sutherland, Peter D., John W. Sewell, and David Weiner. *The WTO and Global Governance.* Overseas Development Council Commentary, October 2000. Available at http://www.odc.org/commentary/wtorpt.1.

Tesón, Fernando R. "Kantian Liberal Internationalism." In *International Society: Diverse Ethical Perspectives,* edited by David R. Mapel and Terry Nardin, 103–13. Princeton, NJ: Princeton University Press, 1998.

Thakur, Ramesh, and William Maley. "The Ottawa Convention on Landmines: A Landmark Humanitarian Treaty in Arms Control?" *Global Governance* 5 (July–September 1999): 273–302.

Third World Network Statement. "Transparency, Participation and Legitimacy of the WTO," WTO Symposia on Trade and Environment and Trade and Development, Geneva, 15–18 March 1999. Available at www.globalexchange.org.

Thompson, Dennis, and Amy Gutmann. *Democracy and Disagreement.* Cambridge: Harvard University Press, 1996.

Thompson, Janna. *Justice and World Order: A Philosophical Inquiry.* London: Routledge, 1992.

———. "Community, Identity and World Citizenship." In *Re-imagining Political Community: Studies in Cosmopolitan Democracy,* edited by Daniele Archibugi, David Held, and Martin Köhler, 179–97. Stanford, CA: Stanford University Press, 1998.

Tickell, Oliver. "Funding Dispute Could Hold Up Biodiversity Treaty." *Nature* 367, no. 27 (January 1994): 309.

Tickell, Oliver, and Nicholas Hildyard. "Green Dollars, Green Menace." *Ecologist* 22 (May–June 1992): 82–3.

Tilly, Charles. "Reflections on the History of European State-Making." In *The Formation of National States in Western Europe,* edited by Charles Tilly, 3–84. Princeton, NJ: Princeton University Press, 1975.

Tolba, Mostafa K., with Kowona Rummel-Bulska. *Global Environmental Diplomacy: Negotiating Environmental Agreements for the World, 1973–1992*. Cambridge: MIT Press, 1998.

Trade Knowledge Network. "Trade and Sustainable Development from a Southern Perspective." Ottawa, Ontario, 31 May—1 June 2000. Available at http://iisd1.iisd.ca/pdf/ka_ottowa_June00.pdf.

Udall, Lori. "The World Bank's Revised Information Policy and New Inspection Panel: Public Accountability or Public Relations?" In *Beyond Bretton Woods, Alternatives to the Global Economic Order,* edited by John Cavanagh, Daphne Wysham and Marcos Arruda, 145–54. Boulder, CO: Pluto Press, 1994.

———. "The International Narmada Campaign: A Case of Sustained Advocacy." In *Toward Sustainable Development, Struggling over India's Narmada River,* edited by William F. Fisher, 201–27. New York: M. E. Sharpe, 1995.

———. "The World Bank and Public Accountability: Has Anything Changed?" In *The Struggle for Accountability, The World Bank, NGOs and Grassroots Movements,* edited by Jonathan A. Fox and L. David Brown, 391–436. Cambridge: MIT Press, 1998.

United Nations Conference on Trade and Development, and World Trade Organization.. "Strengthening the Participation of Developing Countries in World Trade and the Multilateral Trading System." UNCTAD TD/375, 6 May 1996.

United Nations. "Vienna Declaration and Program of Action." Adopted by the World Conference on Human Rights, 25 June 1993. A/CONF.157/23 (July 12).

United Nations, Office of the United Nations High Commissioner for Human Rights. *Fact Sheet No. 19, National Institutions for the Promotion and Protection of Human Rights,* 1993. Available at http://www.unhchr.ch/html/menu6/2/fs19.htm.

———. "National Plans of Action for the Protection and Promotion of Human Rights," 1999. Available at http://www.unhchr.ch/html/menu2/plan_action.htm.

———. "Regional Arrangements for the Promotion and Protection of Human Rights in the Asian and Pacific Region," c. 2002. Available at http://www.unhchr.ch/html/menu6/apw.htm.

United Nations, Economic and Social Council. "Consultative Relationship between the United Nations and Non-Governmental Organizations." Resolution 1296 (XLIV), 23 May 1968.

———. "Consultative Relationship between the United Nations and Non-Governmental Organizations." Resolution 1996/31, 25 July 1996.

United States Trade Representative. "General Council Informal Consultations on External Transparency, Submission from the United States of America," October 2000. Available at http://www.ustr.gov/wto/wtosub.html.

United States Agency for International Development. "New Partnerships Initiative: NGO Empowerment," 1995. Available at http://www.usaid.gov/pubs/npi/corerept/npi-ngo.htm.

Van Dyke, L. Brennan, and John Barlow Weiner. *An Introduction to the WTO Decision on Document Restriction.* International Centre for Trade and Sustainable Development, 1997. Available at http://www.ictsd.org/html/number1.1.

Van Ness, Peter. "Addressing the Human Rights Issue in Sino-American Relations." *Journal of International Affairs* 49 (winter 1996): 309–32.

Van Praag, Nicholas. "The Global Environment Facility, Instrument Establishing." *International Legal Materials* 33 (September 1994): 1273. Document available at www.dc.enews.com/magazines/ilm/archive.

Varney, Wendy, and Brian Martin. "Net Resistance, Net Benefits: Opposing MAI." *Social Alternatives* 19 (January 2000): 47–51.

Vienna Plus Five Global NGO Forum on Human Rights. "Final Declaration." Ottawa, Canada (22–24 June 1998). Available at http://www.hri.ca/vienna+5/final-report.shtml#declaration.

Vig, Norman J., and Regina S. Axelrod, eds. *The Global Environment, Institutions, Law, and Policy*. Washington, DC: Congressional Quarterly, 1999.

Vincent, R. J. *Human Rights and International Relations*. Cambridge: Cambridge University Press, 1986.

Viroli, Maurizio. *Jean-Jacques Rousseau and the "Well-Ordered Society."* Cambridge: Cambridge University Press, 1998.

Wade, Robert. "Greening the Bank: The Struggle over the Environment, 1970–1995." In *The World Bank, Its First Half Century*, vol. 2, edited by Devesh Kapur, John P. Lewis, and Richard Webb, 611–734. Washington, DC: Brookings Institution, 1997.

Walker, R. B. J. *Inside/Outside: International Relations as Political Theory*. Cambridge: Cambridge University Press, 1993.

Walsh, Kenneth, for Swiss Coalition of Development Organizations, Environmental Defense Fund, Center for International Environmental Law, and World Wildlife Fund-International. "The GEF—Five Years after Rio: Time to Take Stock, GEF Council Meeting, April 30–May 1, 1997." (22 April 1997). Available at www.hartford-hwp.com.

Walt, Stephen M. *The Origins of Alliances*. Ithaca: Cornell University Press, 1987.

Walter, Andrew. "NGOs, Business, and International Investment: The Multilateral Agreement on Investment, Seattle, and Beyond." *Global Governance* 7 (January–March 2001): 51–73.

Waltz, Kenneth N. *Theory of International Politics*. Reading, MA: Addison-Wesley, 1979.

Walzer, Michael. *Thick and Thin: Moral Argument at Home and Abroad*. Notre Dame, IN: University of Notre Dame Press, 1994.

Wang, Hongying, and James N. Rosenau. "Transparency International and Corruption as an Issue of Global Governance." *Global Governance* 7 (January–March 2001): 25–50.

Wapner, Paul. *Environmental Activism and World Civic Politics*. Albany, NY: State University of New York Press, 1996.

Warkentin, Craig. *Reshaping World Politics: NGOs, the Internet, and Global Civil Society*. New York: Rowman & Littlefield, 2001.

Wasserstrom, Robert, and Susan Reider. "Lessons from Conoco's Experiences in Ecuador's Rain Forest." *Oil and Gas Journal* 95 (18 August 1997): 24–5.

Weiss, Thomas G., and Leon Gordenker, eds. *NGOs, the United Nations, and Global Governance*. Boulder, CO: Lynne Rienner, 1996.

Wendt, Alexander. "Anarchy Is What States Make of It: The Social Construction of Power Politics." *International Organization* 46 (spring 1992): 391–425.

———. "Collective Identity Formation and the International State." *American Political Science Review* 88 (June 1994): 384–96.

———. "Constructing International Politics." *International Security* 20 (summer 1995): 71–81.

———. "Identity and Structural Change in International Politics." In *The Return of Culture and Identity in IR Theory*, edited by Yosef Lapid and Friedrich Kratochwil, 47–64. Boulder, CO: Lynne Rienner, 1996.

Werksman, Jacob. "Consolidating Governance of the Global Commons: Insights from the Global Environment Facility." *Yearbook of International Environmental Law* 6 (1995): 27–63.

Whalley, John. "Dealing with the North: Developing Countries and the Global Trading System." Center for the Study of International Economic Relations Research Monograph. London, Ontario: University of Western Ontario, 1987.

Willetts, Peter, ed. *The Influence of Non-Governmental Organisations in the U.N. System.* Washington, DC: Brookings Institution, 1996.

Williams, Bruce A., and Albert R. Matheny. *Democracy, Dialogue, and Environmental Disputes: The Contested Languages of Social Regulation.* New Haven, CT: Yale University Press, 1995.

Wiseberg, Laurie. "NGO Self-Examination is the Missing Link in ECOSOC Review." *Human Rights Tribune* 2 (March–April 1994). Available at http://www.hri.ca/cftribune/.

———. "Consultative Status Review Stalled: NGO Disharmony Cause for Concern." *Human Rights Tribune* 3 (June–July 1995). Available at http://www.hri.ca/cftribune/.

World Commission on Environment and Development. *Our Common Future.* New York: Oxford University Press, 1987.

World Resources Institute, United Nations Environment Programme, United Nations Development Programme, and World Bank (1998). *World Resources: A Guide to the Global Environment, 1998–99.* New York: Oxford University Press, 1998.

World Trade Organization "Agreement Establishing the World Trade Organization," 1994. Available at http://www.wto.org/english/docs_e/legal_e/04-wto.wpf.

———. "Understanding of Rules and Procedures Governing the Settlement of Disputes" (DSU), Annex 2, The Uruguay Round Final Act, 1994. Available at http://www.wto.org/english/docs_e/legal_e/final_e.htm.

———. "Guidelines for Arrangements on Relations with Non-Governmental Organizations—Decision Adopted by the General Council on 18 July 1996." WT/L/162, 23 July 1996.

———. "Procedures for the Circulation and Derestriction of WTO Documents—Decision Adopted by the General Council on 18 July 1996—Revision." WT/L/160/Rev.1, 26 July 1996.

———. "United States—Import Prohibition of Certain Shrimp and Shrimp Products—Report of the Panel." WT/DS58/R, 15 May 1998.

———. "Improving the Transparency of WTO Operations. Communication from the European Communities." WT/GC/W/92, 14 July 1998.
———. "Transparency in WTO Work: Proposal by the United States." WT/GC/W/88, 14 July 1998.
———. "Ruggiero Announces Enhanced WTO Plan for Cooperation with NGOs." Press/107, 17 July 1998.
———. "United States-Import Prohibition of Certain Shrimp and Shrimp Products: Report of the Appellate Body." WT/DS58/AB/R, 12 October 1998.
———. "Transparency in WTO Work: Procedures for the Circulation and Derestriction of WTO Documents, Revised Proposals by the United States and Canada." WT/GC/W/106, 13 October 1998.
———. "Challenge of Integrating LDCs into the Multilateral Trading System, Sun City, South Africa, 11–25 June 1999." WT/GC/W/251, 13 July 1999.
———. "General Council—Minutes of Meeting, 17 and 20 July 2000." WT/GC/M/57, 14 September 2000.
———. "Improving the Functioning of the WTO System, Submission to the General Council by the European Community." WT/GC/W/412, 6 October 2000.
———. "General Council Informal Consultations on External Transparency." Submission to the General Council by the United States, WT/GC/W/413/Rev. 1, 13 October 2000.
———, Sub-committee on Least-Developed Countries. "Integrated Proposal for a Pilot Scheme." WT/LDC/SWG/IF/13, 13 February 2001.
———. "General Council—Minutes of Meeting, 30 January and 8 February 2001—Addendum." WT/GC/M/61/Add. 1, 14 February 2001.
———. "WTO Secretariat Activities with NGOs." WT/INF/30, 12 April 2001.
———. "Symposium on Issues Confronting the World Trading System, 6–7 July 2001, Geneva, Switzerland." Available at http://www.wto.org/english/forums_e/ngo_e/ngo_symp_2001_e.htm.
———. "Eleventh Summit of the Heads of State and Government of the Group of Fifteen, Jakarta, Indonesia, 30–31 May." WT/L/404, 9 July 2001.
———. "Zanzibar Declaration, Meeting of the Ministers Responsible for Trade of the Least Developed Countries, Zanzibar, Tanzania, 22–24 July 2001." WT/L/409, 6 August 2001.
———. "General Council—Minutes of Meeting, 18 and 19 July 2001." WT/GC/M/66, 8 October 2001.
———. "Ministerial Declaration, Fourth Ministerial Meeting, 14 November 2001, Doha, Qatar." WT/MIN(01)/DEC/1. Adopted 20 November 2001.
———. "The Doha Development Agenda and Beyond." WTO Symposium, Geneva, Switzerland (April 29–May 1).
———. "Procedures for the Circulation and Derestriction of WTO Documents, Decision of May 14, 2002." WT/L/452, 16 May 2002.
Young, Zoe. "NGOs and the Global Environmental Facility: Friendly Foes?" *Environmental Politics* 8 (spring 1999): 242–67.
Young, Zoe, and Sonja Boehmer-Christiansen. "Green Energy Facilitated? The Uncertain Function of the Global Environment Facility." *Energy & Environment* 9, no. 1 (1998): 35–59.

Zacher, Mark W. "The Decaying Pillars of the Westphalian Temple: Implications for International Governance." In *Governance without Government: Order and Change in World Politics,* edited by James N. Rosenau and Ernst-Otto Czempiel, 58–101. Cambridge: Cambridge University Press, 1992.

Zaelke, Durwood, and David Hunter. Statement and Testimony, "The World Bank Inspection Panel and the Need to Create an International Framework Agreement for Administrative Procedures." *World Bank Disclosure Policy and Inspection Panel*, Hearing, U.S. House of Representatives, Committee on Banking, Finance and Urban Affairs, 103rd Congress, 2nd session, 21 June 1994: 152–63.

Zürn, Michael. "The Rise of International Environmental Politics: A Review of Current Research." *World Politics* 50 (July 1998): 617–49.

Index

SUNY series in Global Politics
James N. Rosenau, Editor

LIST OF TITLES

American Patriotism in a Global Society—Betty Jean Craige

The Political Discourse of Anarchy: A Disciplinary History of International Relations—Brian C. Schmidt

From Pirates to Drug Lords: The Post—Cold War Caribbean Security Environment—Michael C. Desch, Jorge I. Dominguez, and Andres Serbin (eds.)

Collective Conflict Management and Changing World Politics—Joseph Lepgold and Thomas G. Weiss (eds.)

Zones of Peace in the Third World: South America and West Africa in Comparative Perspective—Arie M. Kacowicz

Private Authority and International Affairs—A. Claire Cutler, Virginia Haufler, and Tony Porter (eds.)

Harmonizing Europe: Nation-States within the Common Market—Francesco G. Duina

Economic Interdependence in Ukrainian-Russian Relations—Paul J. D'Anieri

Leapfrogging Development? The Political Economy of Telecommunications Restructuring—J. P. Singh

States, Firms, and Power: Successful Sanctions in United States Foreign Policy—George E. Shambaugh

Approaches to Global Governance Theory—Martin Hewson and Timothy J. Sinclair (eds.)

After Authority: War, Peace, and Global Politics in the Twenty-First Century—Ronnie D. Lipschutz

Pondering Postinternationalism: A Paradigm for the Twenty-First Century?—Heidi H. Hobbs (ed.)

Beyond Boundaries? Disciplines, Paradigms, and Theoretical Integration in International Studies—Rudra Sil and Eileen M. Doherty (eds.)

Why Movements Matter: The West German Peace Movement and U. S. Arms Control Policy—Steve Breyman

International Relations—Still an American Social Science? Toward Diversity in International Thought—Robert M. A. Crawford and Darryl S. L. Jarvis (eds.)

Which Lessons Matter? American Foreign Policy Decision Making in the Middle East, 1979—1987—Christopher Hemmer (ed.)

Hierarchy Amidst Anarchy: Transaction Costs and Institutional Choice—Katja Weber

Counter-Hegemony and Foreign Policy: The Dialectics of Marginalized and Global Forces in Jamaica—Randolph B. Persaud

Global Limits: Immanuel Kant, International Relations, and Critique of World Politics—Mark F. N. Franke

Power and Ideas: North-South Politics of Intellectual Property and Antitrust—Susan K. Sell

Money and Power in Europe: The Political Economy of European Monetary Cooperation—Matthias Kaelberer

Agency and Ethics: The Politics of Military Intervention—Anthony F. Lang, Jr.

Life After the Soviet Union: The Newly Independent Republics of the Transcaucasus and Central Asia—Nozar Alaolmolki

Theories of International Cooperation and the Primacy of Anarchy: Explaining U. S. International Monetary Policy-Making After Bretton Woods—Jennifer Sterling-Folker

Information Technologies and Global Politics: The Changing Scope of Power and Governance—James N. Rosenau and J. P. Singh (eds.)

Technology, Democracy, and Development: International Conflict and Cooperation in the Information Age—Juliann Emmons Allison (ed.)

The Arab-Israeli Conflict Transformed: Fifty Years of Interstate and Ethnic Crises—Hemda Ben-Yehuda and Shmuel Sandler

Systems of Violence: The Political Economy of War and Peace in Colombia—Nazih Richani

Debating the Global Financial Architecture—Leslie Elliot Armijo

Political Space: Frontiers of Change and Governance in a Globalizing World—Yale Ferguson and R. J. Barry Jones (eds.)

Crisis Theory and World Order: Heideggerian Reflections—Norman K. Swazo

Political Identity and Social Change: The Remaking of the South African Social Order—Jamie Frueh

Social Construction and the Logic of Money: Financial Predominance and International Economic Leadership—J. Samuel Barkin

What Moves Man: The Realist Theory of International Relations and Its Judgment of Human Nature — Annette Freyberg-Inan